Designing Applications for Google Cloud Platform

Create and Deploy Applications Using Java

Ashutosh Shashi

Apress®

Designing Applications for Google Cloud Platform: Create and Deploy Applications Using Java

Ashutosh Shashi
Duluth, GA, USA

ISBN-13 (pbk): 978-1-4842-9510-6 ISBN-13 (electronic): 978-1-4842-9511-3
https://doi.org/10.1007/978-1-4842-9511-3

Managing Director, Apress Media LLC: Welmoed Spahr
Acquisitions Editor: Celestin Suresh John
Development Editor: James Markham
Coordinating Editor: Mark Powers
Copy Editor: Kim Wimpsett

Cover designed by eStudioCalamar

Cover image by Bolivia Inteligente on Unsplash (www.unsplash.com)

Distributed to the book trade worldwide by Apress Media, LLC, 1 New York Plaza, New York, NY 10004, U.S.A. Phone 1-800-SPRINGER, fax (201) 348-4505, email orders-ny@springer-sbm.com, or visit www.springeronline.com. Apress Media, LLC is a California LLC and the sole member (owner) is Springer Science + Business Media Finance Inc (SSBM Finance Inc). SSBM Finance Inc is a **Delaware** corporation.

For information on translations, please e-mail booktranslations@springernature.com; for reprint, paperback, or audio rights, please e-mail bookpermissions@springernature.com.

Apress titles may be purchased in bulk for academic, corporate, or promotional use. eBook versions and licenses are also available for most titles. For more information, reference our Print and eBook Bulk Sales web page at www.apress.com/bulk-sales.

Any source code or other supplementary material referenced by the author in this book is available to readers on GitHub (https://github.com/Apress). For more detailed information, please visit www.apress.com/source-code.

Printed on acid-free paper

Table of Contents

About the Author

Ashutosh Shashi is a TOGAF 9 certified enterprise architect, a seasoned software engineer, and a cloud architect with more than 18 years of experience in the industry. He has worked on multiple projects using various technologies and platforms, from small startups to large enterprise systems. He has helped many organizations design and build robust and scalable applications on Google Cloud Platform (GCP). Apart from GCP, he has extensive experience and expertise in AWS and Azure cloud platforms. Ashutosh lives in Duluth, Georgia. He enjoys hiking and spending time with his family in his free time. He also loves to travel and explore different cultures.

About the Technical Reviewer

Chandra Rajasekharaiah is a technology leader, cloud transformation enthusiast, supply chain specialist, and published author. He has led multimillion-dollar enterprise initiatives in technology transformation and cloud migration. He has helped enterprises modernize giant legacy monoliths to microservices-based applications and has deployed on the cloud and across multiple datacenters. He is currently a distinguished engineer for a large automotive parts retailer, focusing on modernizing supply chains.

Introduction

As a software architect with many years of experience, I have worked with various cloud platforms, including Google Cloud Platform (GCP). I have noticed that many developers and architects face challenges when designing and building applications on GCP using Java. They need help understanding the various services offered by GCP, which ones will be best suited for their application, and how to use them effectively to build robust and scalable applications.

This realization prompted me to write this book as a comprehensive guide for developers, architects, and technical managers looking to design and build applications using Java for GCP. This book is based on my practical experience working with GCP and aims to bridge the gap between theory and practice, providing readers with a hands-on approach to learning how to build applications on GCP. This approach allows developers and architects to better understand GCP and its services and enables them to design and build better applications.

This book introduces GCP, outlining its various features, capabilities, and benefits. Then, I explain how you can choose the best tool on GCP to develop scalable, reliable, and cost-effective applications and how it can help organizations accelerate their digital transformation efforts.

This practical guide will provide developers and architects with the tools and knowledge they need to design and build applications on GCP using Java. Through this book, I hope readers overcome any challenges they encounter when using GCP and that they gain the confidence and skills they need to build robust and scalable Java applications.

Source Code

All source code used in this book can be downloaded from `https://github.com/Apress/designing-applications-google-cloud-platform`.

CHAPTER 1

Introduction

This chapter will introduce Google Cloud Platform (GCP) services and how they can be used to build, deploy, and scale applications. This chapter will guide you in setting up a GCP environment and give a brief overview of the most common GCP services. By the end of this chapter, you will be able to understand the basics of GCP, create a GCP project, and know which GCP services you can use to build and deploy applications.

You'll want to create a login on Google or use your existing Google account to start a free GCP trial to follow along with the exercises in this book.

Start a Free Trial on GCP

To start a free trial on GCP, you can follow these steps:

1. Go to the GCP website at `https://cloud.google.com/` and click the Start Free button at the top-right corner of the web page.
2. Sign in using your Google account or create a new one if you don't have a Google account.
3. Fill out the details with your personal and billing information. You must provide a valid credit card to verify your identity, but you will get charged if you upgrade to a paid account.
4. Review the terms and conditions of the free trial and click the "Agree and continue" button.
5. Once you have created your account, you can start using GCP services for free for 90 days. You will receive $300 in credits for any GCP service during this time. Remember that some services may not be eligible for the free trial, so check the details before using them.

A. Shashi, *Designing Applications for Google Cloud Platform*, https://doi.org/10.1007/978-1-4842-9511-3_1

6. Explore the GCP dashboard and try some of the services. Many resources are available to help you get started, including documentation, tutorials, and community forums.

Remember to monitor your usage and billing during the trial period to avoid unexpected charges. If you decide to upgrade to a paid account, you can do so anytime by adding a billing account to your project.

Once the trial starts, you can see the trial status and remaining balance at the top of the GCP console, as shown in Figure 1-1.

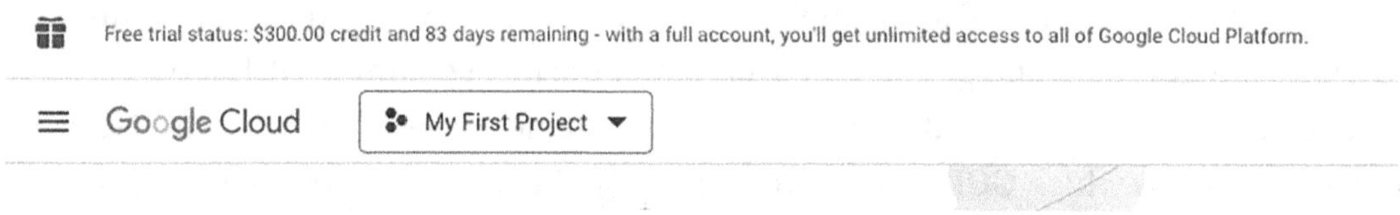

Figure 1-1. *Monitoring your usage and billing*

The GCP project "My First Project" will be created automatically as soon as you start the free trial. You can create more projects as needed.

A project in GCP is used to organize resources. Each project in GCP has its own set of resources and billing, and you can track billing based on the project.

In GCP, a *project* is like a box or a folder containing all the resources, services, and configurations related to a specific application, system, or workload. A project serves as a boundary for resources to ensure they are isolated and can be managed independently.

A project organizes resources in GCP, defines resource ownership and access, manages billing and usage, and enables collaboration among team members. You can think of a project as a logical grouping of resources, which makes it easier to manage, secure, and monitor them.

Figure 1-2 shows a single GCP project that contains Compute Engine (VMs) that can run applications and software, Cloud Storage that can store files and data, Cloud SQL that provides managed database, a load balancer that can distribute traffic between VMs, two firewall rules that can control access to the VMs, and a DNS server that can map domain names to the IP addresses, billing service allows you to manage spending and costs, IAM allows you to control access to your resources and services by adding or removing users, groups, or roles.

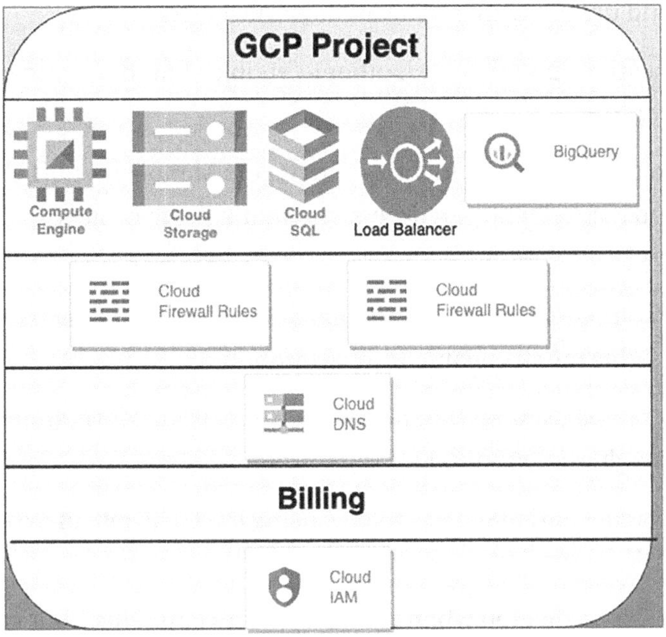

Figure 1-2. *A GCP project*

It is not possible to use GCP without a project. You must create at least one project to access GCP services and resources. When you sign up for a GCP account, you automatically create a default project, which is used for billing and other administrative purposes. You can also create additional projects for your workloads and applications.

Projects in GCP can be linked to each other in different ways. For example, you can link projects to enable shared resources, such as a shared VPC network or a billing account. You can also link projects to control access to resources across multiple projects or to grant permissions to users or service accounts.

Here are some key things to know about GCP projects:

- Projects must use GCP services and resources.
- Each project has a globally unique ID, name, and number across all GCP services.
- A project can contain multiple resources, such as compute instances, storage buckets, and databases.
- Projects can be organized into folders and hierarchies to manage resource ownership and access.

- Billing and usage are managed at the project level.
- Projects can be linked to each other to enable shared resources and access control.
- Each project has its own Identity and Access Management (IAM) policies to control who can access and manage the project's resources.
- You can configure monitoring, logging, and alerting for each project to get insights into its health and performance.
- Projects can be used for different purposes, such as development, testing, staging, or production.
- You can create and manage projects using the GCP console, the Cloud SDK, or the API.
- Projects can be deleted when they are no longer needed, but you need to remove all the associated resources and data before doing so.

When working with GCP projects, keeping track of their configuration and usage and following best practices for security, scalability, and cost optimization are important. You should also consider using tools such as Terraform, Cloud Deployment Manager, or Kubernetes Engine to manage your infrastructure as code and to ensure consistency and reproducibility across multiple projects and environments.

Creating a New Project

To create a new project, click the existing project (My First Project) in the top-left corner of the GCP console. A window like the one shown in Figure 1-3 will appear.

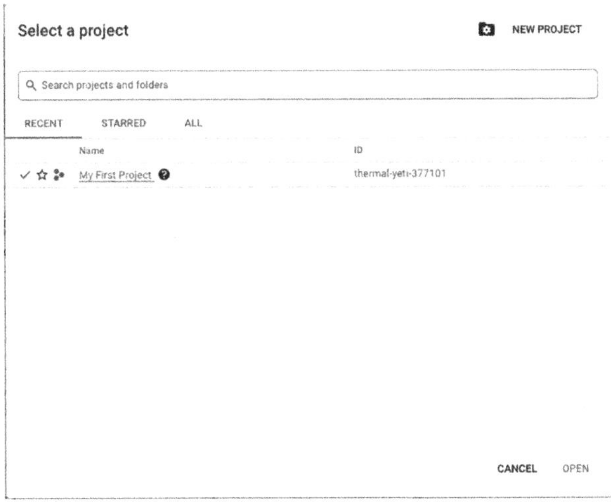

Figure 1-3. *Selecting a project*

You can click the New Project button in the top-right corner to create a new project. A window like the one shown in Figure 1-4 will appear.

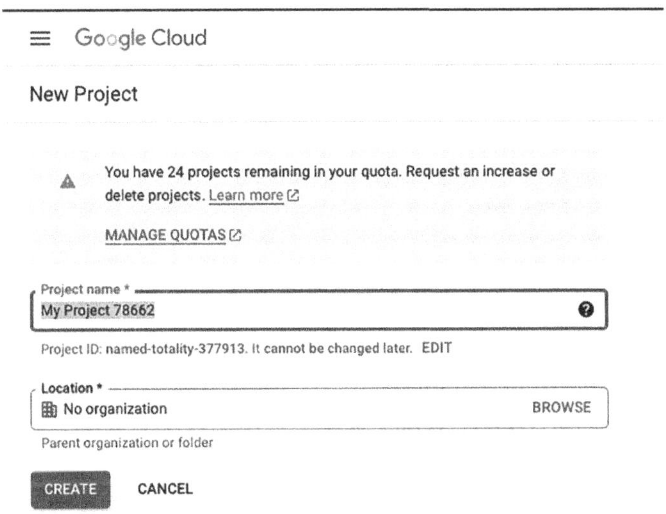

Figure 1-4. *Creating a new GCP project*

Here you can see the message that you have only 24 projects remaining. By default, GCP allows you to create 25 projects; if you need to create more projects, you can request to increase the quota. The name of the project must be between 4 and 30 characters.

Note A *quota* in GCP is a flexible limit, but a *limit* is a hard cap on the amount of a resource you can use.

You can name the project as you choose to reflect the purpose of the project. The project ID is the globally unique identifier for your project. You cannot change the project ID after the project is created. The projects can be associated with the organization you can select for location. If your project name is globally unique, the project ID will be the same as a project name, or else the project ID can be created automatically by adding numbers in front of the project name. You can set your custom project name project ID by clicking in front of the project ID, as shown in Figure 1-5.

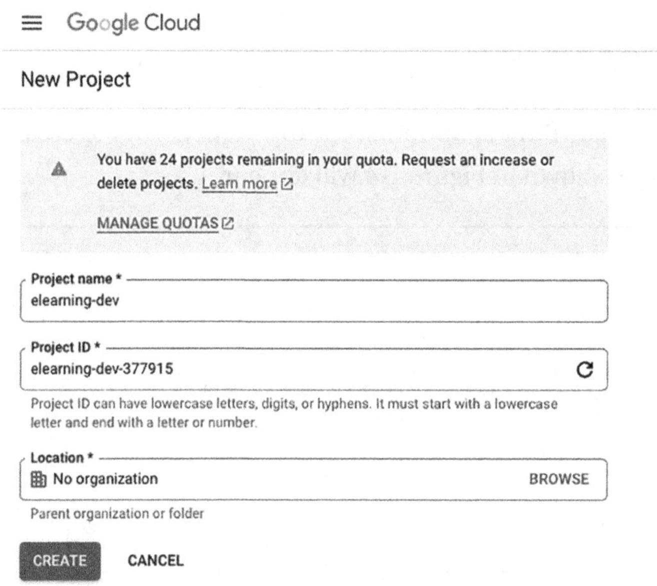

Figure 1-5. *Project ID for GCP project*

After you click Create, you will see it in your activity list. Whenever you create any resource in GCP, you can see it in your activity list, as shown in Figure 1-6.

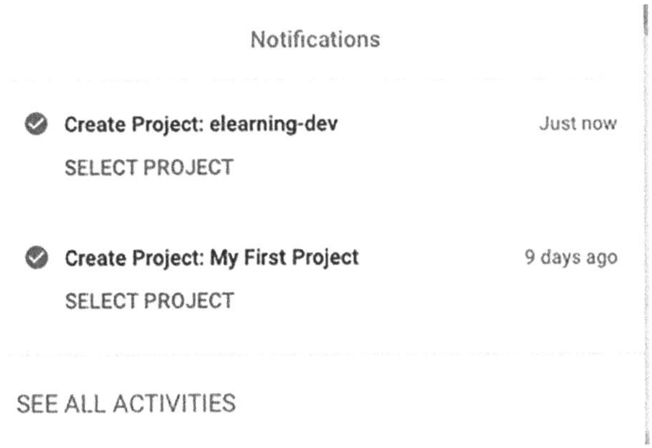

Figure 1-6. *GCP project activities*

For example, if you use GCP for the EdTech application, you can create a project for all your development environments and another project for all the production environments. You can have a separate project for analytics and marketing. By doing that, you can easily see the expenses for nonprod, prod, and analytics for your EdTech applications.

Once the new project is created, you can choose the project you are working on by clicking the project button at the top-left corner of the GCP console, as shown in Figure 1-7. If you don't see your project on the Recent tab of the window, you can click the All tab to see all the projects. To see the project, you need permission for it.

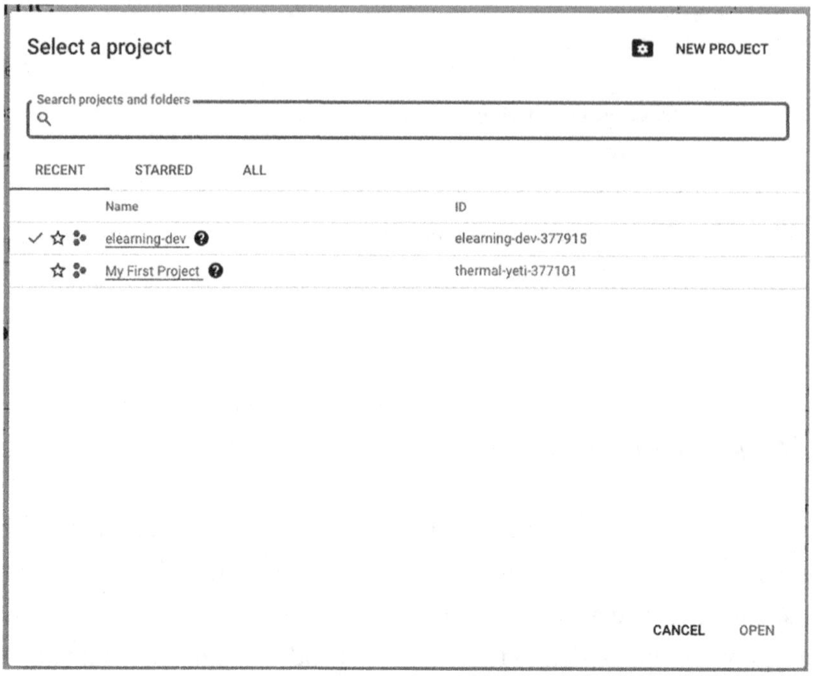

Figure 1-7. *Recent projects*

Select the services from the GCP console in the left pane or search for the service name with the top search button, like the one shown in Figure 1-8.

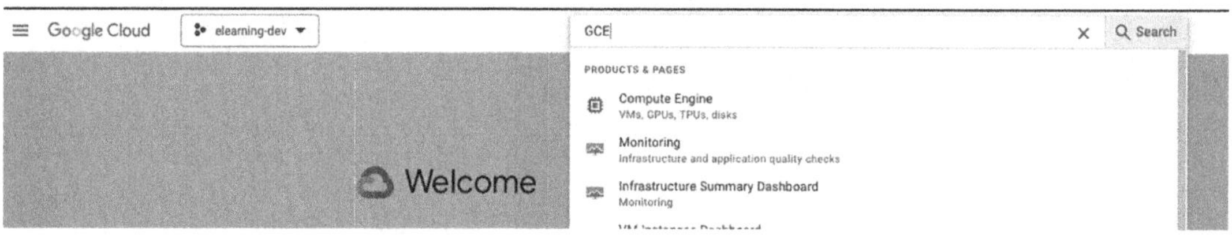

Figure 1-8. *Searching for GCP services*

Overview of GCP and Its Services

GCP architecture refers to the design and layout of infrastructure and services that make up Google Cloud Platform. At a high level, the GCP architecture includes computing, storage, database, networking, and security. It is designed to be scalable, reliable, and secure. It uses multiple layers of abstraction and isolation to ensure that applications and services can run independently and securely on the same infrastructure. It also provides tools and services that allow developers to automate development, monitor performance, and troubleshoot issues in real time.

GCP *regions* and *zones* are the specific geographic locations of GCP resources. A GCP region is a specific location where resources are hosted. The regions comprise one or more availability zones (AZs), physically separated locations called *data centers*. AZs are designed to be independent of each other, so if one AZ experiences an outage, it does not affect the availability of resources in another AZ within the same region. GCP regions and zones are important because they affect the performance and availability of your applications. When you create a GCP resource, you need to specify the region and zone where you want to create the resource.

GCP pricing is based on the pay-as-you-go model, meaning that you pay only for the resources and services you use. The cost depends on several factors, including the type and amount of resources used, the duration of use, and the location of resources. The price may vary by region and AZ, with some regions and AZs costing more than others. GCP provides committed use discounts by committing the use of Compute Engine and cloud storage for a certain amount of uses over a period of time.

GCP provides various services, including computing, storage, networking, big data, machine learning, the Internet of Things (IoT), security, and application development. Let's run through some of the most popular services.

Google Compute Engine

Google Compute Engine (GCE) is the part of GCP that provides scalable, highly available, and high-performance virtual machines for running applications and services. It enables customers to create, configure, and manage virtual machines (VMs) running on the Google infrastructure. GCE offers a range of configurable options, including customizable machine types, disk storage options, and operating systems, including popular Linux distributions and Microsoft Windows. GCE also provides advanced networking features such as load balancing, firewalls, and automatic backups, making it an ideal platform for deploying and managing applications and services.

The integration of GCE with other GCP services, such as Google Kubernetes Engine, Google Cloud Storage, Google Cloud SQL, and Cloud Pub/Sub, is not limited but can depend on the network connectivity and configuration. The ability of integration makes it easy to build complex, multitier applications.

Let's look at an example of a GCE instance in a different region or AZ than the other GCP services it needs to communicate with. In this case, there may be latency and performance issues. If network configuration is not set up properly, it can affect the connectivity and integration between GCE instances and the other GCP services. To optimize integration between GCE instances and the other GCP service, it is important to consider network connectivity and configuration as part of your architecture design, which can include selecting the appropriate region and availability zone, setting up proper network configuration, and using services such as load balancing and cloud CDN to improve performance and availability.

When you search and select GCE the first time, you must enable it by clicking the Enable button, as shown in Figure 1-9. You will not see this option if you are part of the organization and it is already enabled for the selected project.

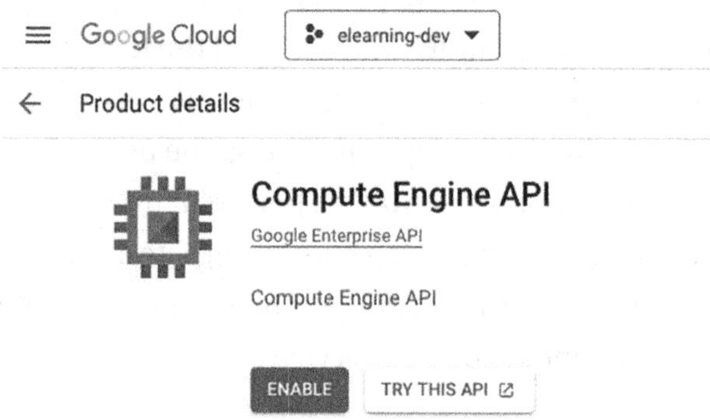

Figure 1-9. *Enabling Compute Engine for first time*

When you click the Enable button, you will see it being enabled, as shown in Figure 1-10.

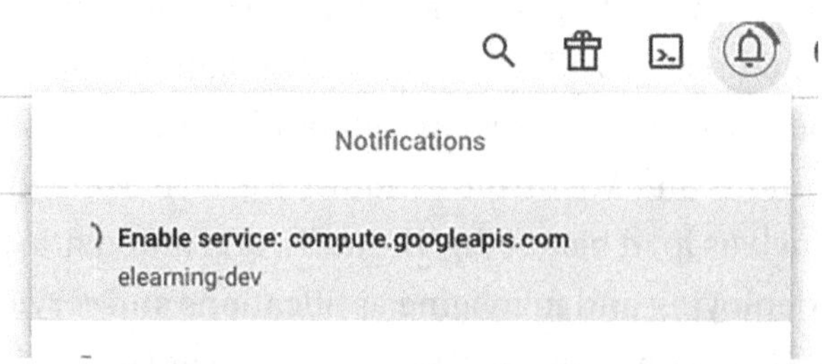

Figure 1-10. *Enabling the Compute Engine API*

Enabling the Compute Engine API will take some time.

Once the API is enabled, you will see the Compute Engine dashboard, as shown in Figure 1-11. From here, you can create virtual machines. By clicking Create Instance, you can create a VM instance. You can migrate your VMs directly from on-prem or other clouds using Google Cloud's Migrate to Virtual Machines feature. Supported sources include on-prem VMware, Amazon EC2, and Microsoft Azure. To migrate, you can click the Import VM button. You can see these two buttons at the top of the screen.

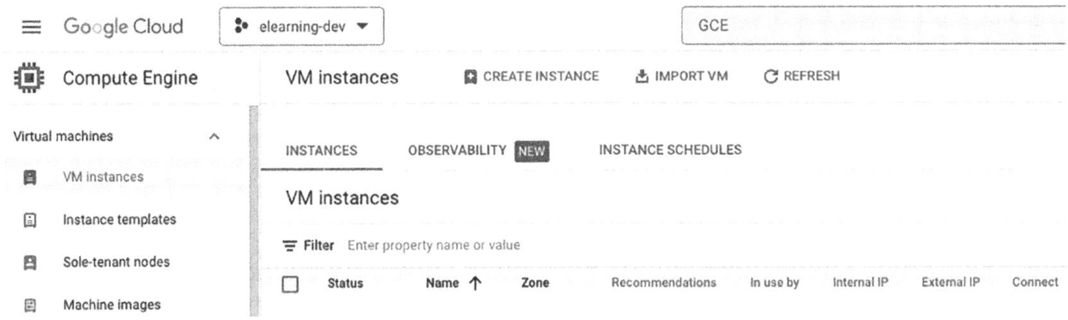

***Figure 1-11.** Compute Engine dashboard*

There are various configurations and instance options available to create a compute instance. Importing an existing VM is a separate topic outside this book's scope.

You can create a VM with the desired configurations such as machine type, operating system, disk type, and size. The best practice is to use a VM template to create a VM for a similar purpose. You can choose the ready-to-go deployable VMs from the marketplace; the Google Cloud Marketplace is a platform for discovering, deploying, and managing preconfigured software solutions on the Google Compute Engine. You will see these options when you click the "Create an instance" button, as shown in Figure 1-12.

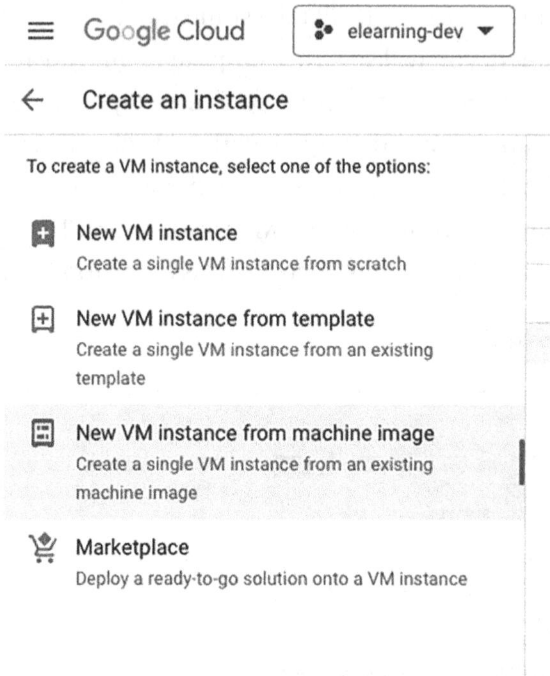

Figure 1-12. *Creating an instance*

GCE can be used for variety of use cases, including batch processing workloads such as rendering and data processing, high-performance computing workloads such as scientific simulation and machine learning, big data processing such as processing and analyzing large datasets, and high-performance, scalable infrastructure for gaming workloads.

Google Kubernetes Engine

Google Kubernetes Engine (GKE) is a fully managed Kubernetes service offered by GCP that makes it easy to deploy, manage, and scale containerized applications using Google infrastructure. GKE provides a complete solution for deploying, managing, and scaling containers, allowing developers to focus on writing code and delivering features. It also provides features such as automatic upgrades, automatic scaling, and self-healing so that developers can focus on their applications, not the underlying infrastructure. Additionally, GKE integrates with other GCP services, such as cloud load balancing, cloud Operations Suite, cloud monitoring and Logging, and cloud DNS, making it easy to manage a complete application stack in a single platform.

A *containerized application* is an application that has been packaged with all of its dependencies into a single unit called a *container*. Containers are isolated from each other and the host operating system, making them a more efficient and secure way to deploy applications. Think of a container as a box containing everything your application needs to run, such as the code, libraries, and settings. This makes it easy to deploy applications to different environments, such as on-premises, in the cloud, or in a hybrid environment. Containers are also more efficient than traditional virtual machines. Virtual machines require a full operating system, while containers require only the application's resources. This can save money on hardware costs and improve performance. Containers are more secure than traditional virtual machines. Containers are isolated from each other and the host operating system, making it more difficult for malware to spread, which makes containers an ideal choice for applications that need to be highly secure.

Like the GCE, you need to enable the Kubernetes Engine API if you are using it for the first time. Figure 1-13 shows the Enable button.

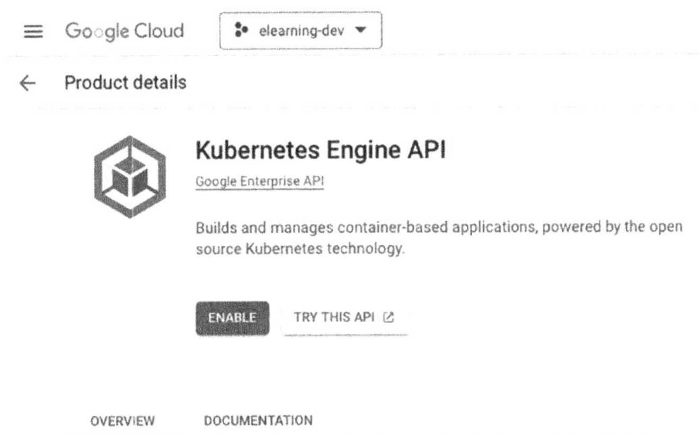

Figure 1-13. *Enabling the Kubernetes Engine API*

After you click the Enable button, GCP will take some time to enable it. After it's enabled, you will see the GKE dashboard. Again, if you are part of the organization and GKE is already enabled for the given project, you will see the GKE dashboard straightaway.

In the left pane, you will see options for the cluster, Workload, Services and Ingress, Applications, Secret and ConfigMaps, etc.

As shown in Figure 1-14, GCP provides two options to create a Kubernetes cluster and deploy a container: a pay-per-pod Kubernetes cluster called Autopilot, where GKE manages your nodes with minimal configuration required. The other option is a pay-per-node Kubernetes cluster called Standard, where you configure and manage your nodes.

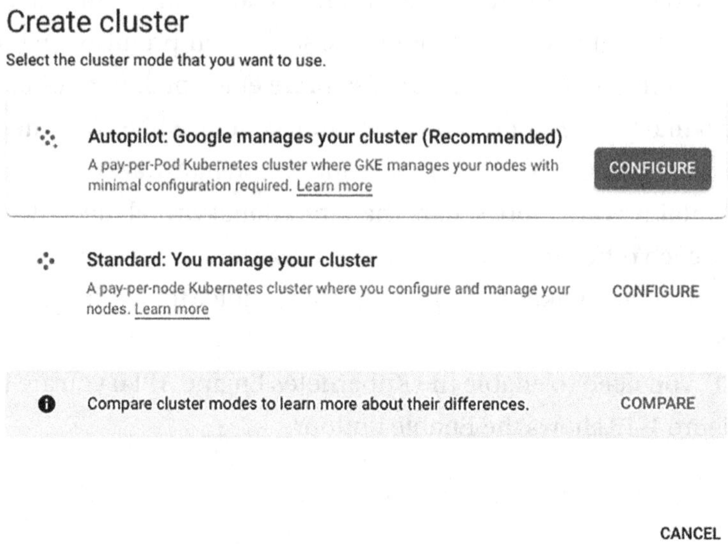

Figure 1-14. *Creating a Kubernetes cluster*

You can have multiple clusters with different configurations for different types of workloads. For example, you might create one GKE cluster for a production application that requires high availability and scalability, with multiple nodes spread across multiple zones. You might create another GKE cluster for a development or testing environment with fewer nodes and simpler configurations, as illustrated in Figure 1-15.

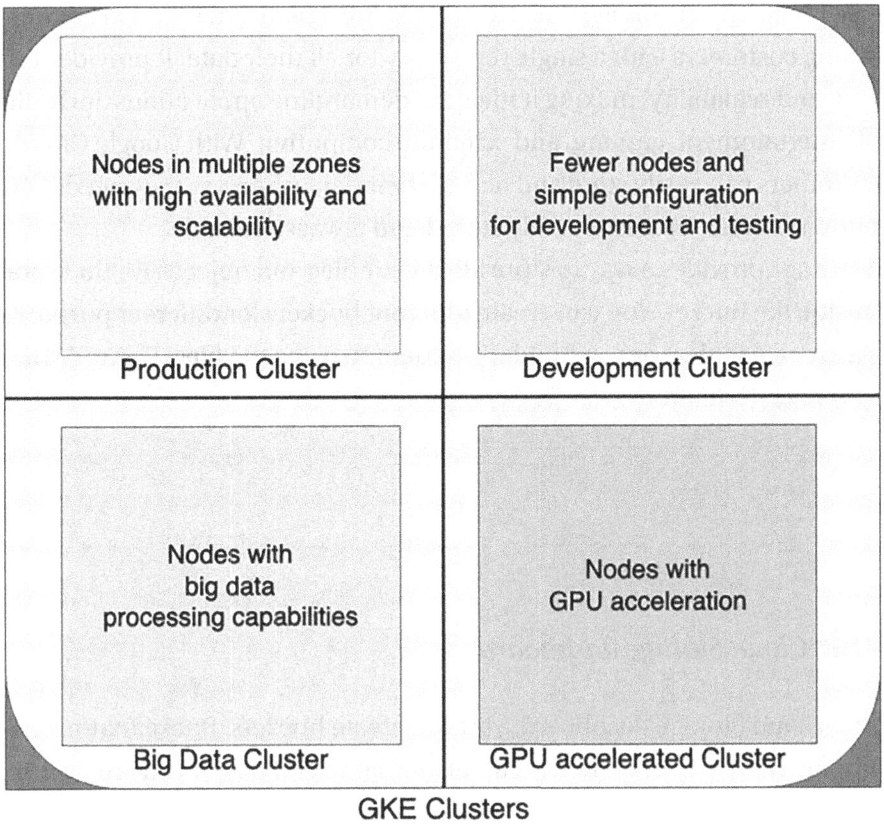

Figure 1-15. *GKE clusters*

You can also create GKE clusters with different machine types, network configurations, and storage options, depending on the specific requirements of your workloads. This allows you to optimize your GKE clusters for performance, cost-effectiveness, and other factors. You might have one GKE cluster for batch processing workloads and another GKE cluster for web applications. This can help prevent resource contention and improve overall performance and reliability.

Google Cloud Storage

Google Cloud Storage (GCS) is a scalable and highly durable object storage service provided by Google Cloud Platform. It provides customers with high-performance access to unstructured data, making it an ideal solution for storing and serving large amounts of data such as images, videos, backups, backups, and logs. Google Cloud

Storage is a unified object storage that provides a single platform for unstructured data, providing customers with a single repository for all their data. It provides high performance and scalability, making it ideal for demanding applications, including media and entertainment, gaming, and scientific computing. With Google Cloud Storage, customers can easily store and access their data wherever they need it, with the peace of mind that their data is securely stored and always available.

Cloud Storage provides a way to store all of your files and objects. All the storage is arranged inside the bucket. You can create different buckets for different purposes, and then you can create folders and subfolders in them to place the files. Figure 1-16 shows the Cloud Storage dashboard.

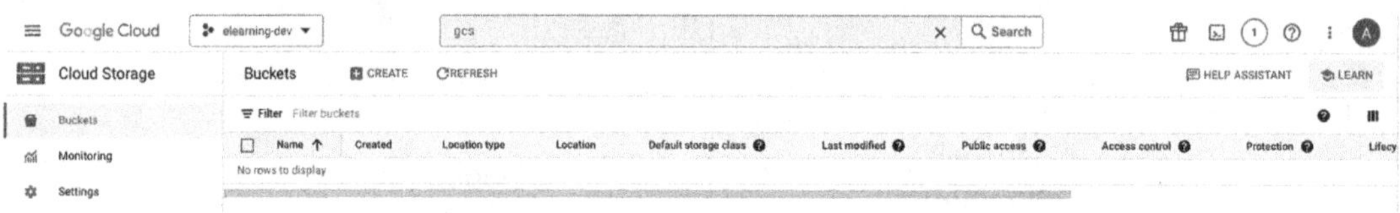

***Figure 1-16.** Cloud Storage dashboard*

From the Cloud Storage dashboard, you can create buckets. Bucket names are globally unique. No two bucket names can be the same globally. If you are deleting your bucket and want to create a new bucket with the same name you are deleting right now, you can do that.

The bucket name should not be carrying any sensitive information, as bucket names are publicly visible. You can add labels to your bucket to group together similar buckets.

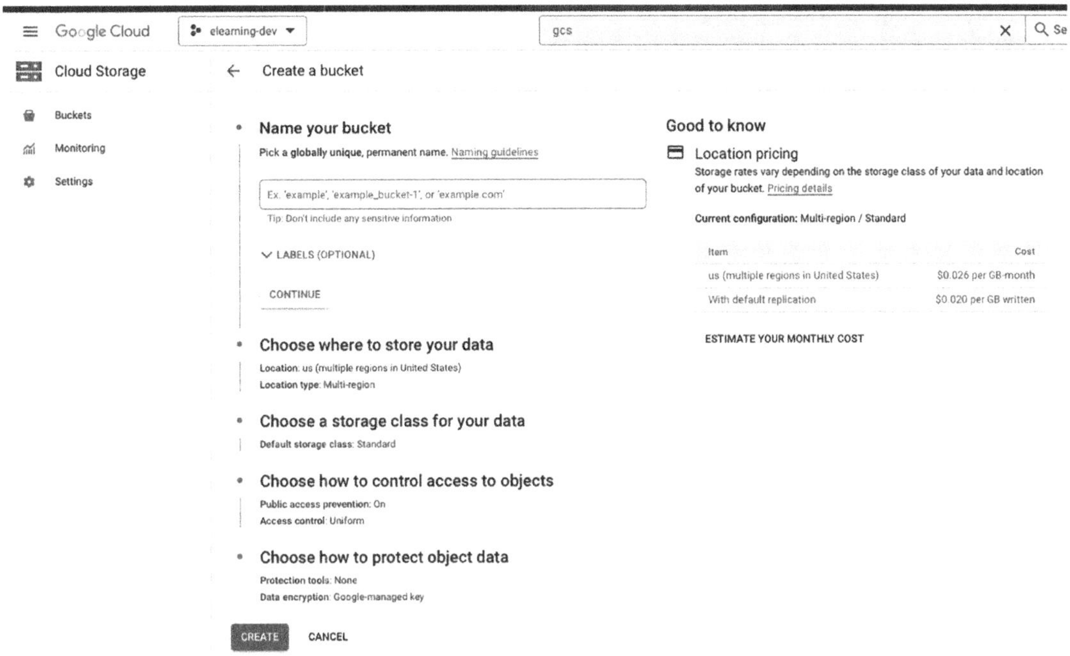

Figure 1-17. *Creating a Cloud Storage bucket*

While creating a bucket, as shown in Figure 1-17, you can choose the location of the bucket as single or multiregion. You can choose the storage class, access control, who can access it, and whether to use data encryption to protect your data. In GCP, you can do encryption either with Google Managed Key or with Customer Managed Key.

Choose the appropriate storage class while creating a storage bucket for your data. GCS offers four storage classes: standard, nearline, coldline, and archive. Each storage class has its own set of characteristics, such as performance, availability, durability, and cost. While creating a bucket, you can choose a storage class to set the default storage class for the bucket, as shown in Figure 1-18.

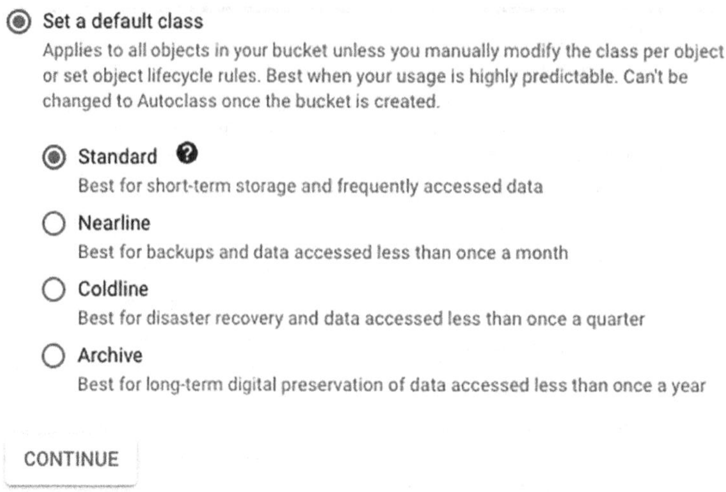
Set a default class
Applies to all objects in your bucket unless you manually modify the class per object or set object lifecycle rules. Best when your usage is highly predictable. Can't be changed to Autoclass once the bucket is created.
Standard
Best for short-term storage and frequently accessed data
Nearline
Best for backups and data accessed less than once a month
Coldline
Best for disaster recovery and data accessed less than once a quarter
Archive
Best for long-term digital preservation of data accessed less than once a year
CONTINUE

Figure 1-18. *Choosing a storage class*

Standard storage is the default storage class and is the most expensive. If you need to access data frequently and quickly, this storage class is best for you. For example, you might use the standard storage class for customer orders and invoices, as you need to be able to access this data quickly and frequently.

Nearline storage is less expensive than standard storage and is a good choice for data that needs to be accessed occasionally but is not critical for your business. For example, you can use nearline storage to back up your website data.

Coldline storage is less expensive than nearline and standard storage and is a good choice for data accessed infrequently and not critical for your business. For example, you might use coldline storage for financial records that are accessed only once a quarter for reporting purposes.

Archive storage is the lowest-cost storage class with the highest access cost and is best for rarely or never accessed data. For example, you might choose the archive storage class for backups that are kept for legal or regulatory reasons.

Google BigQuery

Google BigQuery (GBQ) is a fully managed, serverless, cloud data warehouse that enables super-fast SQL queries using the processing power of Google's infrastructure. It allows organizations to analyze large amounts of data quickly and cost-effectively, making it a popular choice for big data analytics. BigQuery integrates with various other GCP services and tools, including Google Cloud Dataflow, Google Cloud Dataproc, and Google Cloud Storage, making it a flexible and scalable solution for organizations of all sizes. With BigQuery, there's no need to worry about hardware or infrastructure maintenance, as Google manages all the underlying infrastructure. This enables organizations to focus on analysis and insights rather than managing and maintaining hardware.

BigQuery is the enterprise data warehouse where you can export your relevant application data for reporting and analytical purposes. If you go to the BigQuery console, GCP provides public data so that you can explore BigQuery functionality on that data. Figure 1-19 shows the BigQuery dashboard.

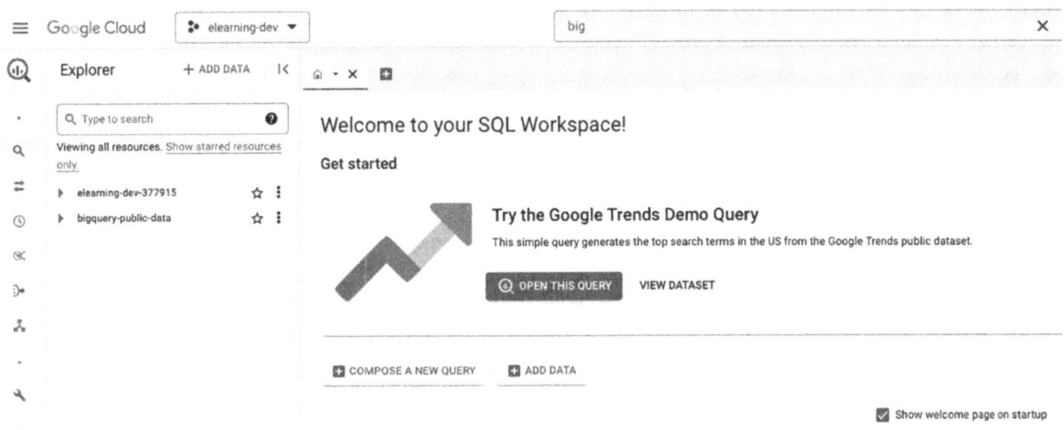

Figure 1-19. *Google BigQuery*

In BigQuery, you can use a query editor to write RDBMS database-like queries. You can add data in BigQuery by uploading data files from the bucket, uploading files from external sources like application logs moved to BigQuery, pushing data through pub/sub to BigQuery, etc. Google provides a sample dataset to try when learning BigQuery. To get this dataset, click to view the dataset in the "Get started" window, as shown on Figure 1-19.

The data in BigQuery is organized in a hierarchical structure. The top level is the *project*, which is a logical container for datasets. The datasets are used to organize tables, and tables are used to store data, as shown in Figure 1-20.

Each table has a schema that defines the structure of the data in the table. The schema includes the names of the columns in the table and the data types of the columns.

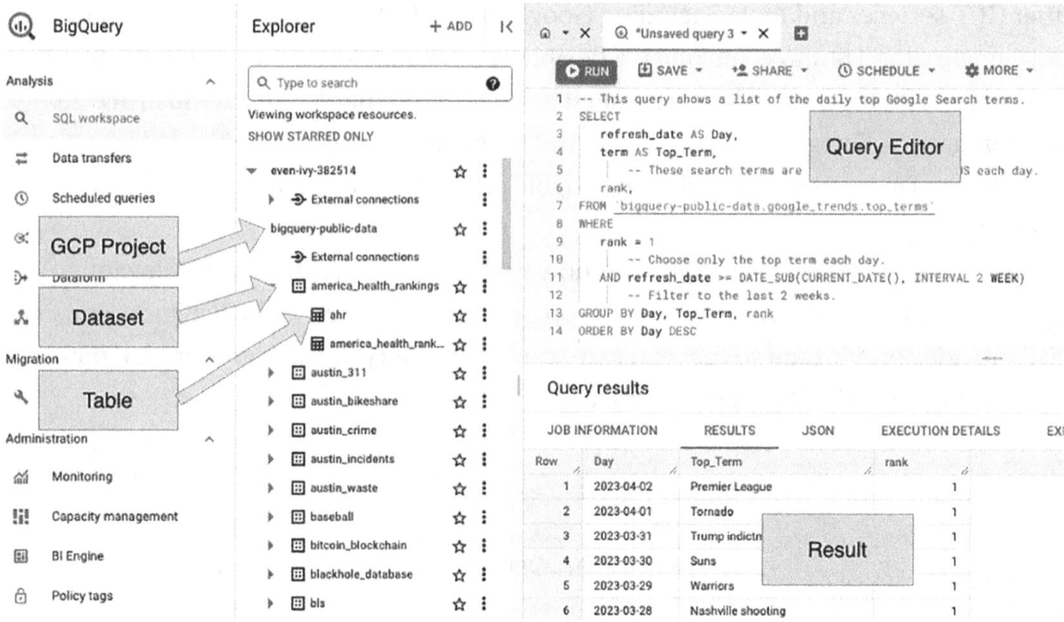

Figure 1-20. *BigQuery Explorer*

BigQuery also supports views within a dataset, which are virtual tables representing a subset of data from one or more tables. Views can provide a different view of the data in the tables or combine data from multiple tables.

Internally, data in BigQuery is organized using a columnar storage format, meaning that data is stored and processed by columns rather than rows. This allows for fast querying and efficient use of resources, especially for large datasets.

BigQuery can be used to integrate data from different sources, which can be useful for creating a single view of your data. It can be used for data warehousing because it can store large amounts of data and is fast at running queries. You can use it to create dashboards and reports that provide insights into your business data. The large amount of data from BigQuery can be used to train machine learning models or perform data analysis to find patterns in your data.

Google Cloud SQL

Google Cloud SQL is a fully managed relational database service provided by Google Cloud Platform. It supports SQL databases such as MySQL, PostgreSQL, and SQL Server. Cloud SQL provides an easy-to-use web interface for managing databases, as well as a number of tools and APIs for integrating with other Google Cloud Platform services. Some of the benefits of using Cloud SQL include automatic backups, high availability, and scalability, allowing you to focus on developing your applications instead of managing infrastructure. Additionally, Cloud SQL is secure and compliant with industry standards, so you can trust that your data is protected. Figure 1-21 shows the cloud SQL dashboard.

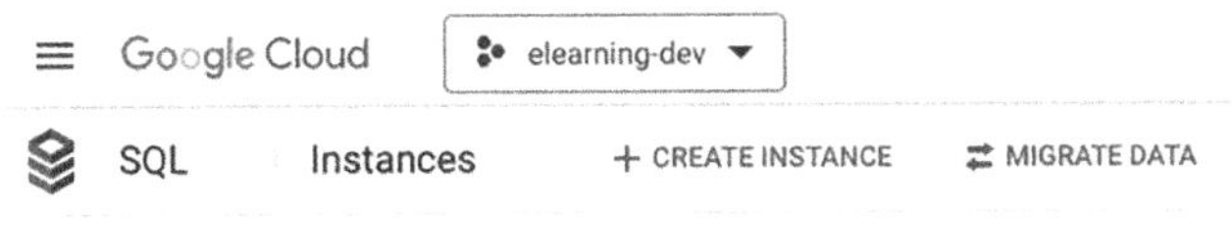

***Figure 1-21.** Cloud SQL*

You can create instances for MySQL, PostgreSQL, or SQL Server in Google Cloud SQL. You can migrate your data to Cloud SQL using the data migration service.

You need to enable the Database Migration API to use the data migration service for migrating data to Cloud SQL, as shown in Figure 1-22.

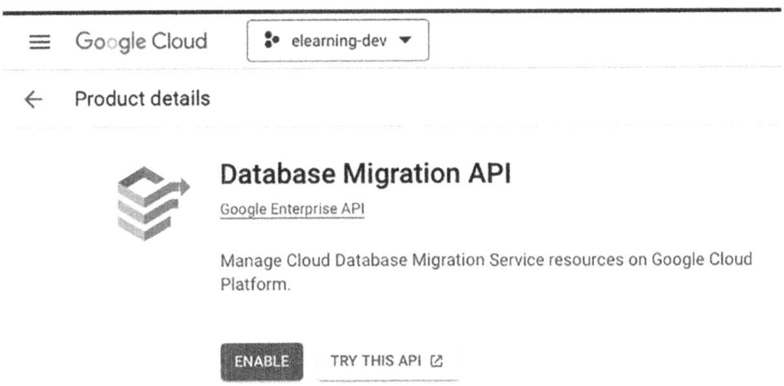

***Figure 1-22.** Database Migration API*

Once it's enabled, you can create a data migration job to start migrating data to GCP. Figure 1-23 shows the Database Migration dashboard.

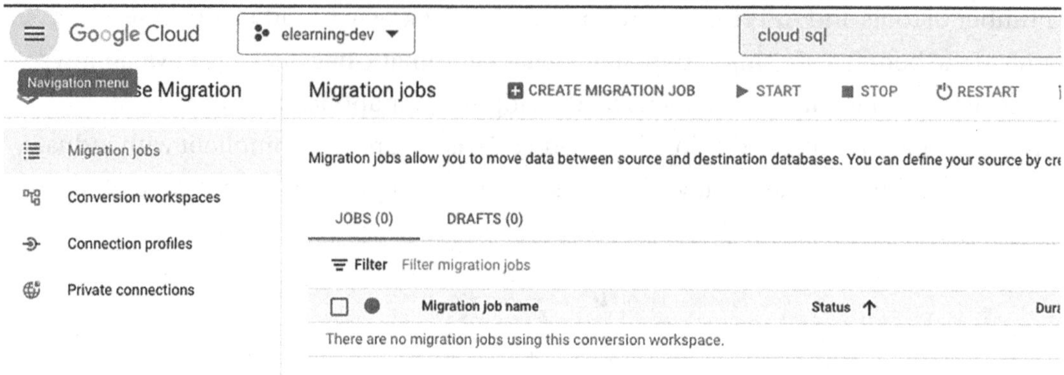

Figure 1-23. *Database Migration dashboard*

The Database Migration Service (DMS) is a fully managed service that allows you to migrate your on-premises databases, or databases running on other cloud platforms, to Google Cloud Platform. With DMS, you can perform one-time or ongoing migrations of your databases with minimal downtime and disruption to your business operations.

DMS is a fully managed service with minimal downtime, it supports live and offline migration, and you can keep running your business while the migration is taking place. It supports migrating multiple on-premises and cloud databases, including MySQL, PostgreSQL, SQL Server, and Oracle to Cloud SQL or Spanner.

If you decided to create a new instance, click the "Create an instance" button. It will ask you which database engine you are trying to create the instance for, as shown in Figure 1-24.

Figure 1-24. *Creating a cloud SQL instance*

For example, if you choose MySQL, it will configure MySQL based on the option you select for your server, such as which region, single zone or multizone, machine type, etc.

GCP introduced a new AlloyDB for an open-source PostgreSQL-compatible database service. AlloyDB offers some features that are not available in Cloud SQL, such as point-in-time recovery and automatic vacuuming and compression.

The choice between Cloud SQL and AlloyDB will depend on your specific needs and requirements. Cloud SQL can be a good choice if you need a MySQL-compatible database service. If you need a PostgreSQL-compatible database service, then AlloyDB can be a good choice. If you need a database service that offers the latest features and technology, then AlloyDB can be a good choice. Cloud SQL is generally less expensive than AlloyDB for workloads that do not require a lot of data processing. However, AlloyDB can be more cost-effective for workloads requiring much data processing.

Google Cloud Spanner

Google Cloud Spanner is a highly scalable, globally distributed, and managed relational database service offered by Google Cloud. It is designed to provide horizontal scalability and strong consistency across all nodes, making it a great choice for applications that require strong consistency and high performance. With its support for SQL, transactions, and secondary indexes, Spanner provides familiar database abstractions, making it easy for developers to use and integrate into existing applications. Spanner's globally distributed architecture, automatic failover, and low latency make it ideal for high-availability and mission-critical applications. With its scalability, reliability, and consistency, Cloud Spanner offers a cost-effective and scalable alternative to traditional relational databases for organizations looking to modernize their data architecture and migrate their applications to the cloud.

Even with the $300, 90-day trial of GCP, you can start a separate free trial for Cloud Spanner for 90 days. You get 10 GB of storage that is not charged against your credits.

By clicking the Start a Free Trial button, as shown in Figure 1-25, you can create a Spanner instance by providing the instance name, instance ID, and location in the configuration.

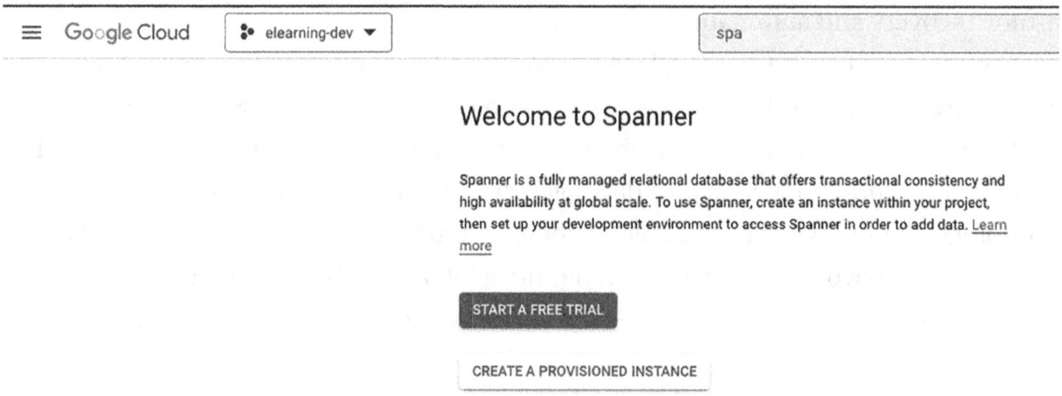

Figure 1-25. *Cloud Spanner*

When creating a Cloud Spanner instance (see Figure 1-26), specify the number of nodes you want to use to run the database. Each node provides a certain amount of computing and storage resources, and the more nodes you use, the more computing and storage resources you have available to run your database.

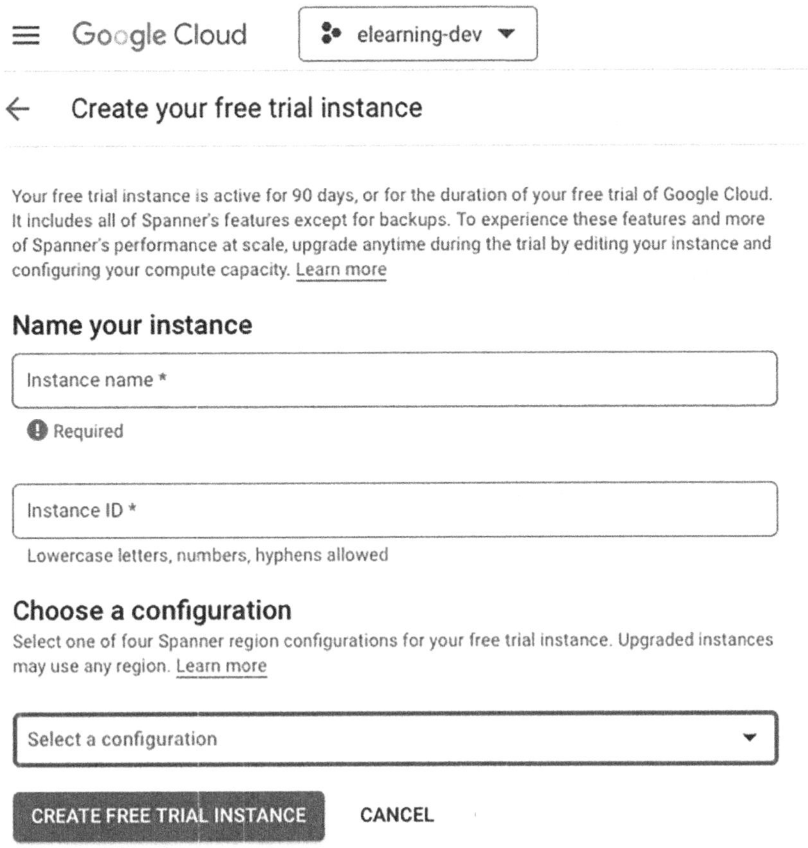

Figure 1-26. *Creating an instance for Spanner*

A node is a unit of computing and storage resources that runs as part of the Cloud Spanner service. A node can be considered a virtual machine optimized for running the Cloud Spanner software.

Cloud Spanner uses a distributed architecture to provide high availability and scalability. The database is partitioned into shards, which are distributed across multiple nodes. Each node stores a portion of the data and processes queries for that portion of the data. This allows Cloud Spanner to handle large databases and complex queries at high speed.

Cloud Spanner also provides strong consistency across all nodes and shards. This means that all clients will see the same data at the same time, even under heavy loads. To achieve strong consistency, Cloud Spanner uses a distributed commit protocol that ensures that all nodes agree on the order in which transactions are committed.

After creating an instance for Cloud Spanner, you can use it without worrying about scaling and still get the benefits of the ACID properties of RDBMSs like with MySQL.

Google Cloud Dataflow

Google Cloud Dataflow is a fully managed service for transforming and analyzing data in real time. It is designed to help developers process and analyze data from various sources, such as batch and streaming data. Cloud Dataflow allows developers to build data processing pipelines using a high-level, simple API that supports both batch and stream processing. It offers a number of features for optimizing the performance and scalability of data processing pipelines, including automatic parallel processing, optimized data movement, and integrated error handling. Additionally, Dataflow integrates with other Google Cloud Platform services such as BigQuery, Cloud Storage, and Cloud Pub/Sub, allowing developers to easily analyze and store data in the cloud.

You can create batch or streaming data jobs, create a data pipeline, and save the state of a streaming pipeline in snapshots. Figure 1-27 shows the Dataflow dashboard.

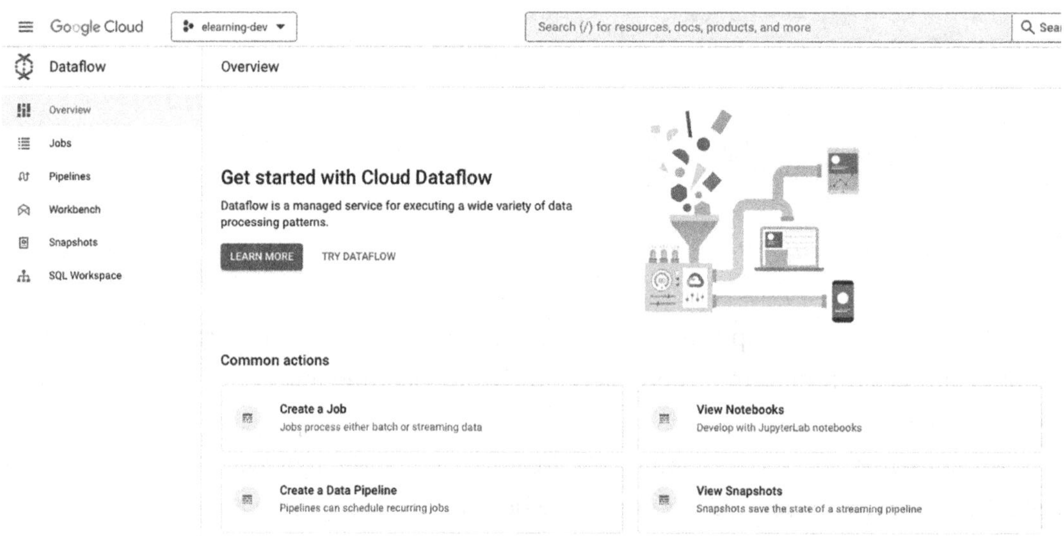

***Figure 1-27.** Cloud Dataflow dashboard*

To create any new job, you need to enable the Dataflow API for your project if it's not already enabled; Figure 1-28 shows the Enable button.

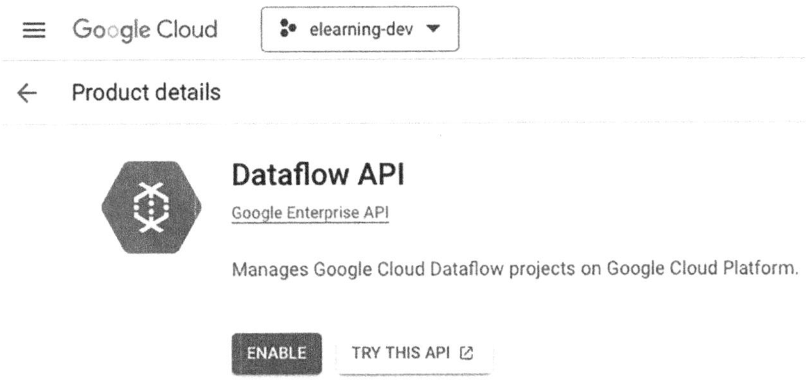

Figure 1-28. *Enabling the Dataflow API*

Dataflow internally used Apache Beam, and it has a few prebuilt templates for creating jobs that cover most common scenarios. You can create a Dataflow job using a prebuilt template or create a template based on your project needs. Figure 1-29 shows how to create a Dataflow job from the template.

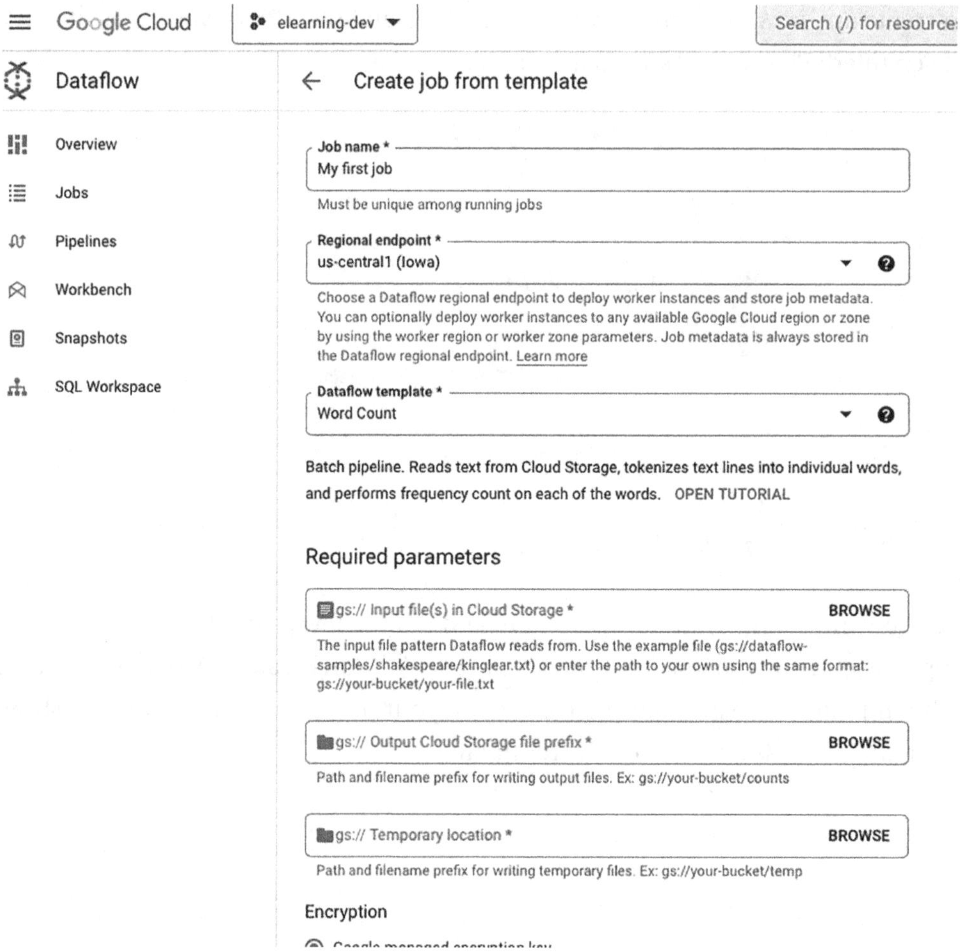

Figure 1-29. *Creating a job from templete*

To create a Cloud Dataflow pipeline, you need to first decide where your data is coming from, like a file or a database. Then, you'll write code in a supported programming language to define how your data will be processed, such as by filtering or grouping. Once your code is written, you'll package it up into a format that can be distributed and executed on the Cloud Dataflow service.

Vertex AI

Vertex AI is a managed machine learning platform for developing, training, and deploying machine learning models. It provides cloud-based infrastructure for running large-scale machine learning workflows and offers various services, including hosting models, training algorithms, and deploying machine learning applications. The platform is designed for data scientists and machine learning engineers who need to quickly and easily build and deploy complex models at scale. With Vertex AI, users can take advantage of Google's infrastructure and expertise in machine learning and focus on their core task of developing models without worrying about managing the underlying infrastructure.

For example, you can use Vertex AI to create a recommendation engine. You can get predictions through batch requests by using the data provided and machine learning. Figure 1-30 shows the Vertex AI dashboard.

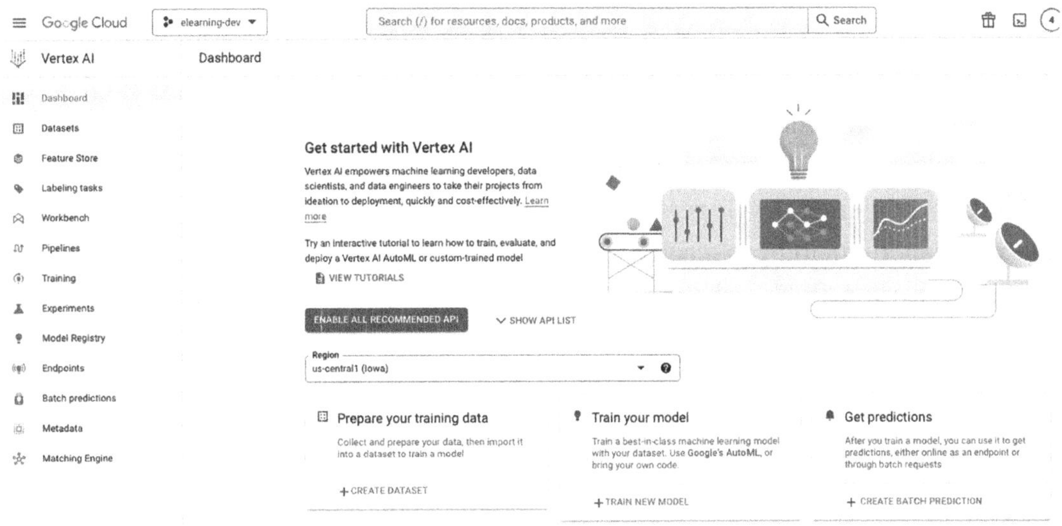

Figure 1-30. *Vettex AI dashboard*

There are machine learning APIs (ML APIs) that have the Cloud Vision API, Video Intelligence API, and Product Search API, as shown in Figure 1-31.

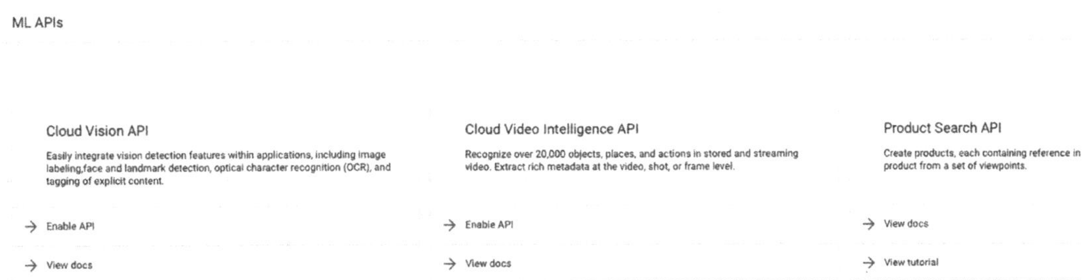

Figure 1-31. *MP APIs*

Vertex AI provides prebuilt models and tools for common machine learning tasks, such as image and text classification. This means you can use these prebuilt models to get started quickly, without needing to develop your own models from scratch.

Google Cloud Translation API

The Google Cloud Translation API is a cloud-based machine translation service offered by Google Cloud. It can translate text between different languages, including English, Spanish, French, German, Chinese, and many others. The API uses advanced machine learning techniques to provide accurate and natural-sounding translations. It is used to translate text in various use cases, including websites, mobile apps, customer service, and document translation. The API is easy to use and can be easily integrated into a wide range of web and mobile applications through a simple API request. With the Google Cloud Translation API, developers can quickly and easily add multilingual support to their applications, helping to reach a wider global audience.

If you are using the Translation API for the first time in your GCP project, you need to enable it, as shown in Figure 1-32.

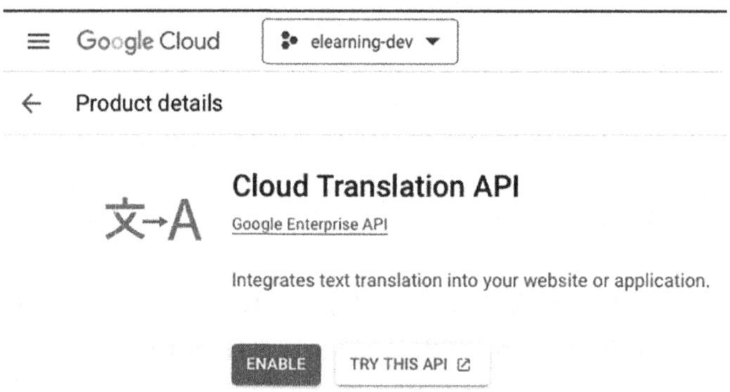

Figure 1-32. *Enabling the Translation API*

Once it's enabled, you can use this API in your project or web application to translate the string or text from one language to another. You can see the traffic on the dashboard, as shown in Figure 1-33.

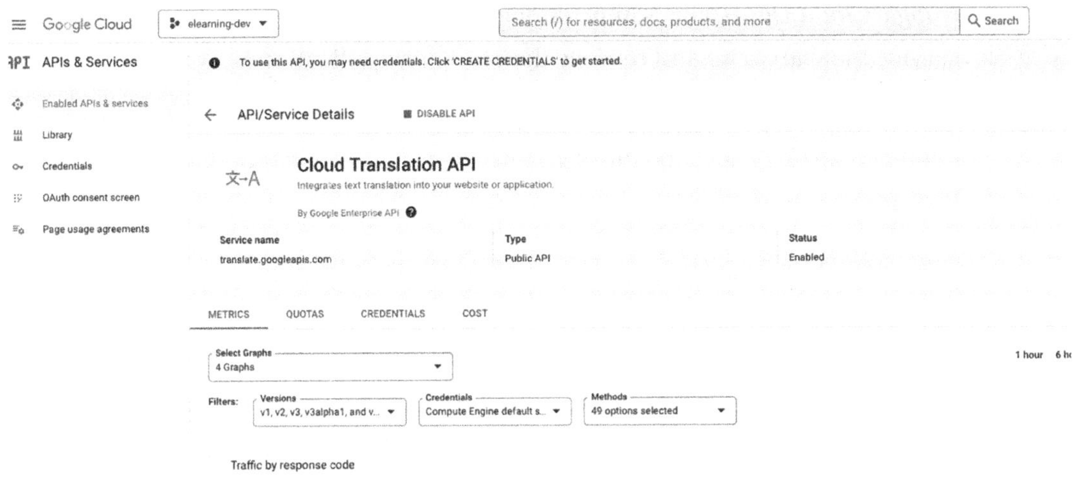

Figure 1-33. *Cloud Translation API dashboard*

The Cloud Translation API supports more than 100 languages and can translate text between any of these languages. You can also customize the translation model to improve the accuracy of translations for your specific use case.

GCP offers many other services to suit different use cases and businesses.

Now that you have a sense of the many services available through GCP, I'm going to give you a high-level overview of the Java programming language.

Overview of Java and Its Capabilities

Java is a popular programming language used to build various applications on the GCP. In addition, the GCP provides many services and tools you can use in conjunction with Java to build, deploy, and scale applications. The following are some examples of GCP services for Java applications:

- *Google App Engine*: A fully managed platform for building and hosting web applications in various languages, including Java.
- *Google Cloud Storage*: A fully managed object storage service that can store and retrieve data for Java applications.
- *Google Cloud SQL*: A fully managed relational database service that can store and retrieve data for Java applications.

- *Google Cloud Datastore*: A fully managed NoSQL document database service that can store and retrieve data for Java applications.
- *Google Cloud Bigtable*: A fully managed, high-performance NoSQL database service that can store and retrieve large amounts of data for Java applications.
- *Google Kubernetes Engine*: You can create a fully managed Kubernetes cluster using GKE. You can deploy containerized java applications to the Google Kubernetes Engine.

The GCP also provides several tools and libraries that can be used to build, deploy, and scale Java applications, including the Google Cloud SDK for Java, which provides a set of command-line tools and libraries for interacting with GCP services. Let's talk about the benefits of using Java for application development for GCP.

The Benefits of Using GCP for Application Development

GCP provides a range of tools and services for developing and deploying Java applications. It offers a scalable, secure, and cost-effective solution for organizations of all sizes. In this book, we will explore the benefits of using GCP for Java development and how to design, build, and optimize Java applications on the GCP platform.

One of the key benefits of using GCP for Java development is scalability. GCP provides automatic scaling and load balancing to ensure that your application can handle spikes in traffic and provide consistent performance. This eliminates the need for manual intervention and allows developers to focus on building new features and improving their applications.

Another benefit of using GCP is security. GCP provides a secure infrastructure and a range of security features, such as access control and encryption, to help keep your applications and data secure. This reduces the risk of data breaches and helps ensure that sensitive information remains confidential.

GCP also offers a range of tools and services for monitoring and logging, making it easier to identify and resolve performance issues. With GCP, you can easily monitor the performance of your applications and get insights into how users are interacting with them. This can help you identify areas for improvement and optimize the performance of your applications.

GCP provides cost-effective and flexible pricing options, allowing you to pay only for what you need. This makes it easier to control costs and provides a more flexible solution for organizations with changing needs.

GCP offers a comprehensive and cost-effective solution for various programming languages including Java development, with a range of tools and services to help organizations build, deploy, and optimize their applications. GCP provides a BOM specifically for Java development called the Google Cloud Libraries BOM. This BOM lists all the libraries and dependencies required for building and running Java applications on GCP, including popular libraries such as Spring, Apache Beam, and others.

In the following chapters, we will explore these benefits in more detail and provide examples and best practices for designing, building, and optimizing Java applications on GCP.

Overview of Microservices

Microservices architecture is a way of building software applications by breaking them down into smaller, independent, and self-contained services, as illustrated in Figure 1-34. Each microservice has its own specific functionality, communicates with other services via APIs, and can be developed, deployed, and scaled independently. The microservices approach allows for faster and more agile development, improved scalability and resiliency, and easier maintenance and evolution of the application.

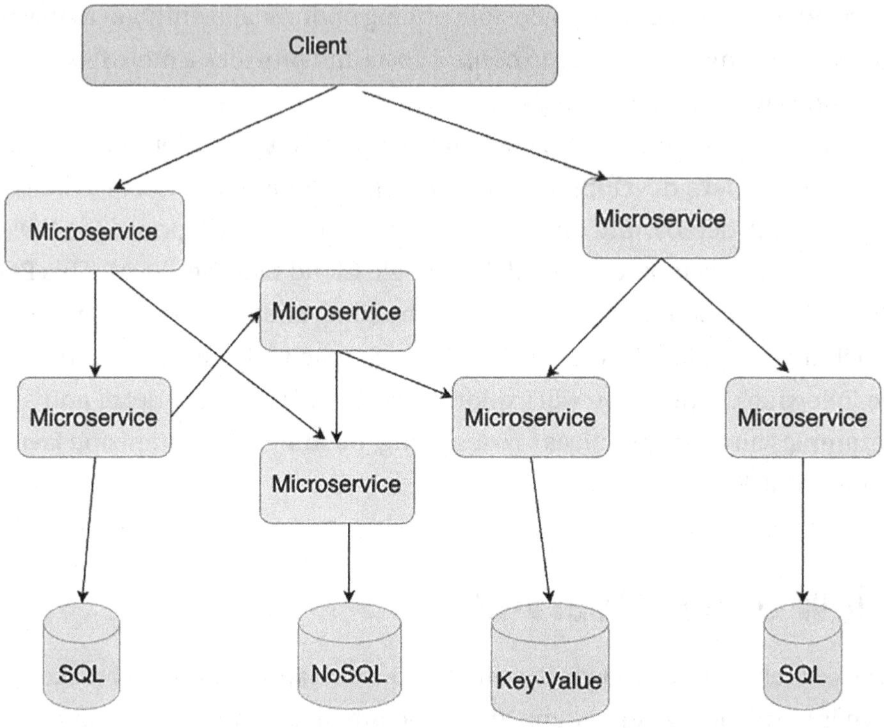

Figure 1-34. *Microservices architecture*

In a microservices architecture, different microservices can be developed using different programming languages and technologies, making it easier to adopt the best tool for the job. Java is a popular choice for developing microservices, as it offers a wealth of tools, frameworks, and libraries for building scalable and reliable applications.

GCP provides a number of services and tools that are well suited for developing and deploying Java-based microservices. For example, Google Kubernetes Engine provides a managed environment for deploying and scaling containerized applications, while Operations Suite provides powerful monitoring and logging capabilities for Java applications running on GCP. Additionally, GCP provides a variety of database options, including Cloud SQL, Cloud Datastore, and Cloud Spanner, which can be used to store data for microservices.

Using GCP for Java development can provide many benefits, including access to a range of powerful and scalable services, a streamlined development and deployment process, and the ability to easily scale and monitor applications.

Summary

In this chapter, I introduced Google Cloud Platform and the benefits it provides for Java development. I explained how GCP offers scalability, security, monitoring and logging, and flexible pricing options, which can help organizations build, deploy, and optimize their Java applications. I also discussed the microservices architecture, which is a way of building software applications by breaking them down into smaller, independent, and self-contained services, and how Java is a popular choice for developing microservices. I concluded by explaining how GCP provides many services and tools that are well suited for developing and deploying Java-based microservices and how using GCP for Java development can provide many benefits, including access to powerful and scalable services, a streamlined development and deployment process, and the ability to scale and monitor applications easily.

Here are some resources for further reference:

- *Cloud-Based Microservices*: `https://link.springer.com/book/10.1007/978-1-4842-6564-2`
- *Google Cloud Documentation*: `https://cloud.google.com/docs`
- *GCP Pricing Calculator*: `https://cloud.google.com/products/calculator`
- *GCP resource hierarchy*: `https://cloud.google.com/resource-manager/docs/cloud-platform-resource-hierarchy`

CHAPTER 2

Setting Up the Development Environment

In this chapter, I focus on setting up a development environment for Java on GCP. I cover the necessary steps to install the Java Development Kit (JDK), an integrated development environment (IDE), and the Google Cloud SDK. I also explain how to create a GCP project, set up credentials, and configure the GCP plugin for different IDEs. Finally, this chapter provides instructions for setting up credentials and configuring the GCP plugin for IntelliJ IDEA, Eclipse, and Visual Studio Code.

To set up a Java development environment for GCP, you will need to perform the following steps:

1. Install the JDK on your local machine. You can download the JDK from the official Oracle website or download Open JDK.

2. Install an IDE of your choice, such as Eclipse or IntelliJ IDEA. These IDEs will provide a user-friendly interface for writing and debugging your Java code.

3. Install the Google Cloud SDK, which provides a command-line interface for interacting with GCP services. The SDK can be downloaded from the Google Cloud website.

4. Install the Google Cloud SDK for Java, which provides a set of libraries and tools for developing Java applications on GCP.

5. Create a new project in your IDE and configure it to use the Google Cloud SDK for Java. This will allow you to use GCP services and libraries in your Java code.

A. Shashi, *Designing Applications for Google Cloud Platform*, https://doi.org/10.1007/978-1-4842-9511-3_2

6. Create a new project in the GCP Console; this will give you credentials to access the GCP services, such as Storage, Bigtable, Datastore, etc.
7. Once your project is set up, you can start writing Java code to interact with GCP services. You can use the Google Cloud SDK for Java to perform tasks such as uploading and downloading data from Google Cloud Storage, querying data from Google Cloud SQL or Google Cloud Datastore, and more.
8. You can also use GCP services such as App Engine, Kubernetes Engine, etc., to deploy your Java application.

Note The previous steps might vary depending on your specific use case and requirements.

Installing the GCP SDK and Java Development Kit

The Google Cloud SDK can be installed on various operating systems, including Windows, macOS, and Linux.

You can install the SDK via a package manager such as `apt-get`, `yum`, etc. Another way to install SDK in a virtual environment is by using the `gcloud` command-line tool to install the SDK in a specific directory.

Here are the general steps to install the SDK on your local machine by downloading it manually:

1. Download the Cloud SDK installer for your operating system from the Google Cloud SDK website.

   For example, you can download the macOS M1 chip by using the following link. You will see the package to download and install it, as shown in Figure 2-1.

   `https://cloud.google.com/sdk/docs/install`

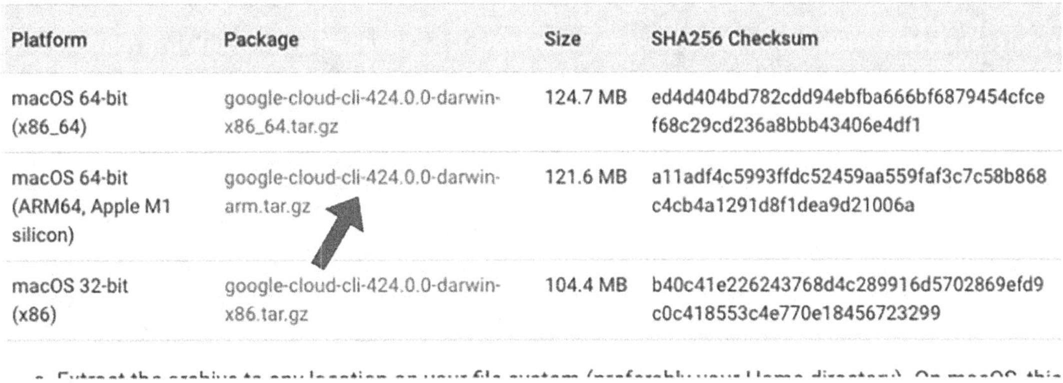

Platform	Package	Size	SHA256 Checksum
macOS 64-bit (x86_64)	google-cloud-cli-424.0.0-darwin-x86_64.tar.gz	124.7 MB	ed4d404bd782cdd94ebfba666bf6879454cfcef68c29cd236a8bbb43406e4df1
macOS 64-bit (ARM64, Apple M1 silicon)	google-cloud-cli-424.0.0-darwin-arm.tar.gz	121.6 MB	a11adf4c5993ffdc52459aa559faf3c7c58b868c4cb4a1291d8f1dea9d21006a
macOS 32-bit (x86)	google-cloud-cli-424.0.0-darwin-x86.tar.gz	104.4 MB	b40c41e226243768d4c289916d5702869efd9c0c418553c4e770e18456723299

Figure 2-1. *Cloud SDK installer*

2. Run the installer and follow the prompts to install the SDK. The installer will also install the `gcloud` command-line tool, which interacts with GCP services, as shown in Figure 2-2.

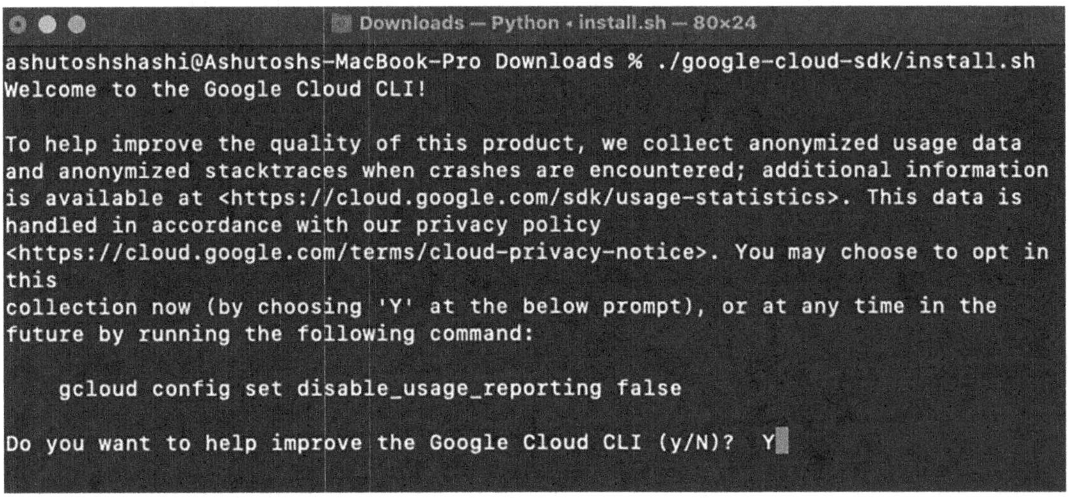

Figure 2-2. *Installing the Google Cloud CLI*

3. After the installation, open a command-line terminal and run the command `gcloud init` to initialize the SDK. This command will prompt you to log in to your Google account and select a project to use with the SDK, as shown in Figure 2-3.

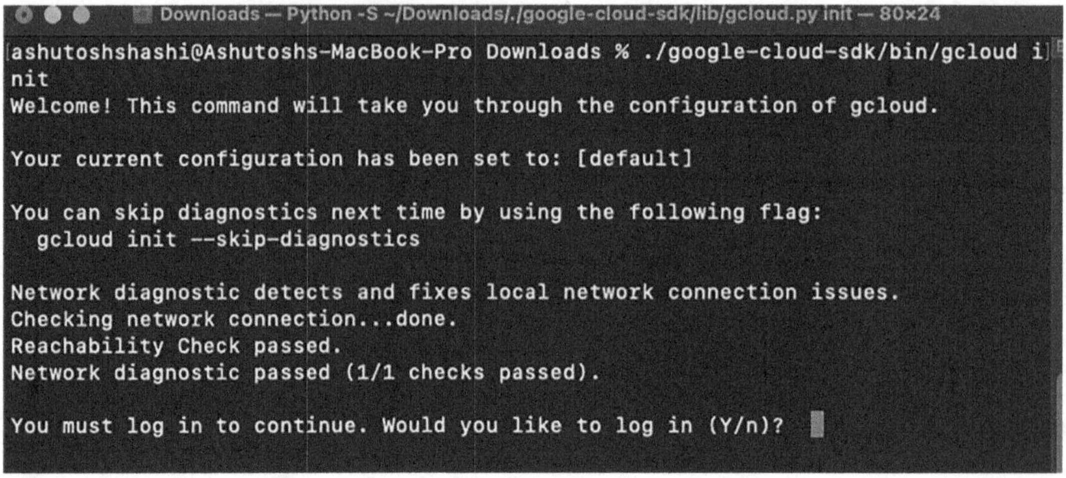

Figure 2-3. *Initialization with the gcloud init command*

4. Verify that the SDK is installed correctly by running the command `gcloud version`. This will display the version number of the SDK and other installed components, as shown in Figure 2-4.

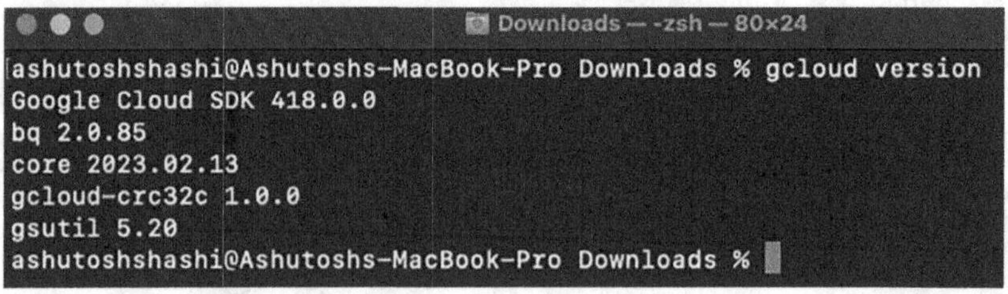

Figure 2-4. *Checking the cloud SDK version*

Note You can refer to the Google Cloud SDK documentation for updated instructions.

Installing Java (Oracle) JDK

To install the latest version of Oracle Java JDK, you can follow these steps:

1. Go to Oracle's official Java website: `https://www.oracle.com/java/technologies/javase-downloads.html`.
2. Click the Download button next to the 17.0.6 version of the JDK.
3. Select the JDK version 17.0.6 for your operating system (Windows, Mac, Linux, etc.).
4. Follow the prompts to complete the installation process.

It is also important to note that you may have to set the `JAVA_HOME` environment variable and add the JDK's `bin` folder to your system's `PATH` variable to use the JDK from the command line.

The Oracle Java JDK is an Oracle proprietary tool. If you are building a business application that will run on your production server, you may need a license from Oracle. If you want to use open-source Java, you can install Open JDK for development.

Installing Java Open JDK

To install the latest version of OpenJDK (the open-source version of the Java Development Kit), you can follow these steps:

1. Go to any vendor site that provides OpenJDK. You can download OpenJDK from `https://adoptium.net/temurin/releases/?version=17`.
2. Click the appropriate link to download the installer for your operating system (Windows, Mac, Linux, etc.).
3. Follow the prompts to complete the installation process.

Alternatively, you can install OpenJDK through a package manager if your operating system supports it. For example, on Ubuntu or Debian-based Linux distributions, you can use the command listed in Listing 2-1 to install the latest version of OpenJDK.

Listing 2-1. OpenJDK Installation Through Linux Package Manager

```
sudo apt-get update
sudo apt-get install openjdk-<version number>-jdk
```

You can install OpenJDK on macOS using the `brew` package manager, as given in Listing 2-2.

Listing 2-2. Installing OpenJDK Using the brew Package Manager

```
brew tap AdoptOpenJDK/openjdk
brew install <version number>
```

It is also important to note that you may have to set the `JAVA_HOME` environment variable and add the JDK's `bin` folder to your system's `PATH` variable to use the JDK from the command line.

Creating a GCP Project and Setting Up Credentials

When you use any application, you need to provide your identity or credentials to access it. Similarly, to use Google Cloud Platform (GCP) services, you need to create a GCP project and set up credentials.

Credentials are a set of access keys or tokens that allow you to authenticate and authorize access to GCP services. For example, an API key can allow an application to access a particular API, while a service account key can grant access to all resources within a project.

When you create a project, you will also create a set of credentials that you can use to authenticate and authorize access to GCP services. These credentials can be managed in the GCP Console or through the Google Cloud SDK.

Creating a Project

Creating a GCP project and setting up credentials are essential steps for accessing and using GCP services securely and effectively. They allow you to authenticate and authorize access to GCP services and manage your resources efficiently.

To create a GCP project, follow these steps:

1. Go to the Google Cloud Console (`https://console.cloud.google.com/`).

2. Click the project drop-down and select or create the project you want to use.

3. Click the hamburger menu (☰) and select APIs & Services ➤ Dashboard.

4. Click the Enable APIs and Services button at the top of the page.
5. Search for the API you want to enable and click it.
6. Click the Enable button.
7. Set up the necessary credentials for the API, such as an API key or OAuth client ID.
8. Use the API in your application by referencing the necessary client library and using the credentials you set up.

Alternatively, use the Google Cloud SDK to create and manage projects using a command line. Follow these steps:

1. Install the Google Cloud SDK.
2. Open the command-line interface (CLI) or terminal.
3. Run the command `gcloud init` to initialize the SDK.
4. Run the command `gcloud projects create <project-name>` to create a new project.
5. Run the command `gcloud projects list` to verify that the project was created.
6. Finally, run the command `gcloud config set project <project-name>` to set the active project.

You can now use the SDK to manage your project, such as creating and managing resources and services.

Note You must have a valid billing account and permission to create a project.

Setting Up Credentials

The API key, OAuth client ID, service account, and user account are all types of credentials that are used to authenticate and authorize access to various services on the Google Cloud Platform. These are all different ways to prove that you have permission to access certain resources on Google Cloud Platform.

An *API key* is a simple string that identifies your application to the GCP services. It's usually used to access public data or services that don't require user authentication.

An *OAuth client ID* is used to authenticate and authorize users to access protected resources on behalf of a user. It is used to enable single sign-on (SSO) between your application and GCP services.

A *service account* is a special account used to programmatically access GCP services and resources. Service accounts are usually used for server-to-server interactions and automation.

A *user account* is an account that identifies an individual user and is used to grant them access to GCP resources. User accounts can be created and managed through the Google Cloud Console.

Setting up credentials on the Google Cloud Platform allows your application to authenticate and authorize with the various GCP services. Here are the general steps to set up credentials on GCP:

1. Go to the Google Cloud Console (`https://console.cloud.google.com/`) and navigate to the project you want to set up credentials.

2. Search for credentials and open IAM service account credentials API, as shown in Figure 2-5.

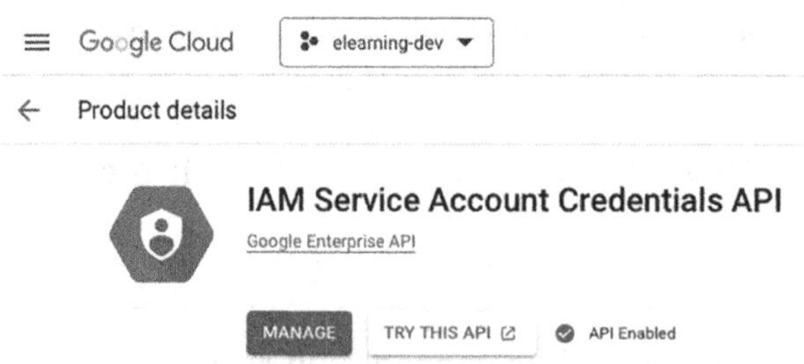

Figure 2-5. *Service Account Credentials API*

Then click Manage. In API and services, you can click Credentials to open the Credentials dashboard, as shown in Figure 2-6.

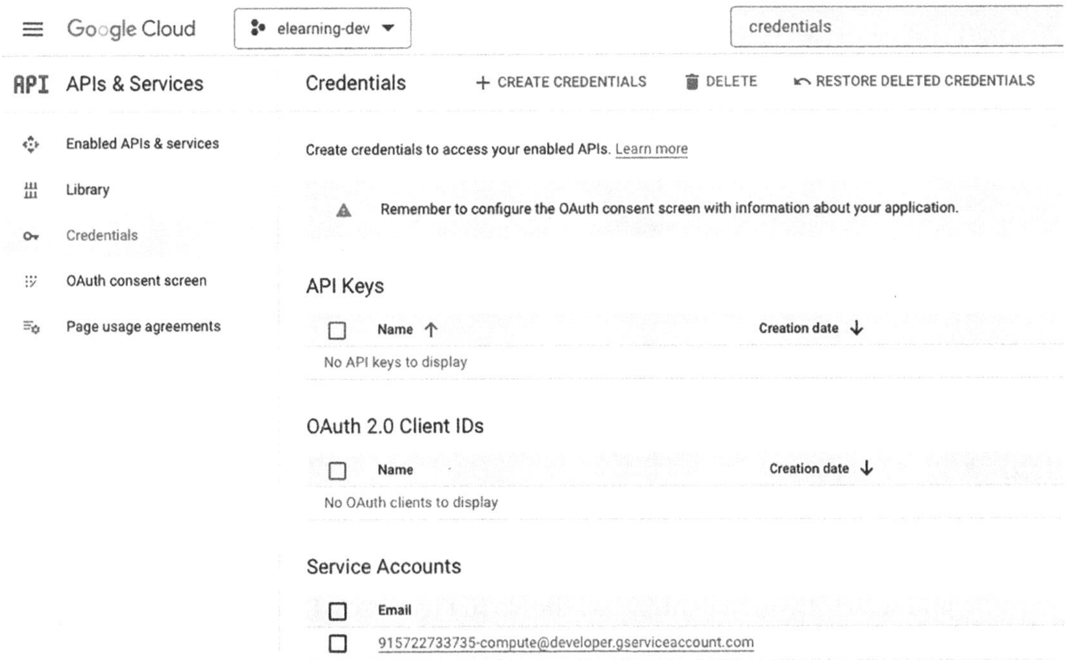

Figure 2-6. *Credentials dashboard*

3. On the Credentials page, you can create different types of credentials, such as an API key, OAuth client ID, or service account key.

4. To create an API key, click the "Create credentials" button and select "API key," as shown in Figure 2-7. The key will be displayed, and you can restrict its usage if desired.

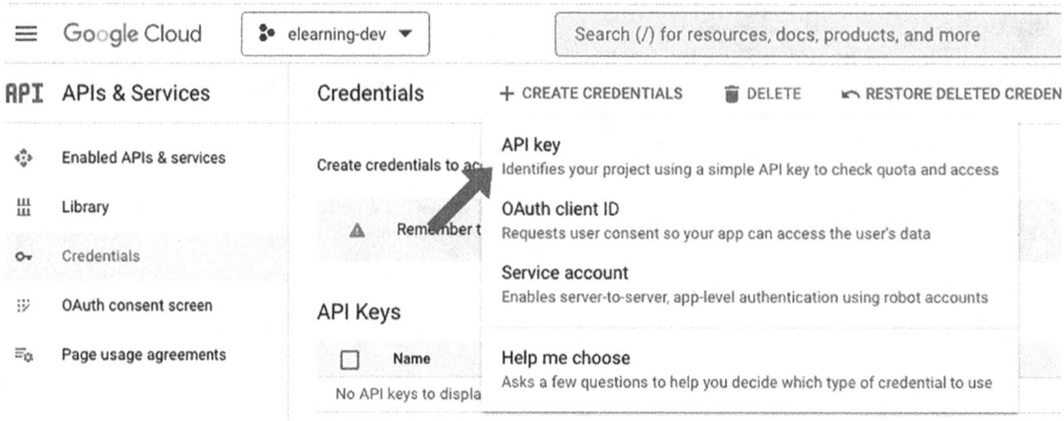

Figure 2-7. *API key*

5. To create an OAuth client ID, click the "Create credentials" button and select "OAuth client ID," as shown in Figure 2-8. Before creating the client ID, you must configure the consent screen and select the application type.

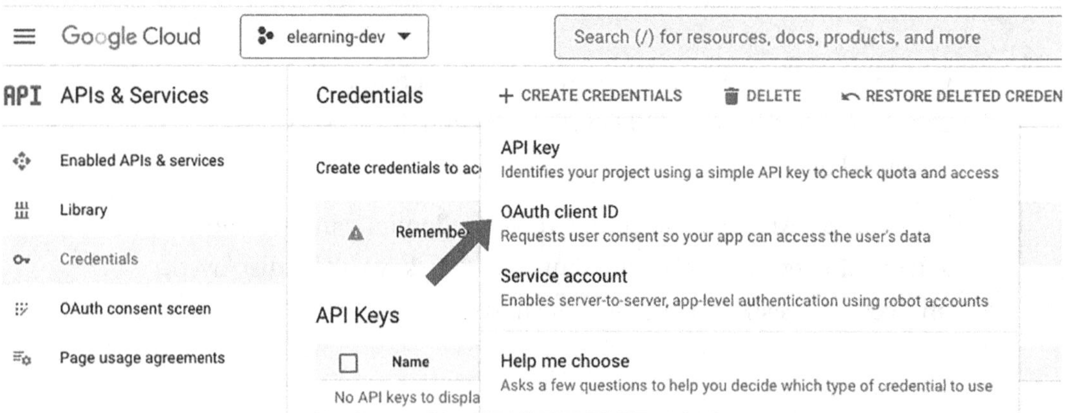

Figure 2-8. *OAuth Client ID*

6. To create a service account key, click the "Create credentials" button and select "Service account key." You will need to select an existing service account or create a new one and then choose the key type and any roles granted to the account.

After creating a service account, it will take you to the IAM & Admin on the GCP Console, as shown in Figure 2-9.

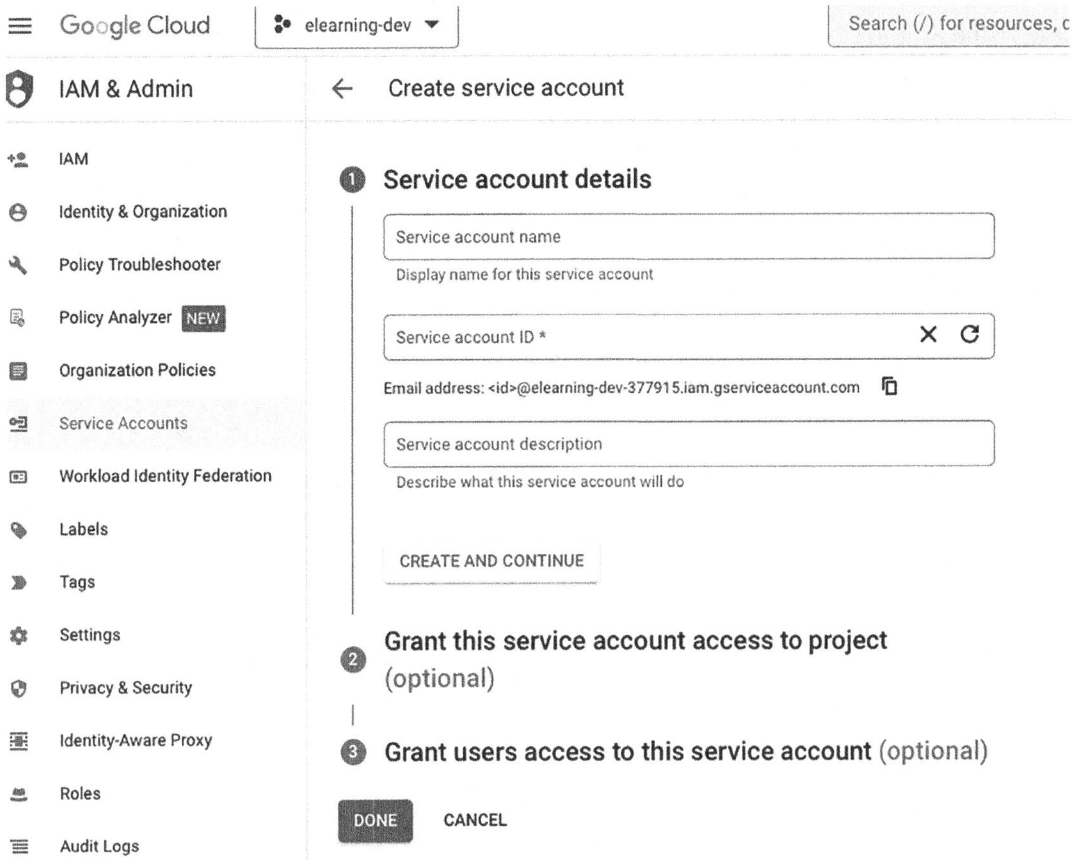

***Figure 2-9.** Creating a service account*

7. Once the credentials are created, you can use them in your application by referencing the necessary client library and using the credentials you set up.

Note Depending on the type of credentials and the service you are trying to use, you may need to grant permissions to the account or key before it can be used.

Setting Up an IDE and Configuring a GCP Plugin

GCP plugins are software tools that can be added to IDEs such as IntelliJ IDEA, Eclipse, and Visual Studio Code to make it easier for developers to interact with GCP services directly from their development environment.

They provide features such as project setup, authentication, debugging, deployment, and management of GCP resources, which helps developers focus on coding and developing their application rather than setting up and configuring GCP services.

GCP plugins make it easy for developers to work with GCP services without leaving their development environment, which improves their productivity and streamlines the development process.

Several IDEs are well-suited for developing Java projects for Google Cloud Platform. The following are some popular options:

- *IntelliJ IDEA*: This popular Java IDE offers strong support for GCP development, including integrating the Google Cloud SDK and deploying applications to App Engine and other GCP services.
- *Eclipse*: Eclipse is another popular Java IDE with a plugin for Google Cloud Development, allowing developers to deploy and manage applications on GCP quickly.
- *Visual Studio Code*: Visual Studio Code is a lightweight and popular code editor that can be used for Java development. It also has a Google Cloud SDK extension that allows developers to deploy and manage their applications on GCP quickly.

Ultimately, the best IDE for your specific needs will depend on your personal preferences and the particular requirements of your project.

Configuring the GCP Plugin

To configure the Google Cloud Platform plugin for your IDE, you will need to follow these general steps:

1. Install the GCP plugin for your specific IDE if it is not installed. This can typically be done through the IDE's plugin marketplace or repository.

2. Open the GCP plugin and sign in to your GCP account.
3. Configure the plugin with your project's credentials, such as the project ID and service account key, and prefer creating a separate service account to configure in your IDE.
4. Set up your desired GCP resources, such as a Cloud SQL instance or a Kubernetes cluster.
5. You may also need to specify the path to the Google Cloud SDK on your local machine if it is not already set.

Note Specific steps may vary depending on your IDE and version of the GCP plugin. You can use dependency manager to add dependency instead of adding GCP plugin to the IDE.

Summary

In this chapter, you learned the essential steps to set up a Java development environment for GCP. You learned to install the Java Development Kit and an IDE of your choice, followed by installing the Google Cloud SDK for Java. Then I explained how to create a GCP project and set up credentials using the Google Cloud Console or the command-line interface. I also covered how to configure the GCP plugin for different IDEs such as IntelliJ IDEA, Eclipse, and Visual Studio Code. Finally, I provided the instructions on how to set up credentials and configure the GCP plugin for each of these IDEs.

Here are some resources for further reference:

- *Google Cloud Java Client Libraries*: `https://cloud.google.com/java/docs/reference`
- *Google Cloud Tools for Eclipse*: `https://cloud.google.com/eclipse/docs`
- *Cloud Code for IntelliJ*: `https://cloud.google.com/code/docs/intellij/install`
- *Cloud Code for VS Code*: `https://cloud.google.com/code/docs/vscode/install`

CHAPTER 3

Google App Engine

In this chapter, you will learn about Google App Engine (GAE), a fully managed platform for developing and deploying web applications and services. GAE allows developers to focus on writing code without worrying about the underlying infrastructure and about scaling the application as traffic increases. The chapter covers the key features of GAE, including the programming languages and frameworks supported, storage options, and deployment methods. You will also learn about scaling and optimizing GAE applications to handle changes in traffic and improve performance. Finally, the chapter covers security considerations and best practices for deploying and managing GAE applications. By the end of this chapter, you will have a comprehensive understanding of Google App Engine and how to use it to develop and deploy web applications.

Google App Engine is a platform-as-a-service (PaaS) offering from Google that allows developers to build and host web applications in a scalable and secure environment. With GAE, developers can build web applications using standard languages and frameworks such as Java, Python, Go, and PHP.

The key feature of GAE is its automatic scaling capabilities, which allows the platform to adjust the number of instances running based on the traffic to the application. This eliminates developers' need to provision and manually manage the underlying infrastructure.

Google App Engine also provides several built-in services and APIs, such as Cloud Datastore (NoSQL), Memcache, and task queues, that can be easily integrated into the application. Additionally, it offers built-in security features such as automatic SSL termination and support for OAuth and OpenID Connect.

GAE also has a free usage tier for small applications and charges for applications that exceed the free usage tier. It is a fully managed platform that simplifies the process of building and deploying web applications while providing high scalability, security, and performance.

A. Shashi, *Designing Applications for Google Cloud Platform*, https://doi.org/10.1007/978-1-4842-9511-3_3

Why Use Google App Engine?

Google App Engine is an excellent choice for web application development in several scenarios.

- *Scalable and high-performance web applications*: GAE's automatic scaling feature ensures that your application can handle many users and requests. Its built-in services and APIs can help you build a high-performance application.
- *Rapid development and deployment*: GAE provides a simple process, allowing developers to focus on writing code without worrying about provisioning and managing infrastructure.
- *Integration with other Google Cloud services*: GAE integrates seamlessly with other Google Cloud services, such as Cloud Storage, Cloud SQL, and BigQuery, allowing developers to build complex, multitier applications.
- *Multilanguage support*: GAE supports multiple languages like Java, Python, Go, PHP, and more, which makes it easy for developers to build web applications using their preferred language.
- *Cost-effective*: GAE has a free usage tier for small applications and charges for applications that exceed the free usage tier.

An example use case of GAE would be a web application for a small business that allows customers to place orders online. The application would need to handle a large number of requests during peak hours and would need to be highly available and scalable. With GAE, the business could easily build and deploy the application. GAE's automatic scaling feature would ensure that the application can handle many users without additional effort.

Use Case of Google App Engine

A good use case for Google App Engine would be a web application that requires high scalability and automatic management. App Engine's PaaS model allows developers to focus on writing code for their applications rather than worrying about the underlying infrastructure. It also allows for easy scaling of resources to accommodate traffic spikes and provides built-in services such as a data store and task queues. Additionally, App Engine integrates well with other Google Cloud Platform services, making it a suitable choice for building a complete, end-to-end solution.

Understanding the Google App Engine Runtime and Service Options

Google App Engine is a platform for developing and hosting web applications in Google-managed data centers. One of the critical features of GAE is the ability to choose a runtime for the application.

GAE Runtime

Runtime is the environment in which the application code runs, and it includes a specific version of a programming language and any necessary libraries or frameworks.

Figure 3-1 shows some of the runtimes currently supported by GAE.

	Second-generation	First-generation
Supported languages	Python 3 Java 11, 17 Node.js PHP 7/8 Ruby Go 1.12+	Python 2.7 Java 8 PHP 5.5 Go 1.11

Figure 3-1. *GAE-supported runtime*

Each runtime has its own set of supported libraries and frameworks, and the choice of the runtime can affect the performance and scalability of the application.

In addition to the runtime, GAE also provides a set of services that can be used by the application, such as a data store for storing data, a task queue for managing background tasks, and a service for sending an email. These services can be accessed using a simple API, abstracting away the underlying infrastructure and allowing developers to focus on writing application code.

GAE also provides built-in support for scaling, load balancing, and automatic failover so that the application can handle many users and traffic without requiring manual configuration or maintenance.

Google App Engine runtime provides a flexible and easy-to-use platform for developing and deploying web applications, with a wide range of language and framework support and built-in services for scaling and infrastructure management.

GAE Service Options

Google App Engine provides a set of services that can be used by applications running on the platform. These services abstract away the underlying infrastructure and provide a simple API for accessing standard functionality, such as data storage and background task processing. The following are some of the main services provided by GAE:

- *Datastore*: This NoSQL data storage service allows you to store and retrieve structured data. It is based on the Google Cloud Datastore and provides automatic scaling and built-in transaction support. You can use the Datastore API to store and retrieve data using a variety of programming languages, including Python, Java, and Go.
- *Cloud SQL*: This service allows you to run a fully managed MySQL or PostgreSQL database on the GAE platform. You can use the standard SQL syntax to perform operations on the database, and it is also fully integrated with other GAE services.
- *Cloud Memorystore*: This service provides a fully managed in-memory data store for GAE applications. It allows you to store data in memory for faster access and is built on top of Redis.
- *Cloud Firestore*: This NoSQL document database service allows you to store, retrieve, and query structured data with real-time synchronization. The data model is based on documents and collections, and the service provides automatic scaling, real-time updates, and offline support.
- *Cloud Storage*: This service allows you to store and retrieve large amounts of unstructured data, such as images, videos, and audio files. It provides automatic scaling and built-in support for data integrity and versioning.

- *Task Queue*: This service allows you to manage background tasks in your application. You can use it to perform tasks asynchronously, such as sending emails, processing images, or updating the datastore.
- *Cloud Pub/Sub*: This service allows you to send and receive messages between GAE applications and other Google Cloud services. It provides a publish-subscribe model for message delivery and can be used for various scenarios, such as event-driven architecture and real-time streaming.
- *Cloud Endpoints*: This service allows you to easily build, deploy, and manage APIs for your GAE applications. It provides built-in support for standard functions such as authentication, monitoring, and logging.
- *Cloud Logging*: This service allows you to collect, search, analyze, and alert on log data from your GAE applications. It provides a unified view of logs from all your GAE services and can be integrated with other Google Cloud services.
- *Cloud Trace*: This service allows you to trace requests propagating through your GAE applications. It provides detailed performance metrics, such as request latency and error rates, and it can be used to identify and fix performance bottlenecks in your application. Cloud Trace provides distributed tracing capabilities for applications running on GAE. Distributed tracing is a technique used to track a request as it travels through multiple services and components of a distributed system. It allows developers to trace a request's path and performance across different services, making identifying and diagnosing issues in a complex system easier.

There are other services are also available, such as Cloud Translation, Cloud Natural Language, Cloud Speech-to-Text, and more. Each of these services provides specific functionality for different use cases and can be used in combination to build powerful, scalable web applications.

Now let us create and deploy a Java web application on Google App Engine.

Building a Web Application for GAE

Developing web applications on Google App Engine involves building and deploying web applications that run on the cloud infrastructure of Google. The process of developing web applications on GAE can be relatively straightforward, especially if you're already familiar with web development and have experience with the tools and technologies used by GAE.

To develop a web application on GAE, you first need to choose a programming language and a runtime environment that are supported by GAE. GAE supports several programming languages, including Java, Python, PHP, Go, and Node.js, and it also provides several runtime environments that you can use to run your web application.

Once you've chosen the programming language and runtime environment, you can begin building your web application using a framework or libraries that are supported by GAE.

After building your web application, you can deploy it to GAE using the GAE command-line tool or the GAE console. The deployment process involves packaging your web application and configuration files into a deployment package and uploading it to GAE. Once your web application is deployed, it can be accessed using a unique URL that is provided by GAE.

Google App Engine (GAE) provides a set of services that can be used by applications running on the platform. These services abstract away the underlying infrastructure and provide a simple API for accessing standard functionality, such as data storage and background task processing.

Creating a Sample Web Application

Creating a sample web application using Java on Google App Engine is a relatively straightforward process. Still, it does require some setup and configuration. Here are the general steps you can follow to create a sample web application:

1. *Install the Google Cloud SDK*: The first step is to install the Google Cloud SDK, a set of tools for working with GAE and other Google Cloud services. You can download the SDK from the Google Cloud website and follow the instructions for installation.

2. *Create a new project*: Once the SDK is installed, you can use the gcloud command-line tool to create a new project.

   gcloud app create --project=[PROJECT-ID]

   This project will contain all the resources needed for your web application, such as the runtime, services, and configuration files. You can use your already created project.

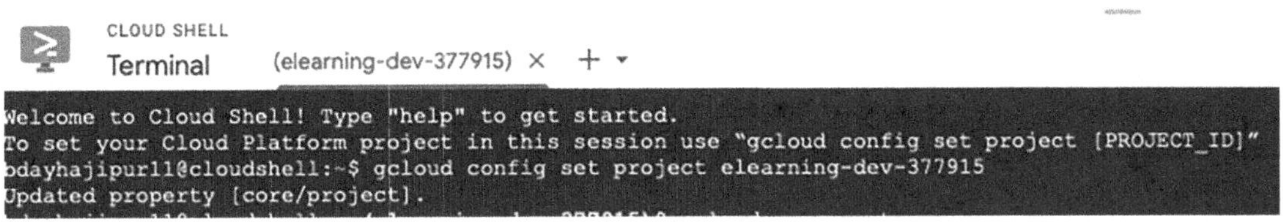

Figure 3-2. *Cloud shell*

3. *Create a new application*: After creating the project, you can use the gcloud command-line tool to create a new application within the project. Figure 3-2 shows the Cloud Shell terminal. This application will be the container for your web application code, and it will have a unique URL that you can use to access it.

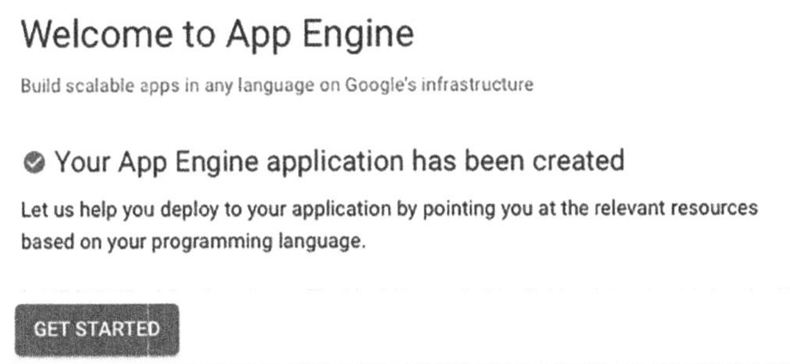

Figure 3-3. *App Engine application creation*

4. *Create a new module*: Once you have created the application, you can create a new module within the application. This module will contain the code for your web application and will be configured to use the Java runtime.

5. *Write the application code*: You can now write the code for your web application using Java. You can use any Java framework or library you like, such as Spring or JSP, but you will also need to use the GAE Java SDK to access the services provided by GAE.

6. Make sure that you have required IAM permission. You can check the Cloud Build Settings page to make sure that the App Engine Admin role and Service Account User role are enabled. If not, you should enable them, as shown in Figure 3-4.

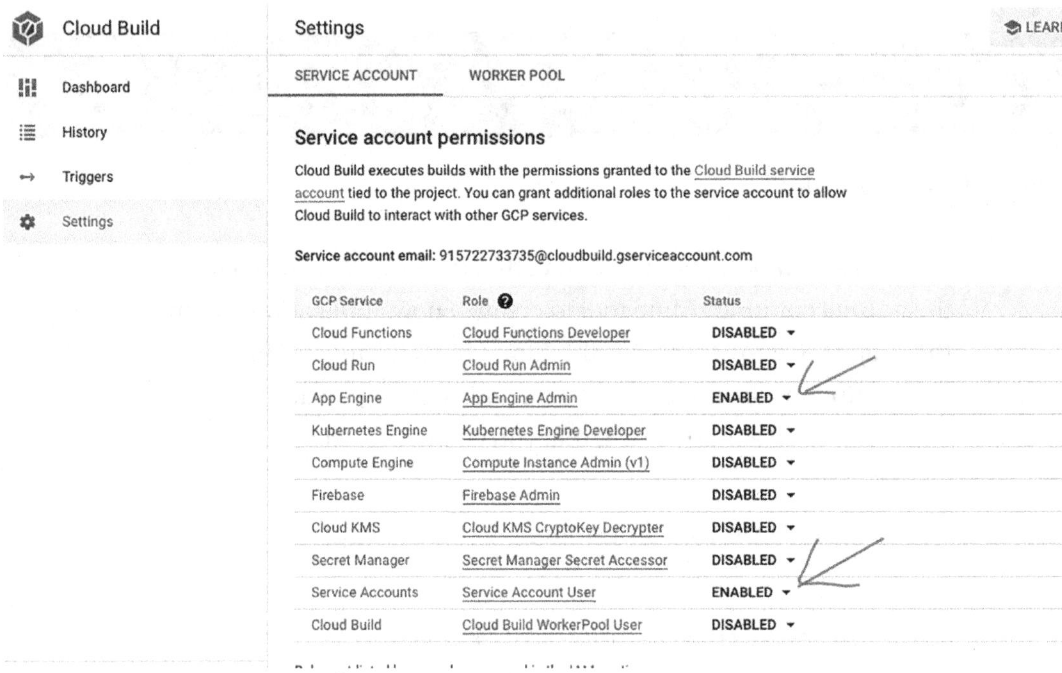

Figure 3-4. *IAM permission*

7. *Deploy the application*: Once the code is written, you can use the `gcloud` command-line tool to deploy the application to GAE. The tool will package the code and configuration files and then upload them to the GAE servers, as shown in Listing 3-1.

Listing 3-1. Deploying the Application on GAE

```
bdayhajipur11@cloudshell:~ (elearning-dev-377915)$ gcloud app deploy
Services to deploy:
```

```
descriptor:                  [/home/bdayhajipur11/app.yaml]
source:                      [/home/bdayhajipur11]
target project:              [elearning-dev-377915]
target service:              [default]
target version:              [20230226t202402]
target url:                  [https://elearning-dev-377915.
                             uc.r.appspot.com]
target service account:      [App Engine default service account]

Do you want to continue (Y/n)?  y

Beginning deployment of service [default]...
Uploading 16 files to Google Cloud Storage
6%
12%
19%
25%
31%
38%
44%
50%
56%
62%
69%
75%
81%
88%
94%
100%
100%
File upload done.
Updating service [default]...done.
Setting traffic split for service [default]...done.
Deployed service [default] to [https://elearning-dev-377915.
uc.r.appspot.com]

You can stream logs from the command line by running:
```

```
  $ gcloud app logs tail -s default

To view your application in the web browser run:
  $ gcloud app browse
bdayhajipur11@cloudshell:~ (elearning-dev-377915)$
```

8. *Test the application*: Once the application is deployed, you can use the URL of your application to access it and test it. You can also use the GAE console to view the logs and monitor the performance of your application, as shown in Figure 3-5.

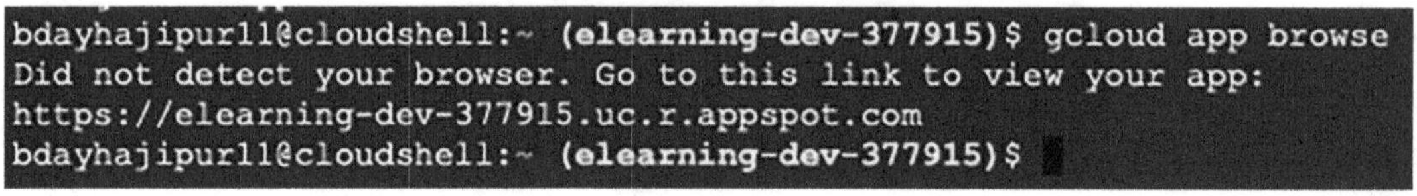

Figure 3-5. *Access deployed app*

You can follow the previous steps to create a sample web application using Java on GAE. The exact details of the process will depend on the specific requirements of your application, such as the framework you choose and the services you need to use.

Google also provides several sample applications with different languages and frameworks that you can use as a starting point and reference. You can find them at `https://github.com/GoogleCloudPlatform/java-docs-samples`.

Deploying a Web Application

Here is a step-by-step example of deploying a web application on the Google App Engine:

1. Create a new project in the Google Cloud Console or use the existing one.
2. Install the Google Cloud SDK and initialize it with your project (not needed if you have already done this).
3. Create a new directory for your web application and navigate to it in the command line.

Clicking Create Application will take you to the Create Application dashboard, as shown in Figure 3-6.

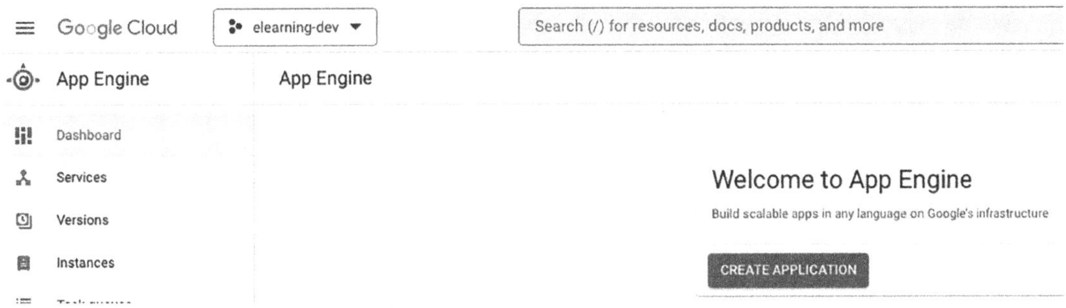

Figure 3-6. *App Engine Dashboard*

Now select the region and select the service account. If no service account is selected, then it will use the default permissions, as shown in Figure 3-7.

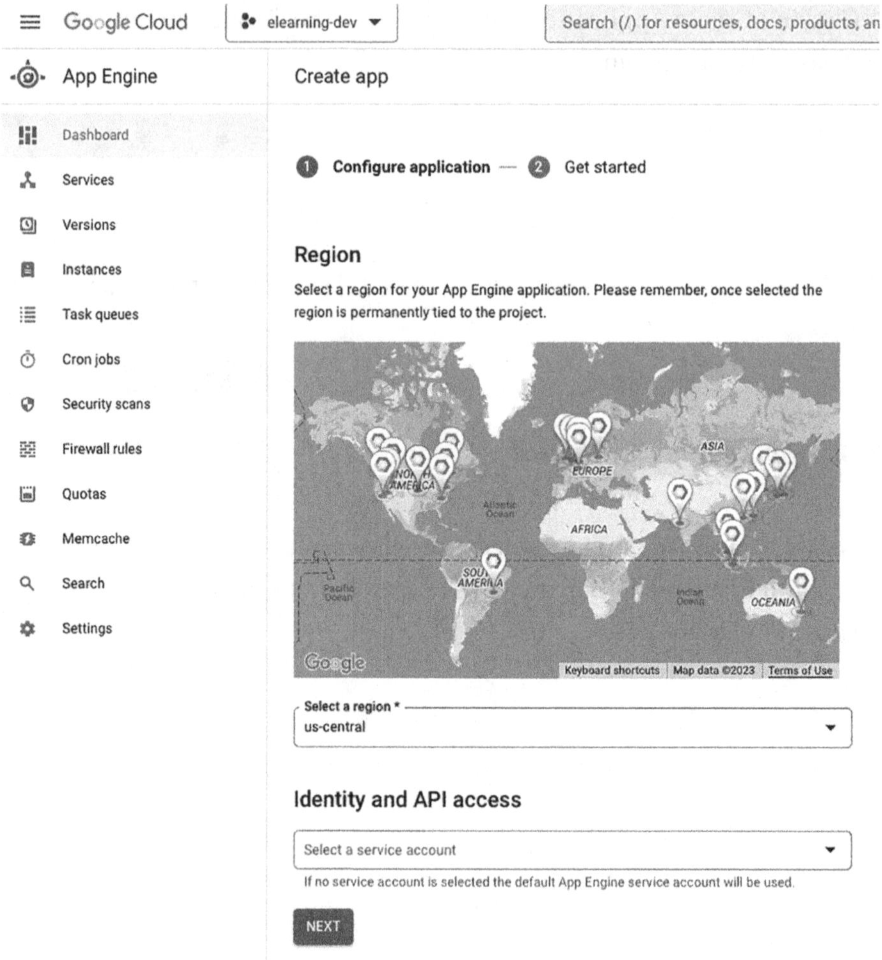

Figure 3-7. *Creating an app*

After clicking the Next button, it will show the app configuration screen, as shown in Figure 3-8.

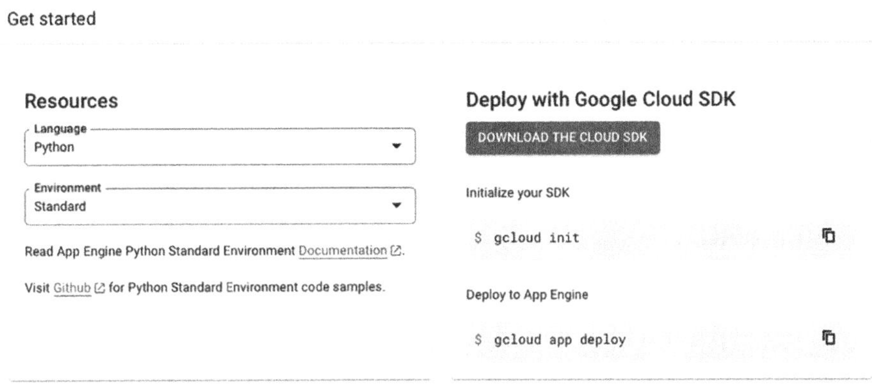

Figure 3-8. *App configuration*

You can select programming language and environment. The Java code sample provided by GCP is in GitHub: `https://github.com/GoogleCloudPlatform/java-docs-samples`.

4. Create a file named `app.yaml` in the root directory of your application. This file will contain the configuration for your App Engine app.

5. Create a file named `main.py` or `app.py` in the root directory of your application. This file will contain the code for your web application.

6. Create a virtual environment and install the dependencies for your application.

7. Run the command `gcloud app deploy` to deploy your application.

8. Once the deployment is complete, navigate to `https://[YOUR_PROJECT_ID].appspot.com` in your browser to access your web application.

Deploying a Java Web Application

The following is a step-by-step guide of deploying a Java web application on the Google App Engine:

1. Create a new project in the Google Cloud Console or use the existing one.

2. Install the Google Cloud SDK and initialize it with your project (not needed if you have already done it).

3. Create a new directory for your web application and navigate to it in the command line.

4. Create a file named `app.yaml` in the root directory of your application. This file will contain the configuration for your App Engine app.

5. Create a file named `web.xml` in the `WEB-INF` directory of your application. This file will contain the web application deployment descriptor.

   The sample application is provided by GCP and is at `https://github.com/GoogleCloudPlatform/java-docs-samples`.

6. Create a file named `appengine-web.xml` in the `WEB-INF` directory of your application. This file will contain the App Engine–specific configuration for your application.

7. Create a new file named `build.gradle` in the root directory of your application. This file will contain the build configuration for your application.

8. Run the command `./gradlew appengineDeploy` to deploy your application.

9. Once the deployment is complete, navigate to the URL `https://[YOUR_PROJECT_ID].appspot.com` in your browser to access your web application.

Setting Firewall and Security Considerations

When you deploy your web application on Google App Engine, you want to make sure that your application is safe and secure from malicious attacks. To do this, you need to take certain security measures, such as setting up firewall rules to allow traffic to your application, controlling access to your application with Identity-Aware Proxy, encrypting data in transit and at rest, using SSL to secure traffic to your app, protecting sensitive data with Cloud Key Management Service, keeping your app and dependencies up-to-date, and using App Engine's built-in security features to secure your application. By following these security measures, you can ensure that your web application is safe and secure for your users.

The following are the key terms is being used in this section:

A *firewall* is a security system that monitors and controls incoming and outgoing network traffic based on predetermined security rules.

Identity-Aware Proxy (IAP) is a service that controls access to cloud applications and VMs without exposing them to the Internet.

OAuth is an authorization protocol that allows applications to access user data from a third-party service without needing to store the user's password.

1. Create firewall rules on GCP Console's "Firewall rules" page to allow traffic to your App Engine app, as shown in Figure 3-9.

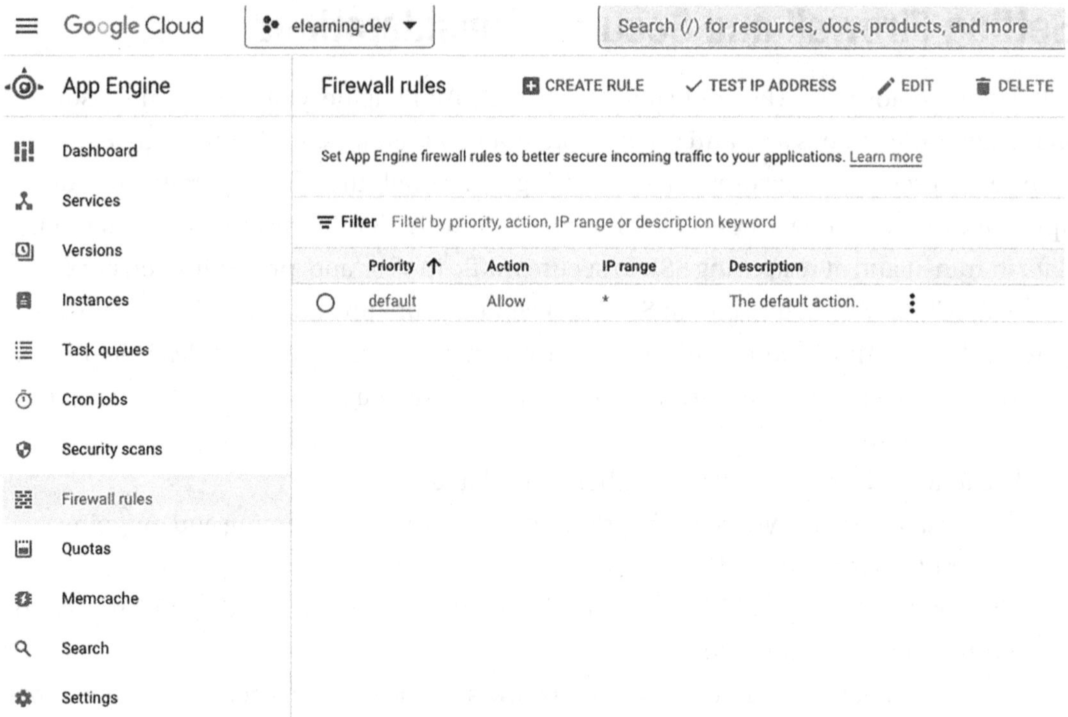

Figure 3-9. *Firewall rule dashboard of GAE*

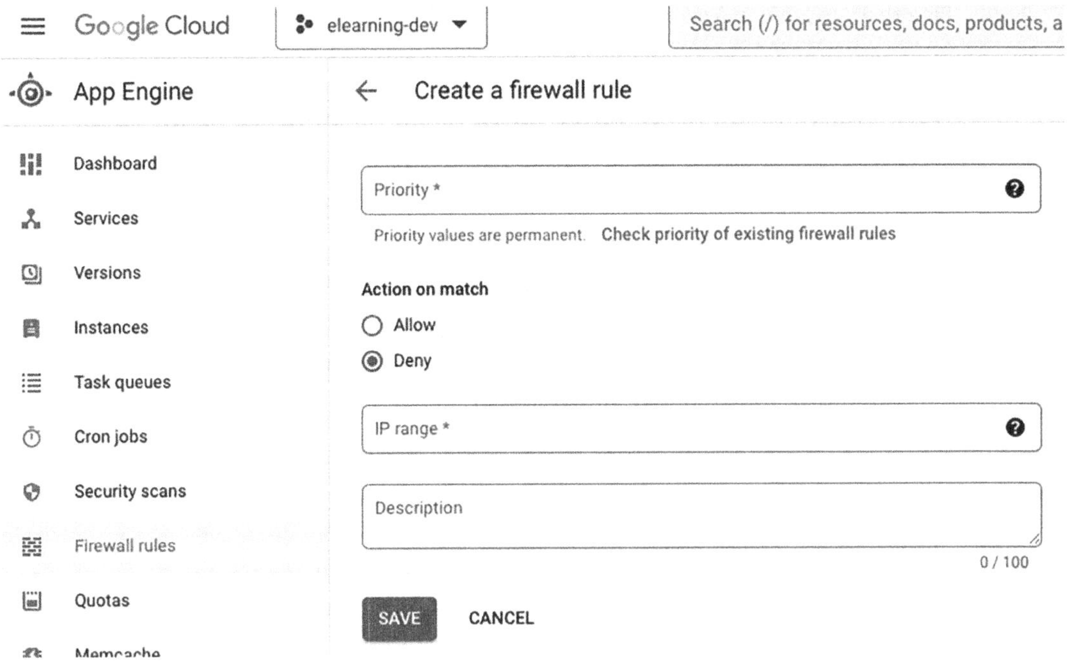

***Figure 3-10.** Creating a firewall rule*

2. Use IAP to control access to your application.

   To use it, you need to enable the API first, if it is not enabled already, as shown in Figure 3-11.

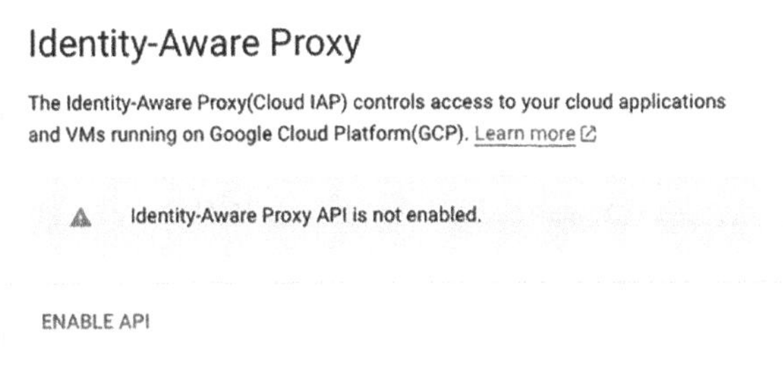

Identity-Aware Proxy
The Identity-Aware Proxy(Cloud IAP) controls access to your cloud applications and VMs running on Google Cloud Platform(GCP). Learn more
Identity-Aware Proxy API is not enabled.
ENABLE API

***Figure 3-11.** IAP*

   Once you enable it, you need to configure OAuth first.

3. Enable encryption for data in transit and at rest.

4. Use Secure Sockets Layer (SSL) to secure traffic to your app.

5. Use the Cloud Key Management Service (KMS) to protect sensitive data.

   Enable the KMS API if it is not already enabled, as shown in Figure 3-12.

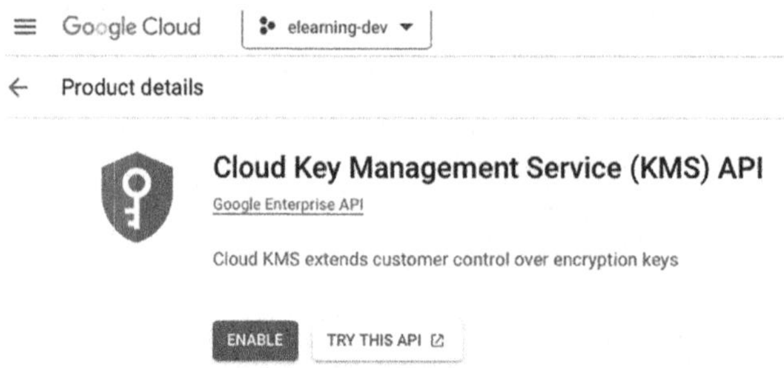

Figure 3-12. *KMS API*

Once it's enabled, it will take you to the dashboard, as shown in Figure 3-13.

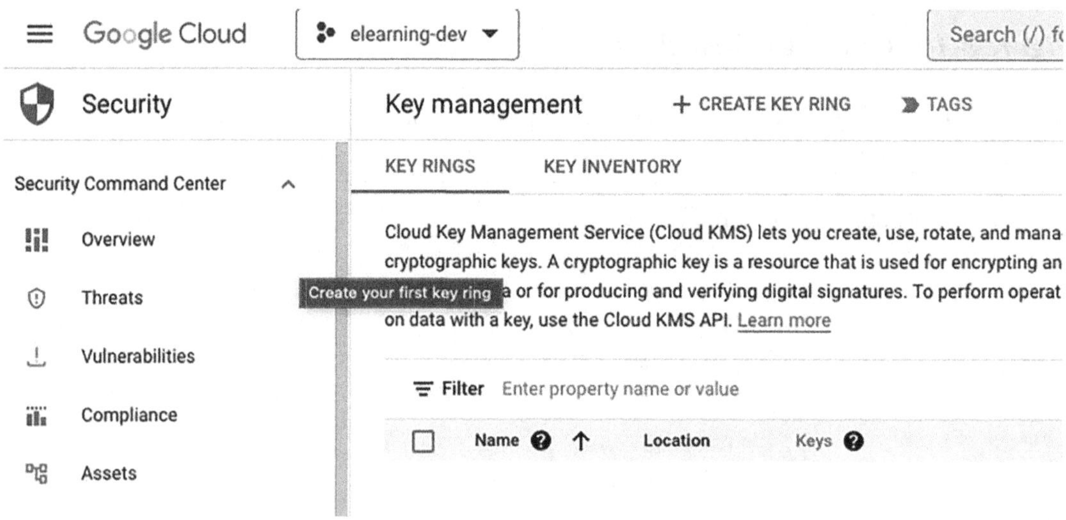

Figure 3-13. *Key management screen*

From the dashboard you can create a key ring (key rings are organized collections of keys) to use it, as shown in Figure 3-14.

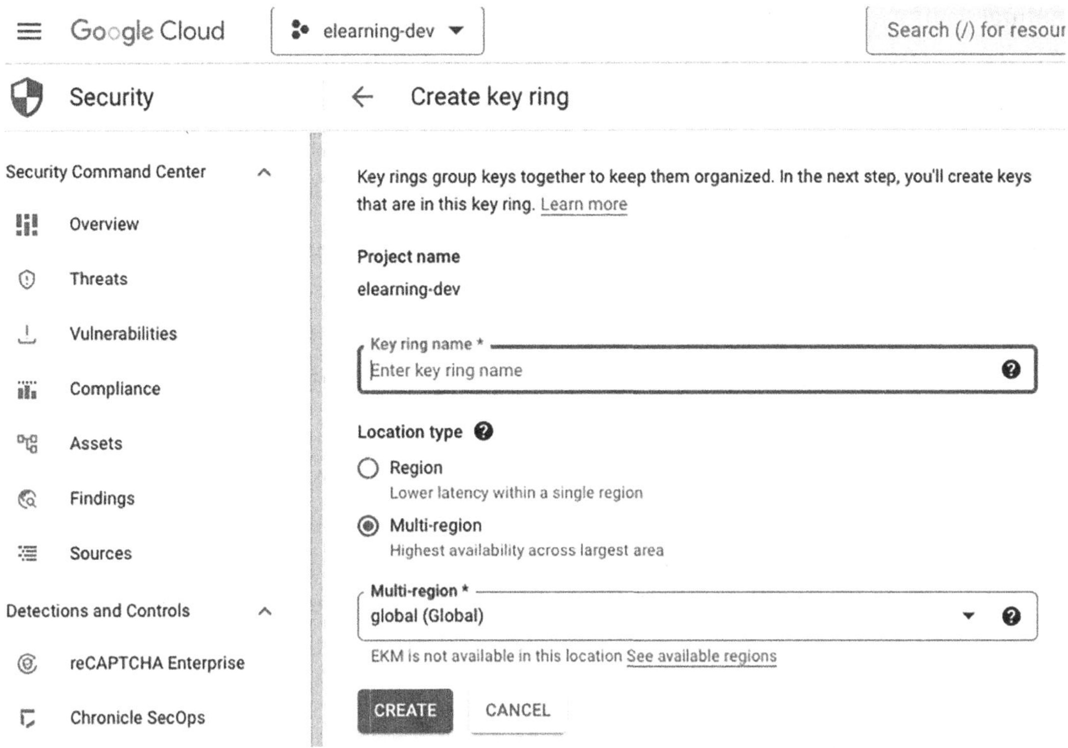

Figure 3-14. *Creating a key ring*

6. Keep your app and dependencies up-to-date.
7. Use App Engine's built-in security features, such as the App Engine security rules to secure your application.

Note The previous steps are complete; however, additional steps or considerations may be specific to your application or environment.

Scaling and Optimizing App Engine Applications

Scaling and optimizing a Google App Engine (GAE) application involves adjusting the application's resources and settings to handle traffic changes and improve performance.

Scaling an application on GAE refers to adjusting the number of instances running to handle changes in traffic. There are two main ways to scale a GAE application:

manual scaling and automatic scaling. Manual scaling involves adjusting the number of instances running, while automatic scaling automatically adjusts the number of instances based on the traffic to the application.

Optimizing a GAE application involves making changes to improve the performance of the application. Here are some ways to optimize a GAE application:

- *Use caching*: Caching can significantly improve the performance of an application by reducing the number of requests to the back end. Caching is the process of temporarily storing frequently accessed data or content to improve the performance and reduce the load on the backend.
- *Optimize the database*: Use indexes, denormalization, and other techniques to improve the performance of database queries. Other techniques to improve the performance of database queries could include optimizing the database schema, using efficient data types, optimizing database queries and transactions, and minimizing the amount of data retrieved.
- *Reduce the number of requests*: Minimize the number of requests made to the back end by reducing the number of round-trips by designing APIs that can retrieve or manipulate multiple related resources in a single HTTP request or using client-side caching.
- *Use the built-in performance tools*: GAE provides several tools to help you identify and fix performance issues, such as the App Engine Performance Dashboard, Cloud Trace, and Cloud Profiler.
- *Use the appropriate instance class*: GAE offers several classes, each with different resources and pricing. Choose the appropriate instance class for your application to optimize performance and costs.
- *Use load balancing*: Use load balancing to distribute traffic across multiple instances and handle increased traffic.
- *Use content delivery network (CDN)*: CDNs can help reduce the application load and improve the application's performance by caching and delivering content closer to the end users.

It's essential to keep in mind that the process of scaling and optimizing an application is an iterative process, and you may need to make multiple changes and monitor the performance of your application to achieve the desired results.

Setting Up Manual and Autoscaling in GAE

Scaling a web application on Google App Engine refers to adjusting the number of instances of the application running to handle changes in traffic. There are two main ways to scale a web application on GAE: manual scaling and automatic scaling.

Manual Scaling

With manual scaling, you manually adjust the number of instances running to handle changes in traffic. To manually scale a GAE application, you can use the App Engine dashboard in the Google Cloud Console. You can set the number of instances running for your application, and App Engine will ensure that that number of instances is running.

Automatic Scaling

Automatic scaling automatically adjusts the number of instances running to handle changes in traffic.

You will need to configure the `app.yaml` file for your application to set up automatic scaling on GAE. In this file, you can set the `automatic_scaling` option to configure the automatic scaling settings for your application.

Here are the options you can set for automatic scaling:

- `min_idle_instances`: The minimum number of idle instances that App Engine should maintain for your application.
- `max_idle_instances`: The maximum number of idle instances that App Engine should maintain for your application.
- `min_pending_latency`: The minimum amount of time that a request should wait before starting a new instance.
- `max_pending_latency`: The maximum amount of time that a request should wait before starting a new instance.

- `target_cpu_utilization`: The target CPU utilization for your application. App Engine will adjust the number of instances to maintain this CPU utilization.

You can also set other options, such as `max_concurrent_requests` and `max_instances`, for more fine-grained control over the scaling of your application.

Once you've configured these options, App Engine will automatically adjust the number of instances running for your application based on the traffic to your application.

It is important to note that in automatic scaling, App Engine will automatically adjust the number of instances running for your application based on the traffic. Still, it may take some time for the changes to take effect.

It is also important to monitor the behavior of your application and adjust the automatic scaling settings as necessary to ensure that your application is performing well and that costs are kept under control.

CHAPTER 4

Data Storage in Google Cloud

In this chapter, we will explore Google Cloud Storage (GCS) and how to use it to store and manage files in a Java application. GCS is a cloud-based object storage service provided by Google Cloud Platform (GCP), which allows users to store and access their data from anywhere in the world. It is a highly scalable and reliable storage solution that offers features such as data encryption, data durability, and data life-cycle management.

We will start by understanding the basics of GCS, including its key concepts and features. We will then learn how to set up a GCS bucket, authenticate with GCS, and install the GCS Java client library. We will also cover how to upload, download, and manage files in a GCS bucket using Java code. By the end of this chapter, you should have a solid understanding of how to use GCS for file storage in a Java application.

Google Cloud offers several data storage solutions for various use cases, including relational databases, NoSQL databases, and object storage. These storage solutions are designed to be highly available, scalable, and reliable, with built-in backup and recovery options.

Organizations need data storage solutions to store and manage their data effectively and efficiently. These solutions enable organizations to access, manage, and analyze data, making it an essential part of any modern business.

With the increasing amount of data generated by organizations, cloud-based data storage solutions have become a popular choice because of their flexibility, scalability, and cost-effectiveness. Google Cloud's data storage solutions are designed to meet the needs of any organization, from small startups to large enterprises, by providing a wide range of options to choose from based on their specific requirements.

A. Shashi, *Designing Applications for Google Cloud Platform*, https://doi.org/10.1007/978-1-4842-9511-3_4

Let's say you have a website where users can create accounts and log in to access certain features. The website needs to store user information such as their name, email, password, and other details. Instead of storing this information on your website's server, you can store it in a cloud database like Google Cloud Datastore.

When a user creates an account or logs in, their information is stored in the cloud database, and when they log out or leave the website, the information remains secure and accessible the next time they log in.

Similarly, suppose you have a mobile application that requires users to input data, such as a fitness app where users can track their workouts and progress. In that case, you can store this data in a cloud database such as Google Cloud Firestore. This ensures that the data is accessible across multiple devices and remains secure.

Using cloud data storage allows you to scale your applications easily, ensures data durability and availability, and provides secure access to your data from anywhere.

Let's talk more about the various storage options in GCP.

Understanding the Various Storage Options in GCP

Google Cloud Platform offers a wide range of storage options to meet different data storage and management requirements. The following are some of the key storage options provided by GCP:

- **Cloud Storage** is a scalable, cost-effective object storage service supporting unstructured data storage. It can be used for various use cases such as backup and archiving, data warehousing, media and entertainment, and web and mobile applications.
- **Cloud SQL** is a fully managed relational database service that supports popular database engines such as MySQL, PostgreSQL, and SQL Server. It is suitable for structured data storage and can be used for various use cases including web and mobile applications, data warehousing, and online transaction processing (OLTP).
- **Cloud Spanner** is a globally distributed, strongly consistent, and fully managed relational database service that supports structured data storage. It is suitable for various use cases such as web and mobile applications, data warehousing, and OLTP.

- **Cloud Bigtable** is a fully managed, NoSQL, wide-column database service that supports structured and semistructured data storage. It can be used for various use cases such as web and mobile applications, data warehousing, and OLAP.
- **Cloud Datastore** is a fully managed, NoSQL document database service that supports structured and semistructured data storage. It can be used for various use cases such as web and mobile applications, data warehousing, and OLAP.
- **Cloud Memorystore** is an in-memory data store service that supports fast access to data. It is suitable for various use cases such as web and mobile applications, data warehousing, and OLAP.

Each of these storage options has its unique features and capabilities. You should choose the one that best fits your needs based on the type of data you are storing, the size of your data, and your application's performance and scalability requirements.

Let's go through each of these options in greater detail, beginning with cloud storage.

Cloud Storage

Google Cloud Storage is a way to store and access large amounts of data in the cloud (over the Internet). It is managed by Google and is designed to be scalable, meaning it can grow as your storage needs grow. It is cost-effective because you pay only for the amount of storage you use. It can store various types of data, such as videos, images, and backups. It can be used for different purposes such as media and entertainment, data warehousing, and web and mobile applications.

A bucket (shown in Figure 4-1) in Google Cloud Storage is like a virtual container where you can store your files, just like you might use a physical container to store things at home. It's a secure and scalable way to store your data in the cloud. You can create, manage, and delete buckets as needed and control who has access to the files in your bucket. Think of it as a big digital box in which you can put your files, and then you can easily access those files from anywhere with an Internet connection.

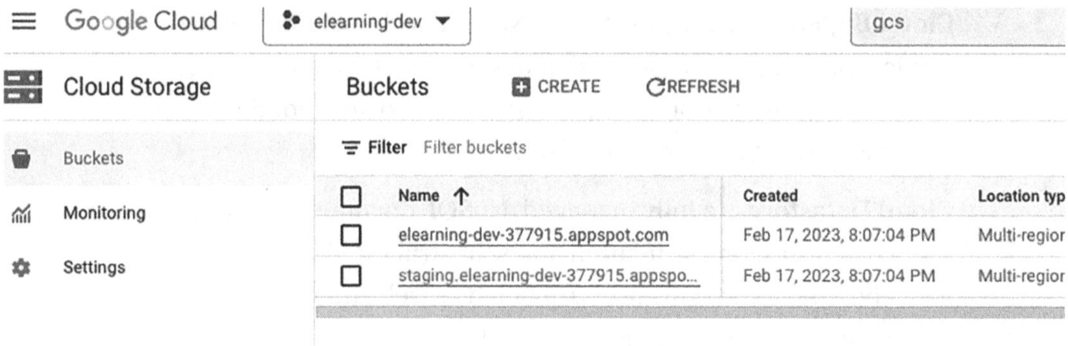

Figure 4-1. *Cloud Storage bucket*

An object in Cloud Storage consists of a file and metadata containing information about the object, such as its name, size, content type, and creation time. Objects can be stored in one of three storage classes:

- *Standard*: This class is intended for frequently accessed data and is suitable for storing data that needs to be retrieved quickly.
- *Nearline*: This class is intended for data accessed less frequently and is suitable for storing data that can be retrieved within a few seconds or minutes.
- *Coldline*: This class is intended for data accessed even less frequently and is suitable for storing data that can be retrieved within several hours.

Google Cloud Storage is an online service that allows you to store and access your data from anywhere in the world using the Internet. It provides an API and web-based interface that lets you perform various operations, such as uploading and downloading data, managing metadata, and controlling access to your data.

Cloud Storage offers several features to help you manage and secure your data, such as access control, versioning, life-cycle management, data integrity, encryption, multiregional location, and backups.

Access control lets you decide who has access to your data by granting permissions to individual users, groups of users, or service accounts. Versioning allows you to keep multiple versions of the same object and revert to an earlier version if needed. Life-cycle management rules can be set up to automatically transition objects to different storage classes or delete them after a certain period. Data integrity techniques, including checksums, ensure that your data is stored and retrieved without errors. You can also encrypt your data both in transit and at rest using either Google-managed keys or customer-managed keys. Cloud Storage also provides the multiregional location feature to store data in multiple regions and backups for data recovery.

Cloud Storage can be used for various purposes such as backup and archiving, data warehousing, media and entertainment, collaborative development, and web and mobile applications. It is a cost-effective solution for storing large amounts of data and can be scaled up or down as needed.

Let's talk about Cloud SQL next.

Cloud SQL

Google Cloud SQL is a fully managed, relational database service provided by Google Cloud Platform. It allows developers and organizations to create and manage databases in the cloud without the need to provision and maintain their hardware. Cloud SQL supports popular database engines such as MySQL, PostgreSQL, and SQL Server.

AlloyDB is a newly introduced fully managed, PostgreSQL-compatible database service for demanding transactional and analytical workloads. It provides enterprise-grade performance and availability while maintaining 100 percent compatibility with open-source PostgreSQL.

You can create a Cloud SQL instance with just a few clicks and choose the size and configuration that best fits your needs. Once your instance is up and running, you can use standard SQL commands to create tables, insert data, and query the database. Figure 4-2 shows the Cloud SQL instance.

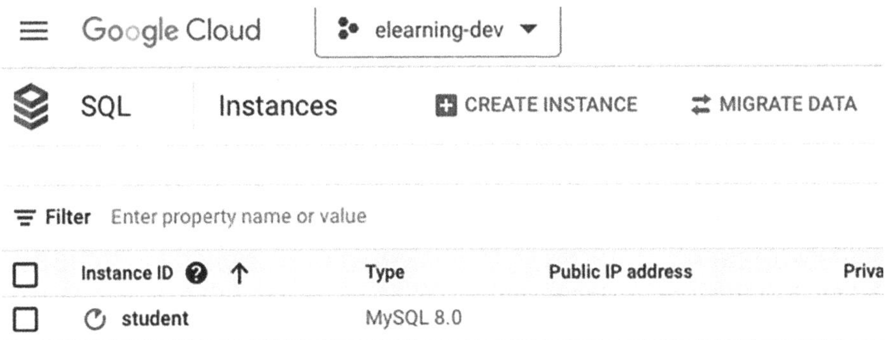

Figure 4-2. *Cloud SQL instance*

Cloud SQL provides several key features and benefits.

- *Automatic backups*: Cloud SQL automatically creates backups of your databases, which can be used to restore your data in case of data loss or corruption. You can also create manual backups at any time.
- *Automatic patching*: Cloud SQL automatically applies security patches and other updates to your database engines without downtime.
- *High availability*: Cloud SQL provides high availability options such as failover replication and read replicas, which can help ensure that your databases are always available, even in the event of a failure.
- *Cloud-native*: Cloud SQL is designed to run in the cloud, which means that it can take advantage of the scalability and performance of GCP.
- *Data encryption*: Cloud SQL supports data encryption both in transit and at rest, using either Google-managed keys or customer-managed keys.
- *Integration with other GCP services*: Cloud SQL can be easily integrated with other GCP services, such as App Engine, Kubernetes Engine, and Cloud Dataflow.
- *Replication and failover*: Cloud SQL allows you to set up replication and failover for your databases across multiple zones or regions. This ensures that your data is always available and protected against disasters or outages in a particular zone or region.

You can create and manage Cloud SQL instances using the Google Cloud Console or the Cloud SQL API. The Google Cloud Console is a web-based interface that allows you to create and manage instances, create and manage databases, and perform other tasks. The Cloud SQL API allows you to create, configure, and manage instances and databases programmatically.

Cloud SQL instances come in two types.

- First generation (also known as MySQL or PostgreSQL)
- Second generation (also known as MySQL or PostgreSQL or SQL Server)

Cloud SQL instances can be used for various purposes, such as the following:

- Storing and managing data for web and mobile applications
- Storing and managing data for data warehousing and analytics
- Storing and managing data for e-commerce and financial systems

Cloud SQL is a fully managed, highly available, and scalable relational database service that makes it easy to create and manage databases in the cloud. It is well-suited for many use cases and can easily integrate with other GCP services.

Let's talk about Cloud Spanner in the next section.

Cloud Spanner

Cloud Spanner is a fully managed, horizontally scalable, relational database service offered by Google Cloud Platform. It provides SQL and transactional consistency across multiple regions, making it a good choice for mission-critical, globally distributed applications. Cloud Spanner supports automatic, synchronous replication, and automatic failover, ensuring high availability and data durability. It also offers strong consistency guarantees, allowing immediate and accurate data retrieval. Additionally, Cloud Spanner supports the use of secondary indexes, stored procedures, and triggers, and it can be accessed using the JDBC and ODBC drivers, as well as a REST API. Cloud Spanner can be used with other Google Cloud services such as Bigtable and Cloud Dataflow to build a complete data processing pipeline.

You can create Cloud Spanner instance through navigating to the Cloud Spanner dashboard. Once you click Create Instance and provide details such as the instance name, instance ID, and the region where you want to create the instance, choose the configuration options, such as the number of nodes, the instance type, and the storage size. And then click Create to create the Cloud Spanner instance.

Once you have created the Cloud Spanner instance, you can start using it to store and retrieve data, as shown in Figure 4-3. You can create tables and define their schemas, insert data into the tables, and query the data using SQL.

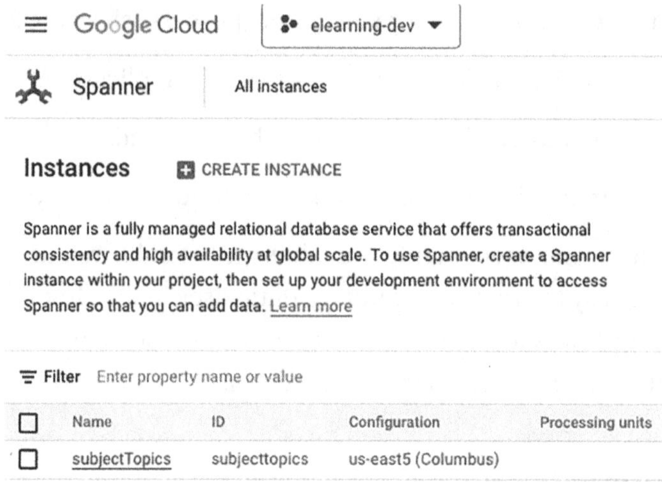

***Figure 4-3.** Cloud Spanner instance*

The following are some key features of Google Cloud Spanner:

- *Horizontally scalable*: Cloud Spanner can automatically scale horizontally to handle increasing workloads without requiring manual sharding or data partitioning.
- *Globally distributed*: Cloud Spanner can replicate data across multiple regions, providing low-latency data access for users worldwide.
- *Strong consistency*: Cloud Spanner provides strong consistency guarantees, ensuring that all queries return the most up-to-date data.
- *Automatic failover*: Cloud Spanner automatically detects and fails over to a replica in the event of a failure, ensuring high availability.
- *SQL support*: Cloud Spanner supports a SQL-based query language, making it easy for developers familiar with SQL to work with the service.
- *Secondary indexes*: Cloud Spanner supports using secondary indexes, which can improve query performance and allow for more efficient data retrieval.

- *Stored procedures and triggers*: Cloud Spanner supports storing procedures and triggers, allowing for complex data processing and manipulation.
- *Access via JDBC/ODBC*: Cloud Spanner can be accessed via JDBC and ODBC drivers, making it easy to integrate with various programming languages and frameworks.

Now we will discuss the use cases of Cloud Spanner.

The Use Cases for Cloud Spanner

Google Cloud Spanner can be used in a variety of use cases; some examples include the following:

- *Online Transaction Processing (OLTP)*: Cloud Spanner is well suited for OLTP workloads that require strong consistency guarantees and low latency, such as e-commerce, financial, and healthcare applications. For example, an e-commerce company could use Cloud Spanner to handle millions of customer orders and financial transactions, ensuring that the data is always up-to-date and accurate. Compared to other databases such as MySQL or PostgreSQL, Cloud Spanner provides stronger consistency guarantees and can handle larger workloads.
- *Gaming*: Cloud Spanner can handle large numbers of concurrent players and real-time data updates, making it suitable for gaming applications that require high availability and low latency. For example, a mobile game developer could use Cloud Spanner to store and retrieve player data and game state, ensuring that the game is always available and responsive. Compared to other databases, such as NoSQL databases, Cloud Spanner provides stronger consistency guarantees and can handle larger workloads.

- *IoT*: Cloud Spanner can handle high-velocity data streams from IoT devices and process and analyze that data in near real time. For example, a manufacturing company could use Cloud Spanner to store and retrieve sensor data from its production line, allowing it to monitor and optimize production in real time. Cloud Spanner provides stronger consistency guarantees and can handle larger workloads than other databases, such as time-series databases.
- *Media and entertainment*: Cloud Spanner can handle high-traffic workloads and can store and serve large amounts of multimedia data, making it suitable for media and entertainment applications. With its strong consistency guarantees, scalability, and globally distributed architecture, Cloud Spanner can provide reliable and fast access to multimedia data for a global audience.
- *Ad Tech*: Cloud Spanner can handle high-traffic and high-velocity data streams, making it suitable for ad tech applications that require real-time data processing and analysis.
- *Supply chain management*: Cloud Spanner can handle large amounts of data and provide real-time visibility into the supply chain, making it suitable for supply chain management applications. For example, a logistics company could use Cloud Spanner to track and manage inventory, shipments, and logistics in real time. Cloud Spanner provides stronger consistency guarantees and can handle larger workloads than other databases, such as traditional relational databases.
- *Healthcare*: Cloud Spanner can handle large amounts of patient data and provide real-time access, making it suitable for healthcare applications such as electronic health record (EHR) systems.
- *FinTech*: Cloud Spanner can handle large numbers of financial transactions and provide real-time access to that data, making it suitable for FinTech applications such as trading platforms and fraud detection systems.

Let's talk about Cloud Bigtable in the next section.

Cloud Bigtable

Google Cloud Bigtable is a fully managed, high-performance NoSQL database service offered by Google Cloud Platform. It is designed to handle large amounts of data and high-traffic workloads and is based on the same technology that powers Google's services, such as Google Search and Google Analytics. It's designed to deliver fast performance with low latency and is based on the same technology that powers Google's services such as Google Search and Analytics. It's a NoSQL database, which means that it can store and manage a wide variety of unstructured and semistructured data, such as time-series data, machine-generated logs, and social media data. Cloud Bigtable is a fully managed service, which means that Google takes care of the infrastructure, security, and maintenance of the service, so you can focus on using it to store and analyze your data.

You can create a Bigtable instance by clicking the Create Instance button on the dashboard. You need to provide name of the instance and number of nodes you want to use in your instance; then click Create. Figure 4-4 shows the Bigtable instance.

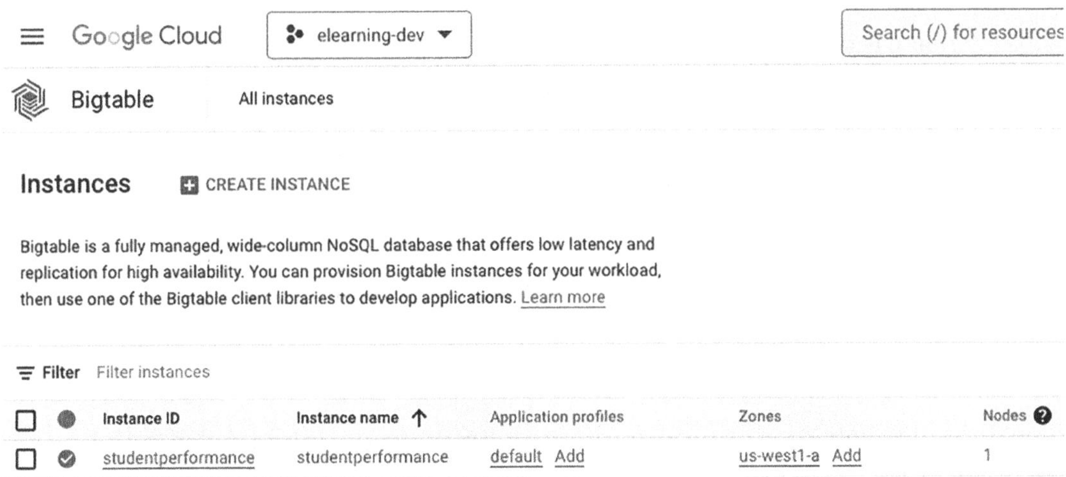

Figure 4-4. *Bigtable instance*

The following are some key features of Cloud Bigtable:

- *Horizontally scalable*: Cloud Bigtable can automatically scale horizontally to handle increasing workloads without requiring manual sharding or data partitioning.

- *Low latency*: Cloud Bigtable provides low-latency data access, making it suitable for high-traffic workloads such as real-time analytics and serving large amounts of data.
- *High performance*: Cloud Bigtable is optimized for high-performance data access, making it suitable for large-scale data processing and analytics.
- *Column-family data model*: Cloud Bigtable uses a column-family data model optimized for high-performance data access and well-suited for storing and retrieving large amounts of data.
- *Automatic data compaction*: Cloud Bigtable automatically compacts data, reducing the amount of storage space required and improving performance.
- *Automatic failover*: Cloud Bigtable automatically detects and fails over to a replica in the event of a failure, ensuring high availability.
- *Cloud-native*: Cloud Bigtable is a cloud-native service, which means that it is designed to run on the cloud and can take advantage of the scalability and elasticity of the cloud.
- *Access via HBase API*: Cloud Bigtable can be accessed via the HBase API, which makes it easy to integrate with various programming languages and frameworks.

We'll talk about the use cases of Cloud Bigtable in the next section.

The Use Cases for Cloud Bigtable

Google Cloud Bigtable can be used in various use cases, and it is best suited for high-performance, large-scale data processing, and storage. The following are some examples:

- *Real-time analytics*: Cloud Bigtable is well-suited for real-time analytics and data processing, such as tracking and analyzing website traffic, social media data, and sensor data. For example, a company could use Cloud Bigtable to track and analyze customer interactions in real time, allowing them to make data-driven decisions and improve customer experience.

- *Internet of Things (IoT)*: Cloud Bigtable is well-suited for handling large amounts of data from IoT devices, such as sensor data, and can process and analyze that data in near real time. For example, a manufacturing company could use Cloud Bigtable to store and retrieve sensor data from its production line, allowing it to monitor and optimize production in real time.
- *Gaming*: Cloud Bigtable can handle large numbers of concurrent players and real-time data updates, making it suitable for gaming applications that require high-performance and low-latency data access. For example, a mobile game developer could use Cloud Bigtable to store and retrieve player data and game state, ensuring that the game is always available and responsive.
- *Ad tech*: Cloud Bigtable is well-suited for handling a large amount of data and providing real-time visibility into the ad tech, such as storing and analyzing ad impressions, bid requests, and other ad-related data. For example, an ad network could use Cloud Bigtable to track and analyze ad performance, allowing them to make data-driven decisions and improve ad targeting.
- *Genomic data*: Cloud Bigtable is well-suited for handling large-scale genomic data and providing real-time visibility into the data. For example, a biotech company could use Cloud Bigtable to store and analyze genomic data, allowing them to make data-driven decisions and improve their research.

Cloud Bigtable is best suited for high-performance, large-scale data processing and storage. It is well-suited for use cases requiring real-time data access and processing, low-latency data access, and high availability.

In the next section, we will discuss Cloud Datastore.

Cloud Datastore

Google Cloud Datastore is a fully managed, NoSQL document database service that is part of Google Cloud Platform. It's designed to help developers store and manage structured data for their web and mobile applications. As a NoSQL database, it provides a flexible and scalable solution for storing data in a nonrelational format. This means that Datastore can handle different data types and structures, such as nested data and arrays, which is useful for storing data that doesn't fit neatly into a traditional relational database.

Datastore is fully managed, meaning that Google takes care of the service's underlying infrastructure, security, and maintenance. This allows developers to focus on building their applications and using Datastore to store and retrieve their data. Datastore is also scalable, allowing developers to start with a small amount of data and then scale up as their application grows.

Datastore is used in many different types of applications, such as e-commerce, social media, and gaming. It is particularly well-suited for applications that need to store and query large amounts of structured data, such as user profiles or product catalogs. Additionally, Datastore provides features such as indexing and querying, which allows developers to search and filter their data quickly and easily.

To create a Google Cloud Datastore instance, open the Datastore dashboard, and create an instance by providing the instance name and storage type, as shown in Figure 4-5.

After you create your Datastore instance, you can access it using the Google Cloud Datastore API or the Cloud Console. You can use the API to perform operations such as reading and writing data, managing indexes, and controlling access to your data. The Cloud Console provides a web-based interface that allows you to interact with your data through a graphical user interface.

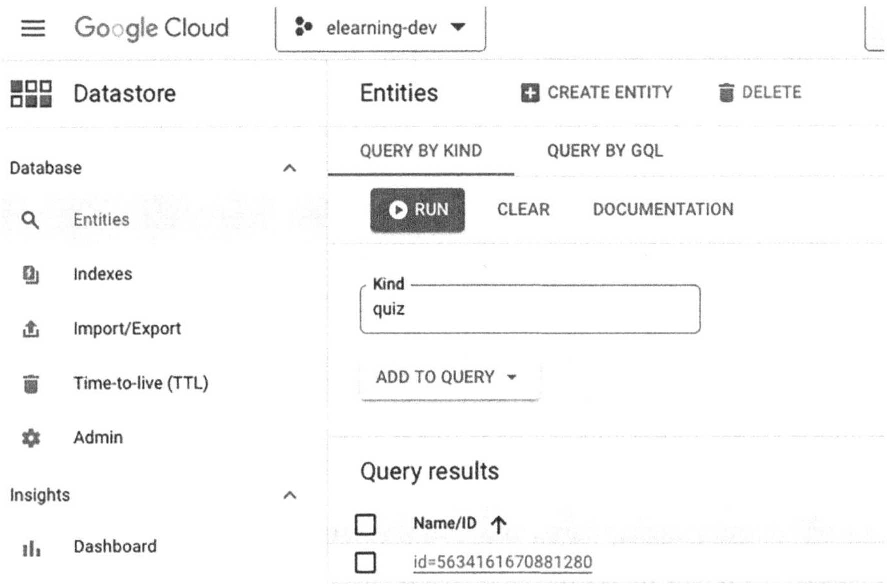

Figure 4-5. *Cloud Datastore*

The following are some key features of Cloud Datastore:

- *Schemaless data model*: Cloud Datastore uses a schemaless data model, which means it does not enforce a fixed schema on the data, allowing for more flexibility in the data structure.
- *Automatic sharding*: Cloud Datastore automatically shards the data to handle increasing workloads without requiring manual data partitioning. Datastore uses the key's value to generate a hash that determines which server the entity is stored on. The hash function used by Datastore is designed to distribute entities evenly across servers to ensure balanced load distribution and optimal performance.
- *High availability*: Cloud Datastore automatically replicates the data to multiple data centers to ensure high availability, even in the event of a failure. It provides a 99.99 percent service-level agreement (SLA) for regional instances and 99.999 percent for multiregional instances.
- *Cloud-native*: Cloud Datastore is a cloud-native service, which means that it is designed to run on the cloud and can take advantage of the scalability and elasticity of the cloud.

- *Access via Google Cloud SDK*: Cloud Datastore can be accessed via the Google Cloud SDK, which makes it easy to integrate with various programming languages and frameworks.
- *Consistency*: Cloud Datastore supports both strong and eventual consistency.
- *Data types*: Cloud Datastore supports many data types, including strings, integers, floating-point numbers, dates, and binary data.

Cloud Datastore can be used in various use cases, such as web and mobile applications, gaming, IoT, e-commerce, and more. It is best suited for use cases requiring flexible and scalable data storage and not requiring complex SQL queries or advanced indexing.

Next, we will discuss the use cases of Cloud Datastore.

The Use Cases for Cloud Datastore

Cloud Datastore is a NoSQL document database provided by Google Cloud Platform for storing and querying data in the cloud. It is designed to handle large amounts of structured and semistructured data. It is a good fit for use cases that involve storing and querying large amounts of data with high availability and low latency.

One example use case for Cloud Datastore is a social media application that needs to store and retrieve user profiles, posts, and comments. The data for each user profile, post, and comment can be stored as a separate document in Cloud Datastore. The application can use the query capabilities of Cloud Datastore to retrieve the data for a particular user or group of users.

Another example use case for Cloud Datastore is an e-commerce application that needs to store and retrieve product information and customer orders. The data for each product and customer order can be stored as separate documents in Cloud Datastore. The application can use the query capabilities of Cloud Datastore to retrieve the data for a particular product or group of products.

Cloud Datastore is a good choice for these use cases because it provides a flexible and scalable solution for storing and querying data in the cloud. It can handle large amounts of data and automatically scale up or down as needed to meet the performance and availability requirements of the application. Additionally, Cloud Datastore provides strong consistency guarantees, automatic indexing, and built-in support for transactions, which makes it well-suited for use cases that involve storing and querying large amounts of data with high availability and low latency.

Datastore can be used in various use cases, including the following:

- Storing and retrieving user data for web and mobile applications.
- Storing and querying data for analysis and reporting.
- Storing and retrieving data for machine learning and artificial intelligence applications.
- Storing and managing metadata for data lakes and data warehouses.
- Storing and managing time series data for IoT applications. In IoT applications, time-series data can include sensor data, logs, and other machine-generated data that needs to be collected, analyzed, and stored in real time.
- Storing and managing data for real-time and offline processing.
- Storing and managing data for backups and disaster recovery. You can use it to store backup copies of critical data from your applications, such as configuration files, user data, and logs. You can also use Datastore to replicate data across multiple regions to ensure data durability and high availability in case of disasters.
- Storing and managing data for content management systems.
- Storing and managing data for e-commerce and online marketplaces.
- Storing and managing data for gaming and social media platforms.

Cloud Datastore can be implemented in many different ways and technologies, such as databases, cloud storage, or even a simple file system.

In the next section, we will talk about Cloud Memorystore.

Cloud Memorystore

Cloud Memorystore is a fully managed in-memory data store service provided by Google Cloud Platform. It is based on the open-source Redis protocol and can store, retrieve, and manipulate data in real time.

You can create Memorystore instance by clicking Create Instance on the Memorystore dashboard. You can select the Redis Memorystore option, choose the instance location and memory size, and provide a name to the instance, as shown in Figure 4-6.

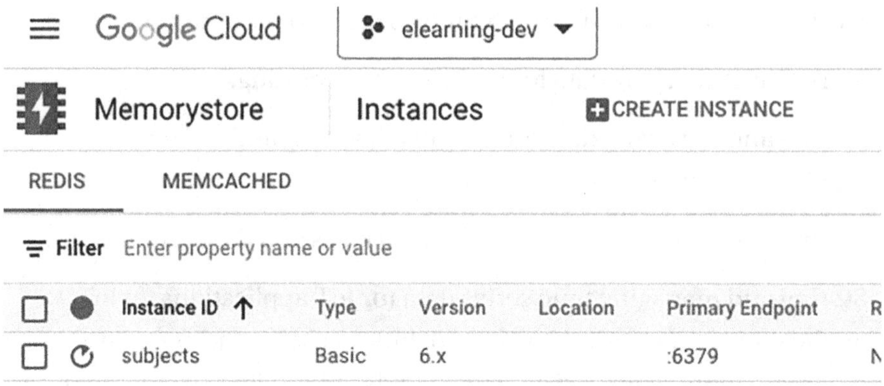

Figure 4-6. *Cloud Memorystore*

Cloud Memorystore is designed for use cases that require low-latency, high-throughput data access, such as gaming, real-time analytics, and session management. It can be used as a cache for frequently accessed data or as a primary data store for real-time data processing.

The following are some of the features of Cloud Memorystore:

- Automatic failover and replication for high availability and disaster recovery
- Scale-up and scale-down capabilities to handle changes in workload
- Encryption of data at rest and transit
- Integration with other GCP services such as Cloud Load Balancing, Cloud Firewall, and Cloud Monitoring and Logging

Cloud Memorystore is also available in two service tiers.

- *Standard Tier*: Offers a balance of performance and cost, with a maximum of 30 GB storage per instance.
- *Memorystore for Redis*: Provides a higher level of performance and larger storage capacity, up to 100 TB

It is helpful for various use cases such as gaming, real-time analytics, session management, caching, and more.

Let's talk about the Memorystore.

Features of Memorystore

Here are some of the main features of Google Cloud Memorystore:

- *In-memory data store*: Cloud Memorystore is an in-memory data store that stores data in random access memory (RAM), providing low-latency and high-throughput data access.
- *Redis compatibility*: Cloud Memorystore is based on the open-source Redis protocol and is compatible with Redis clients, commands, and data structures.
- *Automatic failover and replication*: Cloud Memorystore automatically replicates data across multiple zones for high availability and disaster recovery.
- *Scale-up and scale-down capabilities*: Cloud Memorystore can automatically scale up or down to handle changes in workload.
- *Encryption*: Cloud Memorystore encrypts data at rest and in transit to provide an additional layer of security.
- *Integration with other GCP services*: Cloud Memorystore can be integrated with other GCP services such as Cloud Load Balancing, Cloud Firewall, and Cloud Monitoring and Logging.
- *Standard and Memorystore for Redis tiers*: Cloud Memorystore is available in two service tiers, Standard and Memorystore for Redis. The Standard tier offers a balance of performance and cost, while the Memorystore for Redis tier provides a higher level of performance and larger storage capacity.
- *Flexible deployment options*: Cloud Memorystore can be deployed on-premises, in a hybrid environment, or in the cloud.
- *Cloud Memorystore for Firebase*: Cloud Memorystore for Firebase enables fast and secure access to Cloud Memorystore from Firebase client-side SDKs, allowing for real-time data access and easy scaling.

- *Monitoring and logging*: Cloud Memorystore provides detailed monitoring and logging capabilities to help you understand the performance and usage of your data store.

Now we will talk about the use cases of Memorystore in the next section.

Use Cases of Memorystore

Cloud Memorystore can be used in various use cases; here are a few examples:

- *Caching*: Cloud Memorystore can be used as a cache for frequently accessed data, such as web page content, images, and session data. Caching data in memory can significantly reduce response times and improve the overall performance of your application.
- *Gaming*: Cloud Memorystore can store game state, player data, and leaderboards in real time. The low-latency and high-throughput capabilities of Cloud Memorystore make it well-suited for handling the large amounts of data and high-concurrency requirements of gaming applications.
- *Real-time analytics*: Cloud Memorystore can store and process large amounts of data in real time. This can be useful for use cases such as log analysis, fraud detection, and customer behavior tracking.
- *Session management*: Cloud Memorystore can store session data for web applications. Storing session data in memory can improve the performance and scalability of your application.
- *E-commerce*: Cloud Memorystore can store and retrieve data for e-commerce applications, such as product information, user profiles, and shopping cart data.
- *IoT*: Cloud Memorystore can store and manage time-series data for IoT applications, such as sensor data, device status, and telemetry data.
- *Social media*: Cloud Memorystore can store and retrieve data for social media platforms, such as user profiles, posts, and comments.
- *User-session data*: Cloud Memorystore can store user-session data, such as user profiles, shopping carts, and order history.

- *Use as a message broker*: Cloud Memorystore can also be used as a message broker, which can help decouple the sender and receiver of a message. It can also help implement a pub-sub pattern, where a message is sent to all subscribers.

Cloud Memorystore can be used in many other ways depending on the specific needs of your application.

Now you should have a better understanding of Cloud SQL and Cloud Spanner. Let's compare both in the next section.

Cloud SQL vs. Cloud Spanner

Deciding whether to use Cloud SQL or Cloud Spanner for your application can depend on several factors, including your data model, performance requirements, and use case. Here are a few key points to consider when deciding:

- *Data model*: Cloud SQL is a relational database management system (RDBMS) that uses tables, rows, and columns to organize data. It is best suited for applications that require a traditional relational data model. Cloud Spanner, on the other hand, is a globally distributed, relational database service that uses a combination of a relational and a nonrelational data model. It is best suited for applications that require a highly scalable, globally distributed data model.
- *Performance*: Cloud SQL is a good choice for applications that require high performance but do not need to scale globally. Cloud Spanner, on the other hand, is a good choice for applications that require high performance and global scalability.
- *Use case*: Cloud SQL is typically used for small-to-medium applications with moderate read-write traffic and can handle structured and semistructured data. Cloud Spanner is typically used for large-scale applications with high read-write traffic and can handle structured and semistructured data.

- *Consistency and availability*: Cloud SQL provides eventual consistency and is best for use cases that can handle some inconsistency. Cloud Spanner, on the other hand, provides strong consistency and is best for use cases that require strong consistency. Cloud Spanner's strong consistency and automatic failover features make it well-suited for applications that require high availability and disaster recovery.
- *Cost*: Cloud Spanner is significantly more expensive than Cloud SQL. This is because of the additional features and functionalities that Cloud Spanner provides, such as global scalability, strong consistency, and automatic failover.

The best choice for your application may depend on various factors. It's recommended to evaluate both options thoroughly, based on your specific use case, and make the decision that best aligns with your business requirements. To fully leverage the capabilities of Cloud Spanner, the application should be designed to be stateless and deployed in multiple regions. Cloud Spanner is designed to provide strong consistency and high availability, which means it can handle real-time data operations across multiple regions. This requires the application to be designed with the capability to handle requests from any region and to be able to recover from failures in one region by failing over to another region. Organizations can achieve highly available, globally consistent, and scalable systems by designing applications to leverage Cloud Spanner's capabilities.

Now let's talk about the situations when using Cloud Spanner over Cloud SQL.

When to Use Cloud Spanner Instead of Cloud SQL

A real-world example of a use case where Cloud Spanner may be more suitable over Cloud SQL is for a large, global e-commerce platform.

An e-commerce platform must handle many transactions and user queries simultaneously, as well as a high volume of data. It needs to be globally available and able to handle data inconsistencies. Additionally, it needs to ensure that customers' financial information is secure and available at all times and that customers' orders are processed correctly.

In this scenario, Cloud Spanner could be a good fit because it provides globally distributed data storage, which allows the platform to store data across multiple regions and automatically replicates data for high availability and disaster recovery. It also provides strong consistency, ensuring that all database nodes see the same data simultaneously. It is useful when the application requires a consistent data view across all nodes. This is important for an e-commerce platform, as it needs to maintain a single version of the truth for customers' financial information and orders.

Cloud SQL, on the other hand, may not be the best fit for this use case because it does not provide the same level of global scalability and strong consistency as Cloud Spanner. Additionally, Cloud Spanner does not have the same security features and automatic failover capabilities.

In this example, the e-commerce platform would benefit from the global scalability and strong consistency of Cloud Spanner, which would allow it to handle a high volume of data, ensure data availability and consistency, and provide a secure and reliable platform for customers.

In the next section, we will talk about the situation when Cloud SQL is better to use over Cloud Spanner.

When to Use Cloud SQL Instead of Cloud Spanner

A real-world example of when Cloud SQL/AlloyDB may be more suitable over Cloud Spanner is when a small nonprofit organization needs to store and manage its donor information. The organization may have a small number of donors, and the data that needs to be stored includes basic information such as donor name, contact information, donation history, and donation preferences. The organization may have a moderate amount of traffic to its website, with a small number of donors updating their information or making donations at any time.

In this case, Cloud SQL would be more suitable than Cloud Spanner because the organization's needs are relatively simple and do not require the high scalability and global consistency features provided by Cloud Spanner. Cloud SQL provides a familiar and easy-to-use relational database management system that can handle the organization's moderate amount of traffic, and the organization's budget may not be able to support the costs associated with Cloud Spanner. Additionally, the organization may not have much database experience, so using Cloud SQL would be less intimidating and easier to manage.

Another example of a small e-commerce website that serves customers in only a specific region may not require the global scalability and high availability provided by Cloud Spanner. Instead, Cloud SQL could be a more cost-effective and simpler option for storing and managing its data.

Cloud SQL is also a good choice if the application's data is structured and doesn't require complex transactions or strict consistency guarantees. Cloud SQL is a fully managed relational database service that supports popular database engines like MySQL and PostgreSQL, making it a straightforward option for developers who are familiar with these technologies.

In short, Cloud SQL is a cost-effective and easy-to-use option for small organizations that need to store and manage relatively simple structured data and have a lower scale of read and write operations. It is suitable for cases where budget and database management expertise are limited and where the organization's needs are not as demanding as those of large-scale businesses.

If your application requires complex SQL queries or has a large number of joins between tables, Cloud SQL may be a better fit. Additionally, suppose your application requires support for certain database features that are not currently available in Cloud Spanner, such as stored procedures or user-defined functions. In that case, Cloud SQL may be the better choice.

Let's compare Cloud Spanner with Cloud Datastore in the next section.

Cloud Spanner vs. Cloud Datastore

Deciding between Cloud Spanner and Cloud Datastore for your application can depend on several factors, including your data model, performance requirements, and use case. Here are a few key points to consider:

- *Data model*: Cloud Spanner can be set up as a globally distributed, relational database service that combines a relational and a nonrelational data model. It is best suited for applications that require a highly scalable, globally distributed data model and structured data. Cloud Datastore, on the other hand, is a NoSQL document database service that uses a flexible, hierarchical data model. It is best suited for applications that require a flexible, denormalized data model and semistructured or unstructured data.

- *Performance*: Cloud Spanner is a good choice for applications that require high performance but do not need to scale globally. Cloud Datastore, on the other hand, is a good choice for applications that require high performance and global scalability.
- *Use case*: Cloud Spanner is typically used for large-scale applications with high read-write traffic and can handle structured data. Cloud Datastore is typically used for small-to-medium size applications with moderate read-write traffic and can handle semistructured and unstructured data.
- *Consistency and availability*: Cloud Spanner provides strong consistency and is best for use cases that require strong consistency. Cloud Datastore, on the other hand, provides eventual consistency and is best for use cases that can handle some level of inconsistency. Cloud Spanner's strong consistency and automatic failover features make it well-suited for applications that require high availability and disaster recovery.
- *Cost*: Cloud Spanner is generally more expensive than Cloud Datastore. This is because of the additional features and functionalities that Cloud Spanner provides, such as global scalability, strong consistency, and automatic failover.

The best choice for your application may depend on various factors. It's recommended to evaluate both options thoroughly, based on your specific use case, and make the decision that best aligns with your business requirements.

In the next section, we will talk about the situation when using Cloud Datastore over Cloud Spanner.

When to Use Cloud Datastore Instead of Cloud Spanner

Cloud Datastore is a NoSQL document database that is suitable for storing and retrieving semistructured data, such as JSON or XML documents. It is a fully managed service and provides scalability, automatic sharding, and a flexible schema.

On the other hand, Cloud Spanner is a relational database that provides stronger consistency and is designed to handle structured data at a global scale. It is suitable for use cases that require transactional consistency across multiple regions and high availability. However, Cloud Spanner may be more complex and expensive to set up and maintain compared to Cloud Datastore.

If the data you want to store is semistructured and you don't need global consistency or transactional capabilities, then Cloud Datastore may be a better choice. It is simpler to use and can scale automatically as your data grows. However, if you need strong consistency and transactional capabilities across multiple regions, then Cloud Spanner may be a better choice, even though it may require more effort and resources to set up and maintain.

For example, consider a company that develops a mobile application that allows users to log and track their outdoor activities, such as hiking, biking, running, etc. The application must store many location data, including GPS coordinates, timestamps, and user-generated comments. The data is semistructured, meaning it does not fit well into a traditional relational database structure. The application also needs to handle a high volume of write operations, as users constantly update their activities in real time.

In this case, Cloud Datastore would be more suitable than Cloud Spanner because the stored data is semistructured, and the application does not require complex data transactions or joins. Cloud Datastore is a NoSQL document database designed to handle semistructured data, providing automatic scaling and high availability. Additionally, Cloud Datastore is easy to use and does not require significant database management expertise.

Another advantage of using Cloud Datastore, in this case, is that it is built on top of Google's infrastructure and is designed to handle high write loads; this is essential for the mobile application as it needs to handle a large amount of location data updates in real time.

For another example, consider a social media platform that allows users to create and share content, such as text, images, and videos. The platform must store user information, such as name and contact information, and store the content users create and share. The platform also needs to handle a moderate amount of traffic, with many users creating and viewing content at any given time.

In this case, Cloud Datastore would be more suitable than Cloud Spanner because the platform's needs are relatively simple and do not require the high scalability and global consistency features provided by Cloud Spanner. Cloud Datastore is a NoSQL document database service designed to handle unstructured data and is easy to scale. Additionally, Cloud Datastore is a cost-effective solution for this use case, as it does not require the same complexity and resources as Cloud Spanner.

Another advantage of using Cloud Datastore, in the previous case, is the ability to handle many user requests and store the data in a flexible and scalable way. It can handle many users' data and perform queries over it, which is necessary for the social media platform to provide personalized recommendations and promotions to their users.

In short, Cloud Datastore is suitable for organizations that store and manage unstructured, semistructured, or nonrelational data and do not require complex data transactions or joins. It is particularly useful for cases where the organization must handle a high volume of write operations and the data needs to fit better into a traditional relational database structure. It is a cost-effective and easy-to-use option for cases where the organization's needs are less demanding than those of large-scale businesses that do not require the scalability and global consistency provided by Cloud Spanner.

Now let's talk about the situations when Cloud Datastore is better than Cloud SQL in the next section.

When to Use Cloud Datastore Instead of Cloud SQL

An actual use case where Cloud Datastore may be more suitable over Cloud SQL is when a company needs to store and manage semistructured or unstructured data, such as JSON, and does not require the relational structure provided by Cloud SQL.

For example, consider a gaming company that develops and publishes mobile games. The company needs to store player information, such as player name, level, achievements, and the in-game events and actions players take. The company also needs to handle many players and events at any given time.

In this case, Cloud Datastore would be more suitable than Cloud SQL because the company's data is semistructured, and the relational structure provided by Cloud SQL is not necessary. Cloud Datastore is a NoSQL document database service designed to handle unstructured data and is easy to scale, making it a good fit for this use case. Additionally, Cloud Datastore allows the company to index and query data in various ways, making it easy to scale. It can handle a large number of requests from players.

Another advantage of using Cloud Datastore, in this case, is the ability to handle many players and events in real time and store them in a flexible and scalable way. It can handle many players' data and perform queries over it, which is necessary for the gaming company to provide personalized recommendations and promotions to their players.

For another example, consider an IoT company that needs to store and manage sensor data from many devices. The sensor data is unstructured and includes various data types, such as text, images, and videos, and it can be of different formats and structures. The company also needs to handle many read-and-write operations from devices at any time.

In this case, Cloud Datastore would be more suitable than Cloud SQL because the company's needs are demanding and require a high level of scalability. Cloud Datastore is designed to handle unstructured data and can be easily scaled to handle a large amount of data. Cloud Datastore is a NoSQL document database service that does not require the same level of complexity and resources as Cloud SQL, making it a cost-effective solution.

Another advantage of using Cloud Datastore, in the previous case, is the ability to handle many requests from the devices and store the data in a flexible and scalable way. It can handle a large amount of data and perform queries over it, which is necessary for the IoT company to perform data analysis and make predictions.

In short, Cloud Datastore is suitable for cases where the organization needs to store and manage semistructured or unstructured data, such as JSON, and has a large scale of read-and-write operations. It is a cost-effective and easy-to-use option for cases where the organization's needs are not as demanding as those of large-scale businesses, and the organization does not require the relational structure provided by Cloud SQL.

Now let's talk about using Cloud SQL over Cloud Datastore in the next section.

When to Use Cloud SQL Instead of Cloud Datastore

A use case where Cloud SQL may be more suitable over Cloud Datastore is when a company needs to store and manage structured data that follows a specific schema and requires the full functionality of a traditional relational database provided by Cloud SQL.

For example, consider an e-commerce company that needs to store and manage customer information, inventory, and sales data. The data is structured and follows a specific schema, such as customer information having fields like name, address, and contact information. The company also needs to handle a moderate number of read-and-write operations from customers and employees at any time.

In this case, Cloud SQL would be more suitable than Cloud Datastore because the company's needs are relatively complex and require the full functionality of a traditional relational database. Cloud SQL is a fully managed relational database service that supports SQL, the industry-standard language for managing and querying relational data. It provides features such as transactions, indexes, and stored procedures. Cloud SQL is more cost-effective in this case as it does not require the same level of complexity and resources as Cloud Datastore.

Another advantage of using Cloud SQL, in this case, is the ability to handle complex queries over the data, and it provides a way to enforce data integrity and consistency. This is necessary for the e-commerce company to provide accurate information to the customers and employees and prevent system errors.

For another example, consider a financial company that needs to store and manage financial transactions and customer information. The data is highly structured and needs to follow strict regulations. The company must also handle complex queries and data analysis and run advanced reporting and compliance.

In this case, Cloud SQL would be more suitable than Cloud Datastore because the company's needs are demanding and require full functionality of a traditional relational database. Cloud SQL is a fully managed relational database service that provides advanced features such as support for SQL, encryption at rest, and high-availability options. Additionally, Cloud SQL allows for complex queries and advanced reporting, which is necessary for the financial company to perform data analysis and comply with regulations.

Another advantage of using Cloud SQL, in this case, is handling many complex queries and storing the data in a structured way that guarantees data integrity and consistency. It also has advanced security options and compliance features, which are necessary for the financial company to protect sensitive data and comply with regulations.

In short, Cloud SQL is suitable for cases where the organization needs to store and manage structured data that follows a specific schema and has a moderate scale of read-and-write operations. It is a cost-effective and easy-to-use option for cases where the organization's needs are relatively complex and the organization requires the full functionality of a traditional relational database provided by Cloud SQL.

Now let's see how we can use the Java code to work with Cloud Storage.

Using Java to Interact with Cloud Storage

The following is an example of a Java project that interacts with Cloud Storage using the Google Cloud Storage API:

1. Set up a project in the Google Cloud Console and enable the Google Cloud Storage API.
2. Create credentials for your project, such as an API key or a service account key.
3. Use a library such as the Google Cloud Storage Java Client to interact with the API.

Listing 4-1 shows an example of how you can interact with Google Cloud Storage.

Listing 4-1. Java Code for Interaction with Cloud Storage

```
// Import the Google Cloud Storage Java Client library
import com.google.cloud.storage.Storage;
import com.google.cloud.storage.StorageOptions;

public class CloudStorageExample {

    public static void main(String[] args) {
        // Create a storage client
        Storage storage = StorageOptions.getDefaultInstance().getService();

        // List all of the buckets in the project
        for (Bucket bucket : storage.list().iterateAll()) {
            System.out.println(bucket.getName());
        }
    }
}
```

You can find more details at https://cloud.google.com/storage/docs/reference/libraries#client-libraries-install-java.

You can also use other libraries such as Apache Hadoop, which provide support for interacting with other cloud storage services such as Amazon S3, Microsoft Azure, etc.

The next step is to create a bucket and upload the file to the bucket using Java. Let's discuss this in the next section.

Java Code for Creating a Bucket and Uploading the File to the Bucket

The following is an example of how to create a Java project to connect to a cloud storage service, create a bucket, and upload a file to the bucket using the Google Cloud Storage API:

1. Create a new Java project in your preferred IDE.

2. Add the Google Cloud Storage API dependency to your project's `pom.xml` file, as given in Listing 4-2.

Listing 4-2. POM Dependency for Cloud Storage

```
<dependency>
    <groupId>com.google.cloud</groupId>
    <artifactId>google-cloud-storage</artifactId>
    <version>1.117.0</version>
</dependency>
```

3. In your project, create a new class and import the libraries shown in Listing 4-3.

Listing 4-3. Importing Libraries

```
import com.google.cloud.storage.Bucket;
import com.google.cloud.storage.BucketInfo;
import com.google.cloud.storage.Storage;
import com.google.cloud.storage.StorageOptions;
```

4. In the class, create a method to connect to the cloud storage service and create a new bucket, as given in Listing 4-4.

Listing 4-4. Connect to the Cloud Storage Service

```
public void createBucket(String bucketName) {
    // Connect to cloud storage
    Storage storage = StorageOptions.getDefaultInstance().getService();

    // Create a new bucket
    Bucket bucket = storage.create(BucketInfo.of(bucketName));
    System.out.println("Bucket " + bucket.getName() + " created.");
}
```

5. Create another method to upload a file to the bucket, as given in Listing 4-5.

Listing 4-5. Method to Upload File to the Bucket

```
public void uploadFile(String bucketName, String filePath) {
    // Connect to cloud storage
    Storage storage = StorageOptions.getDefaultInstance().getService();

    // Get the bucket
    Bucket bucket = storage.get(bucketName);

    // Upload a file to the bucket
    bucket.create(filePath, new FileInputStream(filePath),
    Bucket.BlobWriteOption.userProject("your-project-id"));
    System.out.println("File uploaded to bucket.");
}
```

6. In the main method, call the previously created methods with proper arguments to create a bucket and upload a file to the bucket.

Note You must pass your project ID and ensure you have the appropriate credentials to access the cloud storage service.

We have created connection and uploaded file to the bucket; next we will write Java code for downloading files from the bucket.

Java Code for Downloading Files from a Cloud Storage Bucket

Listing 4-6 provides the code that can be used to download a file from a Google Cloud Storage bucket using the `google-cloud-storage` library.

Listing 4-6. Downloading File from Bucket

```
import com.google.cloud.storage.Blob;
import com.google.cloud.storage.BlobId;
import com.google.cloud.storage.Storage;
import com.google.cloud.storage.StorageOptions;

import java.io.File;
import java.io.IOException;

public class DownloadFile {

    public static void main(String[] args) throws IOException {
        // create a storage client
        Storage storage = StorageOptions.getDefaultInstance().getService();

        // specify the bucket and file name
        String bucketName = "my-bucket";
        String fileName = "file.txt";

        // create a blob id
        BlobId blobId = BlobId.of(bucketName, fileName);

        // create a blob object
        Blob blob = storage.get(blobId);

        // download the file
        File file = new File(fileName);
        blob.downloadTo(file.toPath());
    }
}
```

This code uses the `com.google.cloud.storage` package to interact with Google Cloud Storage. It creates a storage client, specifies the bucket and filename, creates a blob object, and then uses the `downloadTo` method to download the file to the local file system.

You will need to have the `google-cloud-storage` library added to your project dependencies, and you need to provide credentials to access the GCS bucket.

Now we will write Java code to manage files in the Cloud Storage bucket.

Java Code for Managing Files in a Cloud Storage Bucket

The code provided in Listing 4-7 is sample Java code for managing files. This code uses the `java.io.File` class to interact with files. It creates a new file, checks if the file exists, gets the file size, and then deletes the file.

Listing 4-7. Managing Files in the Bucket

```
import java.io.File;
import java.io.IOException;

public class FileManager {

    public static void main(String[] args) throws IOException {
        // specify the file name
        String fileName = "file.txt";

        // create a file object
        File file = new File(fileName);

        // create a new file
        file.createNewFile();

        // check if the file exists
        if (file.exists()) {
            System.out.println("File exists");
        }

        // get the file size
        long fileSize = file.length();
        System.out.println("File size: " + fileSize);
```

```
        // delete the file
        file.delete();

        // check if the file was deleted
        if (!file.exists()) {
            System.out.println("File deleted");
        }
    }
}
```

You can also use the `File` class to create directories, list files in a directory, and move, copy, and rename files, as demonstrated in Listings 4-8 and 4-9.

Listing 4-8. Renaming File

```
file.renameTo(new File("newName.txt"));
```

Listing 4-9. Iterating File for Performing Any File Operations

```
File dir = new File("/path/to/directory");
if(dir.isDirectory()){
    File[] files = dir.listFiles();
    for(File f : files){
        //do something with file
    }
}
```

The following section will show you how to use Cloud Storage for file storage.

Using Cloud Storage for File Storage in a Java Application

To use Google Cloud Storage for file storage in a Java application, you can use the GCS Java client library, which provides a set of classes and methods for interacting with GCS.

Here are the general steps for using GCS for file storage in a Java application:

1. *Set up a GCS bucket*: You will need to create a GCS bucket in the Google Cloud Console and set up the appropriate permissions for the bucket.
2. *Authenticate with GCS*: You will need to provide authentication credentials, such as an API key or service account key, to the client library to access the cloud storage.
3. *Install the GCS Java client library*: You can install it via Maven or Gradle and import it into your project.
4. *Upload a file*: Use the provided classes and methods to upload a file to your GCS bucket.
5. *Download a file*: Use the provided classes and methods to download a file from your GCS bucket.
6. *Delete a file*: Use the provided classes and methods to delete a file from your GCS bucket.

You can refer to the GCS Java client library documentation for detailed instructions on how to use the library and its various classes and methods.

Let's talk about setting up the GCS bucket.

Setting Up a GCS Bucket

To set up a Google Cloud Storage bucket, you can follow these steps:

1. Log in to the Google Cloud Console (`https://console.cloud.google.com/`) using your Google account.
2. Select the project in which you want to create the bucket. If you haven't created a project yet, you can create one by clicking the project drop-down in the top bar and selecting New Project.
3. Click the Storage option in the navigation menu on the left. This will take you to the Cloud Storage browser.
4. Click the Create Bucket button.

5. Fill in the required information for the bucket, such as the bucket name, storage class, and location. Make sure the name you choose is unique across all of GCS.

6. Click the Create button to create the bucket.

7. Now you have to set up the appropriate permissions for the bucket, you can set the access control for the bucket by going to the Permissions tab in the bucket's settings and adding members to the bucket.

8. Once you've set up the permissions, you're ready to start using the bucket to store files in your Java application.

Note GCS bucket names are globally unique, so you'll need to choose a unique name that has not been used by anyone else.

Next, we will talk about authenticating with GCS in a Java application.

Authenticating with GCS

To authenticate with Google Cloud Storage in a Java application, you will need to provide authentication credentials, such as an API key or service account key, to the GCS Java client library.

Here are the general steps for authenticating with GCS:

1. *Create a service account*: Go to the Google Cloud Console and navigate to the "IAM & admin" section. Create a new service account and grant it the appropriate permissions for the GCS bucket you want to access.

2. *Download the service account key*: Once the service account is created, you can download the key in JSON format.

3. *Set the environment variable*: Set the `GOOGLE_APPLICATION_CREDENTIALS` environment variable to the path of the downloaded JSON file.

4. *Use the service account key in your code*: In your Java code, use the `Credentials` class from the Google Cloud SDK to load the service account key and create a `Storage` object from it. You can then use this object to interact with GCS.

Alternatively, you can use the `StorageOptions.newBuilder()` class to create a storage client with the service account key and use it to interact with GCS.

It's important to keep the service account key secure and not share it or check it into version control.

You may also use OAuth2 client ID and the secret to authenticate your application. In that case, you can use the Google Cloud SDK library and use the following to get the credentials.

```
GoogleCredentials.getApplicationDefault()
```

To get access to GCS, you need to create service account and download it to use into your code.

Creating a Service Account, Downloading It, and Using It in the Project

Here are the detailed steps for creating a service account, downloading the key, and using it in your Java project to authenticate with Google Cloud Storage:

1. Create a service account:

    - Go to the Google Cloud Console (`https://console.cloud.google.com/`).
    - Select the project that you want to create the service account for.
    - In the navigation menu, click "IAM & admin" and then "Service accounts."
    - Click the Create Service Account button.
    - Give the service account a name and description.
    - Grant it the appropriate permissions for the GCS bucket you want to access, such as Storage Object Admin and Storage Object Creator.
    - Click Create to create the service account.

2. Download the service account key:
   - After creating the service account, you will be taken to the service account details page.
   - Click the Actions button and select Create key.
   - Select the JSON format and click Create.
   - A JSON file containing the key will be downloaded to your computer.
3. Set the environment variable:
   - Set the `GOOGLE_APPLICATION_CREDENTIALS` environment variable to the path of the downloaded JSON file.
4. Use the service account key in your code, as shown in Listing 4-10:
   - In your Java code, use the `Credentials` class from the Google Cloud SDK to load the service account key and create a `Storage` object from it.
   - You can then use this object to interact with GCS.

Listing 4-10. Providing Path of Service Account JSON

```
import com.google.auth.Credentials;
import com.google.auth.oauth2.GoogleCredentials;
import com.google.cloud.storage.Storage;
import com.google.cloud.storage.StorageOptions;

import java.io.FileInputStream;
import java.io.IOException;

public class GCSExample {
    public static void main(String[] args) throws IOException {
        // Load the service account key
        Credentials credentials = GoogleCredentials.fromStream
        (new FileInputStream("path/to/service_account.json"));
        // Create a storage client
        Storage storage = StorageOptions.newBuilder().
        setCredentials(credentials).build().getService();
```

```
        // Use the storage client to interact with GCS
        // ...
    }
}
```

Alternatively, you can use the `GoogleCredentials.getApplicationDefault()` method to get the credentials without setting the environment variable.

It's essential to keep the service account key secure and not to share it or check it into version control.

You can also use the `GoogleCredentials.fromStream` method to load the credentials from a stream, such as a file or a resource in your application.

Next, we will talk about installing GCS client library.

Installing the GCS Java Client Library

To install the Google Cloud Storage Java client library in your application, you will need to add the library as a dependency in your project. The GCS Java client library is available on the Maven Central Repository so that you can add it as a dependency in your build file (e.g., `pom.xml` for a Maven project, `build.gradle` for a Gradle project, etc.).

Here are the general steps for installing the GCS Java client library:

1. Add the GCS Java client library as a dependency in your build file.

   For Maven, add the following dependency to your `pom.xml` file, as shown in Listing 4-11. The version mentioned is at the time of writing this book; check for latest version when you are working on it.

Listing 4-11. Cloud Storage Dependency

```
<dependency>
  <groupId>com.google.cloud</groupId>
  <artifactId>google-cloud-storage</artifactId>
  <version>1.143.0</version>
</dependency>
```

For Gradle, add the following line to your `build.gradle` file:

```
implementation 'com.google.cloud:google-cloud-storage:1.143.0'
```

2. Run the build command to download the dependency and its transitive dependencies.

   For Maven, run the following command:

   ```
   mvn clean install
   ```

   For Gradle, run the following command:

   ```
   gradle build
   ```

The GCS Java client library includes the classes needed to interact with GCS, such as the `Storage` class for creating and managing buckets, and the `Blob` class for creating and managing objects.

You can check the latest version of the library from the maven central repository, `https://mvnrepository.com/artifact/com.google.cloud/google-cloud-storage`.

Make sure to also have the Google Cloud SDK installed in your system and also the environment variable `GOOGLE_APPLICATION_CREDENTIALS` is set properly; if not, the code will throw the exception `com.google.auth.oauth2.GoogleCredentials` not found.

Uploading a File

To upload a file to Google Cloud Storage using the Java client library, you will need to create a `Storage` object that authenticates with your GCS account, create a `Blob` object that represents the file you want to upload, and then use the `Blob.create` or `Blob.createFrom` method to upload the file to GCS.

Listing 4-12 shows an example of how to upload a file to GCS using the Java client library.

Listing 4-12. Uploading File to GCS

```
import com.google.cloud.storage.Blob;
import com.google.cloud.storage.BlobId;
import com.google.cloud.storage.BlobInfo;
import com.google.cloud.storage.Storage;
import com.google.cloud.storage.StorageOptions;
import java.io.File;
```

```
public class GCSUploadExample {
  public static void main(String[] args) {
    // Authenticate with GCS using a service account
    Storage storage = StorageOptions.newBuilder()
        .setCredentials(GoogleCredentials.fromStream
        (new FileInputStream("path/to/credentials.json")))
        .build()
        .getService();

    // Create a BlobId object representing the file you want to upload
    String bucketName = "my-bucket";
    String fileName = "path/to/file.txt";
    BlobId blobId = BlobId.of(bucketName, fileName);

    // Create a BlobInfo object representing the file you want to upload
    BlobInfo blobInfo = BlobInfo.newBuilder(blobId).build();

    // Use the Blob.create method to upload the file to GCS
    File file = new File(fileName);
    Blob blob = storage.create(blobInfo, file);

    // Print the public URL of the uploaded file
    System.out.println("File uploaded to: " + blob.getMediaLink());
  }
}
```

In Listing 4-12, the `StorageOptions.newBuilder().setCredentials()` method is used to authenticate with GCS using a service account. The `BlobId.of()` method is used to create a `BlobId` object that represents the file you want to upload, and the `BlobInfo.newBuilder()` method is used to create a `BlobInfo` object that represents the file's metadata.

The `storage.create(blobInfo, file)` method is used to upload the file to GCS, and the `blob.getMediaLink()` method is used to print the public URL of the uploaded file.

You can also use the `Blob.createFrom` method, which accepts `inputStream` as well.

```
Blob blob = storage.createFrom(blobInfo, fileInputStream);
```

Make sure that the service account you are using has the correct permissions to upload files to the bucket, else you'll get an error.

Downloading a File

To download a file from Google Cloud Storage using the Java client library, you will need to create a `Storage` object that authenticates with your GCS account, create a `Blob` object that represents the file you want to download, and then use the `Blob.downloadTo` method to download the file from GCS.

Listing 4-13 shows an example given in Listing 4-13 of how to download a file from GCS using the Java client library.

Listing 4-13. Downloading File from GCS

```
import com.google.cloud.storage.Blob;
import com.google.cloud.storage.BlobId;
import com.google.cloud.storage.Storage;
import com.google.cloud.storage.StorageOptions;
import java.io.FileOutputStream;
import java.io.IOException;

public class GCSDownloadExample {
  public static void main(String[] args) throws IOException {
    // Authenticate with GCS using a service account
    Storage storage = StorageOptions.newBuilder()
        .setCredentials(GoogleCredentials.fromStream
        (new FileInputStream("path/to/credentials.json")))
        .build()
        .getService();

    // Create a BlobId object representing the file you want to download
    String bucketName = "my-bucket";
    String fileName = "path/to/file.txt";
    BlobId blobId = BlobId.of(bucketName, fileName);

    // Create a Blob object representing the file you want to download
    Blob blob = storage.get(blobId);

    // Use the Blob.downloadTo method to download the file from GCS
```

```
    FileOutputStream outputStream = new FileOutputStream("path/to/download/
    location/file.txt");
    blob.downloadTo(outputStream);
    outputStream.close();
  }
}
```

In the Listing 4-13 example, the `StorageOptions.newBuilder().setCredentials()` method is used to authenticate with GCS using a service account. The `BlobId.of()` method is used to create a `BlobId` object that represents the file you want to download, and the `storage.get(blobId)` method is used to create a `Blob` object that represents the file.

The `blob.downloadTo(outputStream)` method is used to download the file from GCS, and the `outputStream.close()` method is used to close the output stream after the download is complete.

Make sure the service account you are using has the correct permissions to download files from the bucket; otherwise, you'll get an error.

You can also download the file to `byte[]` by using `blob.getContent()` method, and you can download to a specific folder using `blob.downloadTo(Path path)`.

Deleting a File

To delete a file from Google Cloud Storage using the Java client library, you will need to create a `Storage` object that authenticates with your GCS account, create a `BlobId` object that represents the file you want to delete, and then use the `Storage.delete` method to delete the file from GCS.

Listing 4-14 shows an example of how to delete a file from GCS using the Java client library.

Listing 4-14. Deleting a File from GCS

```
import com.google.cloud.storage.BlobId;
import com.google.cloud.storage.Storage;
import com.google.cloud.storage.StorageOptions;

public class GCSDeleteExample {
  public static void main(String[] args) {
    // Authenticate with GCS using a service account
    Storage storage = StorageOptions.newBuilder()
```

```
        .setCredentials(GoogleCredentials.fromStream
        (new FileInputStream("path/to/credentials.json")))
        .build()
        .getService();

    // Create a BlobId object representing the file you want to delete
    String bucketName = "my-bucket";
    String fileName = "path/to/file.txt";
    BlobId blobId = BlobId.of(bucketName, fileName);

    // Use the Storage.delete method to delete the file from GCS
    boolean deleted = storage.delete(blobId);
    if(deleted) {
        System.out.println("File deleted successfully!");
    } else {
        System.out.println("File deletion failed!");
    }
  }
}
```

In the Listing 4-14 example, the `StorageOptions.newBuilder().setCredentials()` method is used to authenticate with GCS using a service account. The `BlobId.of()` method is used to create a `BlobId` object that represents the file you want to delete, and the `storage.delete(blobId)` method is used to delete the file from GCS.

Make sure the service account you are using has the correct permissions to delete files from the bucket; otherwise, you'll get an error.

Also, the `storage.delete(blobId)` method returns a Boolean value, which is `true` if the file is deleted successfully and `false` if the file deletion fails.

Summary

In this chapter, you learned about using Google Cloud Storage to store and manage files in a Java application. We covered the basics of GCS, including creating a bucket, authenticating with GCS, and managing files in a bucket. We also discussed the GCS Java client library, which provides a set of classes and methods for interacting with GCS and installing and using it in a Java application. Finally, we covered how to upload and download files from a GCS bucket using Java code. Overall, this chapter provided a comprehensive guide to using GCS in a Java application.

```
.setCredentials(GoogleCredentials.fromStream(
    new FileInputStream(pathToCredentials.json)))
    .build()
    .getService();
```

[illegible]

Summary

[illegible]

CHAPTER 5

Google Cloud SQL

In this chapter, we discuss how to use Google Cloud SQL to store and manage data in a cloud-based SQL database. We cover various aspects of working with Cloud SQL, such as creating a Cloud SQL instance, connecting to it, and creating tables, as well as inserting, updating, and querying data. We also discuss how to interact with Cloud SQL using the Java programming language.

Google Cloud SQL is a fully managed relational database service provided by Google Cloud Platform (GCP) that allows users to create and manage databases using MySQL, PostgreSQL, or SQL Server database engines. It provides a simple, web-based interface for managing databases and integration with other GCP services such as App Engine, Compute Engine, and Cloud Storage.

With Cloud SQL, users can easily create, configure, and manage databases, with automatic backups, automatic software updates, and built-in monitoring and logging. Users can also choose to create a new database or import an existing one.

Cloud SQL offers a variety of features to help users manage their databases, such as the following:

- *Automatic backups*: Cloud SQL automatically creates and manages backups of your databases so you can easily recover from data loss or corruption.
- *Automatic software updates*: Cloud SQL automatically updates the database software to the latest version, ensuring that your databases are always up-to-date with the latest security and performance enhancements.

A. Shashi, *Designing Applications for Google Cloud Platform*, https://doi.org/10.1007/978-1-4842-9511-3_5

- *High availability*: Cloud SQL is a service provided by Google Cloud Platform that allows you to run databases in the cloud. It is like a digital warehouse for storing information in an organized way. One of the benefits of Cloud SQL is that it is designed to keep your information safe and available, even if something goes wrong. It does this by automatically switching to a backup copy of your database if there is a problem with the main copy.
- *Scalability*: Cloud SQL allows you to easily scale your database up or down as needed, with minimal downtime.
- *Security*: Cloud SQL provides a variety of security features to help protect your databases, such as encryption at rest and in transit, and the ability to control access to your databases using firewall rules.
- *Monitoring and logging*: Cloud SQL provides built-in monitoring and logging capabilities, so you can easily keep track of the performance and activity of your databases.
- *Integration with other GCP services*: Cloud SQL can be easily integrated with other GCP services such as App Engine, Compute Engine, and Cloud Storage, making it easy to build a complete cloud-based solution for your applications.

Cloud SQL is a great option for users looking for a fully managed, high-performance relational database service that is easy to use and integrate with other GCP services.

Automatic Backup of Cloud SQL Database

Automatic backups are a feature of Google Cloud SQL that allow the service to automatically create and manage backups of your databases. These backups are stored in a separate storage location and can be used to recover from data loss or corruption.

The frequency and retention period of the backups can be configured by the user. For example, you can set backups to occur every day, every week, or every month, up to 365 backups. You can also set the retention period for backups, which means that backups older than the retention period you set will be deleted automatically.

Cloud SQL backups are incremental, which means that only changes made to the database since the last backup are included in the new backup. This makes the backup process more efficient and reduces storage costs. That means Cloud SQL takes one full backup of your database instance and then uses incremental backups to capture only the changes made since the last backup. This means the first backup contains all of the data in your database, but subsequent backups capture only the new or changed data, rather than duplicating all the data in each backup.

The backups can be used to restore the entire database or specific tables, and they can also be used to create a new Cloud SQL instance with the same data as the original one.

The automatic backup feature in Google Cloud SQL allows users to automatically create and manage backups of their databases, with configurable frequency and retention period. These backups can be used to recover from data loss or corruption and also to create new Cloud SQL instances with the same data as the original one.

Now we will discuss configuring automatic backup.

Configuring Automatic Backup

To configure automatic backups for a Cloud SQL instance, you can follow these steps:

1. Go to the Cloud SQL instances page in the Google Cloud Console.
2. Click the instance for which you want to configure automatic backups.
3. On the instance details page, click the Backup tab.
4. In the Automatic Backups section, you can configure the following options:
    - *Backup window*: The time window during which backups will be taken. You can choose a predefined window or specify a custom window.
    - *Retention period*: The number of days for which backups will be retained. Once the retention period is reached, backups will be deleted automatically.
5. Click Save to apply the changes.

It's important to note that the backups will be taken only during the backup window you specified and only when the instance is running during that window.

You can also view the status of your backups and download the backups on the Backup tab.

Note When you create a new Cloud SQL instance, automatic backups are enabled by default, and the retention period is set to 7 days.

Automatic Software Updates of Database Software to the Latest Version

The automatic software updates feature of Google Cloud SQL allows the service to automatically update the database software to the latest version. This ensures that your databases are always up-to-date with the latest security and performance enhancements.

When a new version of the database software is released, Cloud SQL will schedule an update window during which the update will be applied. The update window can be customized by the user. The update process is designed to be nondisruptive, meaning that your database will continue to be available during the update process.

It's important to note that automatic software updates apply only to the database software and not the data stored in the database. Also, it's always a good idea to test the updates in a nonproduction environment before applying it to your production databases.

To configure automatic software updates for a Cloud SQL instance, you can follow these steps:

1. Go to the Cloud SQL instances page in the Google Cloud Console.
2. Click the instance for which you want to configure automatic updates.
3. In the instance details page, click the Settings tab.
4. In the Automatic Updates section, you can select the option "Automatically patch minor version upgrades."
5. Click Save to apply the changes.

It's important to note that automatic software updates will apply only to minor version updates and not to major version updates. In the case of major version updates, users will be notified and will have to manually perform the update.

In short, automatic software updates is a feature in Google Cloud SQL that allows the service to automatically update the database software to the latest version, ensuring that the databases are always up-to-date with the latest security and performance enhancements. This feature can be configured in the Cloud SQL instances, and it's nondisruptive, meaning that the database will continue to be available during the update process.

High Availability of Google Cloud SQL

High availability (HA) is a feature that ensures that a system or service is continuously operational and available to users, even in the event of planned or unplanned outages. In the context of Google Cloud SQL, high availability refers to the ability of the service to keep databases running and accessible, even in the event of an unexpected failure or maintenance.

Google Cloud SQL offers several options for achieving high availability.

- *Read replicas*: This feature allows you to create one or more read-only replicas of a master database. The replicas are updated in real time with the master database and can be used to offload read traffic from the master. This helps to improve performance and reduce the risk of overloading the master database.
- *Automatic failover*: This feature automatically switches over to a standby replica if the primary instance fails. This ensures that the service remains available even in the case of an unexpected failure. For high availability, you can set up read replicas in different regions and failover on it if the whole region is down.
- *Multizone deployment*: This feature allows you to deploy your Cloud SQL instances across multiple availability zones within a region. This provides additional protection against failures and outages caused by zone-specific issues, such as power outages or network failures.

- *Cloud SQL for PostgreSQL and MySQL support for replication*: This means that you can use replication to create a highly available setup.
- *Cloud SQL for PostgreSQL and MySQL support Cloud SQL managed replication*; This means you can use replication and managed by Cloud SQL service to create a highly available setup.

It's worth noting that some of these options may come with additional costs, and it's important to evaluate the specific requirements and cost implications of each option before deciding on a high availability solution for your Cloud SQL instances.

Google Cloud SQL offers several options for achieving high availability such as read replicas, automatic failover, multizone deployment, and replication support for both PostgreSQL and MySQL. These options can help to improve performance and reduce the risk of overloading the master database, ensuring service availability even in the case of unexpected failure or maintenance.

Let's talk read replicas in detail in the next section.

Cloud SQL Read Replicas

Read replicas are a feature in Google Cloud SQL that allows you to create one or more read-only copies of a master database. These replicas are updated in real time with the master database and can be used to offload read traffic from the master. This helps to improve performance and reduce the risk of overloading the master database.

When a read replica is created, it initially replicates the data from the master database. After that, it continuously receives updates from the master database through the replication process. This ensures that the replica always has the most recent data.

Read replicas can be used for several purposes, such as the following:

- *Scaling read performance*: By offloading read traffic to replicas, you can improve the overall performance of your database. This is particularly useful for read-heavy workloads or for serving users in different geographic locations.
- *Analytical workloads*: By having read replicas, you can create a separate replica for analytical workloads; this will help to avoid impacting the performance of the primary replica.

- *Backups*: Read replicas can be used as a source for creating backups.
- *Multiregion deployments*: By having read replicas in different regions, you can serve users in different geographic locations with lower latency.

Read replicas are supported for Cloud SQL for MySQL and Cloud SQL for PostgreSQL.

It's important to note that while read replicas can be used to offload read traffic, they cannot be used to offload write traffic. Writes must be directed to the master database. Also, it's important to evaluate the cost implications of creating read replicas, as each replica instance incurs additional charges.

The replicas can be used for several purposes such as scaling read performance, analytical workloads, backups, and multiregion deployments. They are supported for Cloud SQL for MySQL and Cloud SQL for PostgreSQL, but it's important to evaluate the cost implications of creating read replicas as each replica instance incurs additional charges.

Next, we will discuss the automatic failover of Cloud SQL.

Cloud SQL: Automatic Failover

Automatic failover is a feature in Google Cloud SQL that automatically switches to a standby replica if the primary instance fails. This ensures that the service remains available even if there is an unexpected failure.

When a primary instance fails, the system automatically switches to a healthy replica, which becomes the new primary instance. This process is transparent to users and applications and should not disrupt service availability.

Automatic failover is supported for Cloud SQL for MySQL and Cloud SQL for PostgreSQL instances with replication enabled.

When you create a new Cloud SQL instance, you can specify whether you want to enable automatic failover. If you choose to enable automatic failover, you can also specify the number of replicas you want to create, as well as the zone or region where you want to create them.

It's worth noting that automatic failover comes with additional costs, and it's important to evaluate the specific requirements and cost implications of this feature before deciding to enable it for your Cloud SQL instances.

Automatic failover is supported for Cloud SQL for MySQL and Cloud SQL for PostgreSQL instances with replication enabled. When you create a new Cloud SQL instance, you can specify whether you want to enable automatic failover and the number of replicas you want to create. However, it's important to evaluate the specific requirements and cost implications of this feature before deciding to enable it for your Cloud SQL instances.

Multizone Deployment

Multizone deployment is a feature in Google Cloud SQL that allows you to create replicas of a master database across multiple zones within a region. This improves the availability and durability of your database by providing protection against zone-level failures.

When you create a Cloud SQL instance, you can specify the number of zones you want to create replicas in. Google Cloud SQL automatically creates replicas in different zones and keeps them in sync with the master database.

If the primary instance fails, one of the replicas in a different zone will automatically be promoted to primary and take over. This process is transparent to users and applications and should not disrupt service availability.

Multizone deployment is supported for Cloud SQL for MySQL and Cloud SQL for PostgreSQL instances.

It's worth noting that using multiple zones for replication increases the cost of running the Cloud SQL instances. It's important to evaluate the specific requirements and cost implications of this feature before deciding to enable it for your Cloud SQL instances.

This feature is supported for Cloud SQL for MySQL and Cloud SQL for PostgreSQL instances. When creating a new Cloud SQL instance, you can specify the number of zones you want to create replicas in. However, it's important to evaluate the specific requirements and cost implications of this feature before deciding to enable it for your Cloud SQL instances.

Cloud SQL: Scalability

Scalability is the ability of a system, such as a database, to handle an increasing amount of work or load. Google Cloud SQL provides several options for scaling your database depending on your needs.

One way to scale a Cloud SQL instance is by increasing its memory and CPU resources. This can be done by modifying the machine type of the instance. This allows you to handle more concurrent connections and perform more complex queries.

Another way to scale a Cloud SQL instance is by creating read replicas. Read replicas are copies of the primary instance that can be used to handle read-only workloads such as read-heavy workloads. This allows you to offload read traffic from the primary instance and improve performance.

Additionally, Google Cloud SQL allows you to scale out your database by sharding it across multiple instances. This is a more advanced technique, but it allows you to horizontally scale your database and handle very large workloads.

Google Cloud SQL provides several options for scaling your database depending on your needs, such as increasing its memory and CPU resources, creating read replicas, or sharding it across multiple instances. You can modify the machine type of the instance for more concurrent connections and complex queries, create read replicas for read-heavy workloads, offload read traffic from the primary instance, and implement sharding for very large workloads.

Cloud SQL: Security

To secure your Google Cloud SQL instances, you can take several steps.

1. Use Cloud SQL Authentication to control access to your instances. This feature allows you to use Google Cloud Identity and Access Management (IAM) to grant or deny access to specific users or groups.

2. Use Cloud SQL Authorization to control access to specific databases and tables within your instances.

3. Enable encryption for your instances to protect data at rest and in transit. Cloud SQL supports both customer-managed encryption keys and Google-managed encryption keys.

4. Use Cloud SQL Private IP to connect to your instances securely and privately from within your Google Cloud Virtual Private Cloud (VPC) network.

5. Use Cloud SQL backups and replication to ensure that your data is protected and available in the event of a disaster.

6. Regularly check the Cloud SQL audit logs to monitor for unusual activity and ensure compliance with security policies.

To configure security settings, you can use the Cloud SQL web interface, the `gcloud` command-line tool, or the Cloud SQL API. You will need to have the appropriate permissions to configure security settings for your instances.

Security is a continuous process, and you need to regularly review and update your security configurations to ensure that they are meeting your needs and protecting your data.

Authentication

Cloud SQL authentication is a feature of Google Cloud SQL that allows you to control access to your instances using Google Cloud IAM permissions.

With Cloud SQL Authentication, you can grant or deny access to specific users or groups based on their Google Cloud Platform identity. This means you can use the same authentication and authorization mechanisms that you use for other GCP resources to control access to your Cloud SQL instances.

There are two types of authentication methods you can use with Cloud SQL.

- *Cloud IAM authentication*: This method uses Google Cloud IAM to grant or deny access to specific users or groups based on their GCP identity.

- *Database authentication*: This method uses the standard authentication mechanisms provided by the underlying database engine. For example, you can use username and password authentication to grant or deny access to specific users.

You can configure authentication settings for a Cloud SQL instance using the Cloud SQL web interface, the `gcloud` command-line tool, or the Cloud SQL API.

To use Cloud SQL authentication, you need to enable the Cloud SQL API, create a service account with the appropriate permissions, and configure your Cloud SQL instances to use the service account.

Authorization

Cloud SQL authorization refers to the process of controlling access to specific databases and tables within your Cloud SQL instances. This allows you to specify which users or groups have permission to perform specific actions on your instances, such as `SELECT`, `INSERT`, `UPDATE`, or `DELETE`.

Cloud SQL supports two types of authorization methods.

- *Cloud IAM authorization*: This method uses Google Cloud IAM to grant or deny access to specific users or groups based on their GCP identity. You can specify the permissions that each user or group has for a particular Cloud SQL instance or specific database or table.
- *Database authorization*: This method uses the standard authorization mechanisms provided by the underlying database engine. For example, you can create users and roles in MySQL and grant or revoke specific privileges to them.

You can configure authorization settings for a Cloud SQL instance using the Cloud SQL web interface, the `gcloud` command-line tool, or the Cloud SQL API.

Authorization works in conjunction with authentication, and it is a best practice to use both methods together to ensure that only authorized users can access your Cloud SQL instances and perform specific actions on the databases and tables within them.

Encryption

Encryption is a process of converting plain text into ciphertext to protect data from unauthorized access. Google Cloud SQL supports encryption to protect data at rest and in transit.

Encryption at rest:

- Google Cloud SQL supports customer-managed encryption keys (CMEK) and Google-managed encryption keys (GMEK) for encrypting data stored on disk.
- With CMEK, you can manage your own encryption keys, while with GMEK, Google handles the key management for you.
- Both methods use the Advanced Encryption Standard (AES) algorithm with 256-bit keys to encrypt data.

Encryption in transit:

- Cloud SQL supports Transport Layer Security (TLS) to encrypt data in transit between the client and the Cloud SQL instance.
- You can configure the encryption settings for an instance and use the SSL/TLS certificates to establish secure connections.

It is important to keep in mind that encryption does not protect you from security breaches caused by misconfigurations, such as a weak password, so it is important to use encryption in conjunction with other security measures to ensure the overall security of your data.

You can configure encryption settings for a Cloud SQL instance using the Cloud SQL web interface, the `gcloud` command-line tool, or the Cloud SQL API.

Private IP

Cloud SQL Private IP is a feature of Google Cloud SQL that allows you to connect to your instances securely and privately from within your Google Cloud VPC network. With Private IP, your Cloud SQL instances are assigned a private IP address within your VPC network, which means that connections to the instances are made over an internal network, rather than over the Internet. With Cloud SQL Private IP, data stays within Google's network and is not exposed to the public Internet. This provides an additional layer of security for your data, as it is not transmitted over the Internet where it could potentially be intercepted by unauthorized parties.

By using Cloud SQL Private IP, you can do the following:

- Enhance the security of your connections by eliminating the need to open inbound ports on your firewall.
- Improve the performance of your connections by reducing latency and increasing throughput.
- Simplify your network architecture by eliminating the need for a VPN or other network-level security mechanisms.

To use Cloud SQL Private IP, you need to do the following:

- Create a VPC network and a subnet within that network
- Create a Cloud SQL instance with the same VPC network and subnet
- Connect to the Cloud SQL instance using its private IP address

You can use Cloud SQL Private IP in combination with Cloud SQL authentication, authorization, and encryption to create a highly secure and performant connection to your Cloud SQL instances.

Audit Log

Audit logging is a process of recording events that occur within a system, such as user actions, system events, and security-related activities. Google Cloud SQL supports audit logging to help you monitor and analyze the activity on your instances.

Cloud SQL Audit Logs provide detailed information about the activity on your instances, such as the following:

- Who executed a particular query
- What query was executed
- When it was executed
- From where it was executed

You can view the audit logs in the Cloud SQL logs viewer in the Cloud Console or export them to Cloud Logging or BigQuery for further analysis.

To enable Audit Logs for a Cloud SQL instance, you need to follow these steps:

1. Create a Cloud SQL instance.
2. Enable the Cloud SQL Admin API.
3. Create a Cloud Logging sink or BigQuery dataset.
4. Configure the Cloud SQL instance to export the logs to the Cloud Logging sink or BigQuery dataset.

Audit logs can help you detect and troubleshoot issues, detect and prevent security breaches, and comply with regulatory requirements. It is a best practice to regularly review the audit logs and take appropriate actions based on the information they provide.

Cloud SQL: Monitoring and Logging

Google Cloud SQL Monitoring and Logging are important tools that help you understand the performance and activity of your Cloud SQL instances, as well as detect and troubleshoot issues.

Monitoring

The following are the monitoring features:

- Cloud SQL Monitoring allows you to track the performance of your instances, such as CPU and memory usage, number of connections, and disk space usage.
- You can use Cloud SQL Monitoring to set up alerts so you can be notified when certain thresholds are met, such as when the CPU usage exceeds a certain percentage.
- You can view the monitoring data in the Cloud Console or export it to Cloud Monitoring for further analysis.
- To enable monitoring for a Cloud SQL instance, you need to do the following:
    1. Create a Cloud SQL instance.
    2. Enable the Cloud Monitoring API.
    3. Create a Cloud workspace.
    4. Link the Cloud SQL instance to the Cloud workspace.

Logging

The following are the logging features:

- Cloud SQL Logging allows you to record events that occur within your instances, such as queries, errors, and system events.
- You can use Cloud SQL Logging to track user activity, detect and troubleshoot issues, and comply with regulatory requirements.

- You can view the logs in the Cloud Console, export them to Cloud Logging, or BigQuery for further analysis.
- To enable logging for a Cloud SQL instance, you need to do the following:
    1. Create a Cloud SQL instance.
    2. Enable the Cloud SQL Admin API.
    3. Create a Cloud Logging sink or BigQuery dataset.
    4. Configure the Cloud SQL instance to export the logs to the Cloud Logging sink or BigQuery dataset.

Both monitoring and logging are important for ensuring the performance and security of your Cloud SQL instances and should be configured and regularly reviewed as a best practice.

Now let's discuss how to integrate Cloud SQL with other Google Cloud services.

Integration of Cloud SQL with Other GCP Services

Google Cloud SQL can be integrated with other Google Cloud Platform services to create a more powerful and flexible cloud-based infrastructure. These are some examples of how Cloud SQL can be integrated with other GCP services:

- *Cloud Storage*: You can use Cloud Storage to store your backups and binary logs, which can be used to restore your Cloud SQL instances in the case of a failure or data loss.
- *Cloud Load Balancing*: You can use Cloud Load Balancing to distribute incoming traffic to your Cloud SQL instances, which can help you improve performance and availability.
- *Cloud IAM*: You can use Cloud IAM to control access to your Cloud SQL instances and to fine-tune permissions for different users and groups.
- *Cloud data loss prevention (DLP)*: You can use Cloud DLP to automatically discover, classify, and redact sensitive data in your Cloud SQL instances, which can help you protect sensitive information and comply with regulatory requirements.

- *Cloud Dataflow*: You can use Cloud Dataflow to process and analyze the data in your Cloud SQL instances, which can help you gain insights and make data-driven decisions.
- *Cloud App Engine*: You can use Cloud App Engine to host your web applications and connect them to your Cloud SQL instances, which can help you create powerful and scalable web applications.

Integration of Cloud SQL with Cloud Storage

Google Cloud SQL can be integrated with Google Cloud Storage to store backups and binary logs, which can be used to restore your Cloud SQL instances in the case of a failure or data loss. This integration allows you to keep your data safe and recoverable, even in the event of a disaster.

Here is an example of how you can integrate Cloud SQL with Cloud Storage:

1. Create a Cloud SQL instance and a Cloud Storage bucket.
2. In the Cloud SQL instance, go to the Backup tab and set the backup configuration. You can choose to take backups on a daily, weekly, or monthly basis, and specify a retention period.
3. On the Backup tab, select the Cloud Storage bucket where you want to store the backups. You can also choose to encrypt the backups for added security.
4. Once the backups are configured, you can go to the Replication tab in the Cloud SQL instance and set up replication to another region or another Cloud SQL instance.
5. You can also enable binary logging in the Cloud SQL instance, which will allow you to create point-in-time recovery snapshots.
6. Set up replication to another region or another Cloud SQL instance.
7. Once binary logging is enabled, you can create a Cloud Storage bucket to store the binary logs.
8. Go to the Binary Logs tab in the Cloud SQL instance, select the Cloud Storage bucket where you want to store the binary logs, and set the retention period.

9. Once the binary logs are stored in Cloud Storage, you can use them to restore your Cloud SQL instances to a specific point in time.

By integrating Cloud SQL with Cloud Storage, you can ensure that your data is safe and recoverable, even in the event of a disaster. This integration can help you improve the availability and resilience of your Cloud SQL instances and protect your data from data loss or corruption.

The previous steps may change or be different based on the Cloud SQL version you are using. It's always recommended to check the official documentation for the updated instructions.

Integration of Cloud SQL with Cloud Load Balancing

Google Cloud SQL can be integrated with Google Cloud Load Balancing to distribute incoming traffic to your Cloud SQL instances, which can help you improve performance and availability. This integration allows you to create a highly available and scalable Cloud SQL infrastructure that can handle a large number of concurrent connections.

Here is an example of how you can integrate Cloud SQL with Cloud Load Balancing:

1. Create a Cloud SQL instance and a Cloud Load Balancing instance.
2. In the Cloud SQL instance, go to the Connections tab, and set the maximum number of connections. This will help you control the number of connections that can be made to the Cloud SQL instance at any given time.
3. In the Cloud Load Balancing instance, create a new backend service and point it to the Cloud SQL instance.
4. Create a new load balancer and attach the back-end service to it.
5. Once the load balancer is created, you can configure health checks and automatic failover to ensure that the Cloud SQL instance is always available.

6. Configure the load balancer to distribute incoming traffic to the Cloud SQL instance, based on your specific needs.

7. Once the load balancer is configured, you can use it to distribute incoming traffic to the Cloud SQL instance and to ensure that the Cloud SQL instance is always available, even in the event of a failure.

By integrating Cloud SQL with Cloud Load Balancing, you can create a highly available and scalable Cloud SQL infrastructure that can handle a large number of concurrent connections. This integration can help you improve the performance and availability of your Cloud SQL instances and ensure that your data is always accessible to your users.

The previous steps may change or be different based on the Cloud SQL version you are using. It's always recommended to check the official documentation for the updated instructions.

Integration of Cloud SQL with IAM

Google Cloud SQL can be integrated with Google Cloud IAM to control access to your Cloud SQL instances and resources. This integration allows you to grant or deny access to specific users, groups, or services, based on your organization's security policies.

Here is an example of how you can integrate Cloud SQL with IAM:

1. Create a Cloud SQL instance and a project in the Google Cloud Console.

2. In the Cloud SQL instance, go to the Access Control tab and create a new IAM policy.

3. In the IAM policy, specify the roles and permissions that should be granted or denied to specific users, groups, or services. For example, you can grant the Cloud SQL Editor role to a specific group of users or deny access to the Cloud SQL instance to a specific service account.

4. Once the IAM policy is created, you can associate it with the Cloud SQL instance.

5. In the Cloud SQL instance, go to the Access Control tab and add the IAM policy to the Cloud SQL instance.

6. Once the IAM policy is associated with the Cloud SQL instance, the specified roles and permissions will be enforced for the specified users, groups, or services.

By integrating Cloud SQL with IAM, you can control access to your Cloud SQL instances and resources, based on your organization's security policies. This integration can help you improve the security of your Cloud SQL instances and ensure that only authorized users, groups, or services have access to your data.

The previous steps may change or be different based on the Cloud SQL version you are using. It's always recommended to check the official documentation for the updated instructions.

Integration of Cloud SQL with Cloud Data Loss Prevention

Google Cloud SQL can be integrated with Google Cloud DLP to protect sensitive data in your Cloud SQL databases. This integration allows you to automatically discover, classify, and redact sensitive data in your Cloud SQL databases, based on your organization's security policies. It is also needed because of the regulatory requirements.

Here is an example of how you can integrate Cloud SQL with Cloud DLP:

1. Create a Cloud SQL instance and a project in the Google Cloud Console.
2. In the Cloud SQL instance, go to the Security tab, and then click Data Loss Prevention.
3. Click Create new DLP job," and configure it to scan the Cloud SQL instance for sensitive data.
4. In the DLP job configuration, specify the type of data you want to scan for (e.g., credit card numbers, Social Security numbers, etc.), and specify the actions you want DLP to take if sensitive data is detected (e.g., redact, mask, etc.).
5. Once the DLP job is configured, you can run it and view the results in the Cloud DLP logs.
6. You can also set up periodic scans or even real-time scanning of your Cloud SQL databases.

By integrating Cloud SQL with Cloud DLP, you can protect sensitive data in your Cloud SQL databases, based on your organization's security policies. This integration can help you improve the security of your Cloud SQL instances and ensure that sensitive data is protected against data loss or leakage.

The previous steps may change or be different based on the Cloud SQL version you are using. It's always recommended to check the official documentation for the updated instructions.

Integration of Cloud SQL with Cloud Dataflow

Google Cloud SQL can be integrated with Google Cloud Dataflow to process and analyze data in your Cloud SQL databases. This integration allows you to use Dataflow to extract, transform, and load (ETL) data from your Cloud SQL databases, enable continuous streaming, and then process and analyze the data using Dataflow's powerful data processing capabilities.

A use case for integrating Cloud SQL with Dataflow could be in a scenario where a company wants to analyze the customer data stored in their Cloud SQL database to gain insights into customer behavior and preferences. The company could use Dataflow to extract and transform the relevant data from the Cloud SQL database and then use Dataflow's powerful data processing capabilities to perform analysis on the data, such as identifying trends and patterns in customer behavior. This could help the company to make data-driven decisions about their products and services and to better understand their customers' needs and preferences.

Here is an example of how you can integrate Cloud SQL with Cloud Dataflow:

1. Create a Cloud SQL instance and a project in the Google Cloud Console.
2. Create a Dataflow job in the Google Cloud Console, and specify the Cloud SQL instance as the source of the data.
3. In the Dataflow job, specify the SQL query that you want to run on the Cloud SQL instance to extract the data.
4. Use the Dataflow SDK to define the pipeline that will process and analyze the data.

5. Once the pipeline is defined, you can run the Dataflow job to process and analyze the data.

6. The processed data can then be stored in a BigQuery table, Cloud Storage, or another storage option of your choice.

By integrating Cloud SQL with Cloud Dataflow, you can process and analyze data in your Cloud SQL databases using Dataflow's powerful data processing capabilities. This integration can help you gain insights from your data and make better data-driven decisions. It also allows for more flexible processing of your data and can handle large volumes of data with ease.

The previous steps may change or be different based on the Cloud SQL version you are using. It's always recommended to check the official documentation for the updated instructions.

Integration of Cloud SQL with Cloud App Engine

Google Cloud SQL can be integrated with Google Cloud App Engine to create web and mobile applications that use data stored in Cloud SQL.

Here is an example of how you can integrate Cloud SQL with Cloud App Engine:

1. Create a Cloud SQL instance and a project in the Google Cloud Console.

2. Create an App Engine application in the same project and select the runtime environment (e.g., Java, Python, Go, etc.).

3. In the App Engine application, use the Cloud SQL library for the runtime environment to connect to the Cloud SQL instance and interact with the data stored in the instance.

4. Use the Cloud SQL library to perform operations such as reading, writing, updating, and deleting data in the Cloud SQL instance.

5. Once the App Engine application is configured to interact with the Cloud SQL instance, you can deploy it to App Engine, and it will be accessible to users via a URL.

By integrating Cloud SQL with Cloud App Engine, you can create web and mobile applications that use data stored in Cloud SQL. This integration allows you to easily build and deploy applications that can read, write, update, and delete data stored in a Cloud SQL instance. Additionally, App Engine provides automatic scaling, load balancing, and monitoring services that can help you create highly available and scalable applications.

The previous steps may change or be different based on the Cloud SQL version you are using and runtime environment you are using. It's always recommended to check the official documentation for the updated instructions.

Understanding the SQL/NoSQL Options in GCP

Google Cloud Platform offers several options for working with SQL databases.

- *Cloud SQL*: A fully managed relational database service that allows you to create and manage SQL databases, including MySQL and PostgreSQL
- *Cloud Spanner*: A globally distributed, relational database service that offers a SQL-like interface and automatic, synchronous replication for high availability
- *Cloud Bigtable*: A NoSQL, wide-column store database that is designed for large-scale, low-latency data processing
- *Cloud Datastore*: A NoSQL document database that allows you to store, retrieve, and query data using a simple key-value model
- *BigQuery*: A fully managed, cloud-native data warehouse that allows you to run SQL-like queries on large datasets

GCP offers a range of SQL and NoSQL database options to suit different use cases and workloads. Cloud SQL is a fully managed SQL database service, while Cloud Spanner offers a globally distributed SQL database with automatic replication. Cloud Bigtable is a NoSQL wide-column store database designed for low-latency data processing, while Cloud Datastore is a document-based NoSQL database with a simple key-value model. Finally, BigQuery is a cloud-native data warehouse that allows for SQL-like queries on large datasets.

When choosing a SQL option in GCP, it's important to consider the specific requirements of your use case, such as the type of data you need to store, the performance and scalability needs of your application, and the level of control and management you need.

Benefits of Cloud SQL Instead of a Self-Managed, On-Premises Database

Cloud SQL is a fully managed relational database service offered by Google Cloud Platform that allows you to create and manage SQL databases, including MySQL and PostgreSQL. It offers several benefits over self-managed, on-premises databases.

- *Scalability*: Cloud SQL allows you to easily scale your databases up or down to match the needs of your application, without having to worry about the underlying infrastructure.
- *High availability*: Cloud SQL automatically replicates data across multiple zones to ensure that your data is always available, even in the event of a zone failure.
- *Automatic backups*: Cloud SQL automatically takes daily backups of your data, so you don't have to worry about manually backing up your databases.
- *Security*: Cloud SQL provides several security features, such as encryption at rest and in transit, to ensure that your data is protected.
- *Low maintenance*: With Cloud SQL, you don't have to worry about managing and maintaining the underlying infrastructure, such as servers and storage. Google handles all of the underlying infrastructure, so you can focus on developing and deploying your application.
- *Cost-effective*: Cloud SQL can be more cost-effective than running a self-managed database, especially when you have a variable workload. You pay only for the resources you use, and you can easily scale up or down as needed.

- *Integration*: Cloud SQL easily integrates with other GCP services, such as Cloud App Engine, Cloud Dataflow, and BigQuery, making it easy to build and deploy applications that use data stored in Cloud SQL.
- *Flexibility*: Cloud SQL supports different types of SQL databases, allowing you to choose the database that best meets your needs.

Cloud SQL is a great option for organizations that want the benefits of a relational database without the operational overhead and costs of managing and scaling the infrastructure.

Use Case for Cloud SQL

There are several use cases for using Cloud SQL.

- *Traditional relational databases*: Cloud SQL is a good choice for running traditional, relational databases, such as MySQL and PostgreSQL, in a fully managed environment. This allows you to easily scale and manage your databases without having to worry about the underlying infrastructure.
- *E-commerce and retail*: Cloud SQL can be used to store and manage customer data, inventory, and sales information for e-commerce and retail websites.
- *Content management systems*: Cloud SQL can be used to store and manage content for websites and other digital media, such as images, videos, and articles.
- *Business intelligence and analytics*: Cloud SQL can be used to store and manage data for business intelligence and analytics applications, such as data warehousing and reporting.
- *Mobile and web applications*: Cloud SQL can be used to store and manage data for mobile and web applications, such as user profiles, preferences, and transactions.
- *Internet of Things (IoT) and sensor data*: Cloud SQL can be used to store and manage data from IoT devices and sensors, such as temperature, humidity, and other environmental data.

- *Microservices*: Cloud SQL can be used to store and manage data for microservices-based applications, allowing each microservice to have its own database.
- *Multicloud and hybrid cloud*: Cloud SQL can be used as part of a multicloud or hybrid cloud strategy, allowing organizations to store and manage data in the cloud while also maintaining on-premises databases for specific use cases.

These are just a few examples of the many possible use cases for Cloud SQL. With its scalability, high availability, and automatic backups, Cloud SQL can be used for a wide range of applications and workloads.

Here is one real-life use case for using Cloud SQL.

Suppose a company wants to build an e-commerce website that requires a database to store customer orders, product details, and customer information. They decide to use Google Cloud SQL to manage their database as it provides a fully managed SQL database service, which can handle high volumes of traffic and ensure high availability of their database.

They create a Cloud SQL instance using the Google Cloud Console and configure it to use MySQL. They then create a database schema that includes tables for storing customer orders, product details, and customer information. The Cloud SQL instance provides a public IP address that can be used to connect to the database from the Internet.

Next, they create a web application using a programming language like Java or Python. The web application connects to the Cloud SQL instance using the JDBC driver and runs SQL queries to insert, update, and retrieve data from the database. They also use Cloud SQL's built-in backup feature to ensure that their data is safe and can be restored in case of any failure.

As their e-commerce website grows and more users start using it, they decide to add read replicas to the Cloud SQL instance. The read replicas allow them to scale their read performance and improve the responsiveness of their website. They can also use the replicas for running analytical workloads and generating reports.

In addition, they use Cloud SQL's Private IP feature to connect to their database securely and privately from within their VPC network. This ensures that their data is protected and encrypted while it is in transit between the web application and the database.

In this case, by using Cloud SQL, the company is able to build a scalable and highly available database for their e-commerce website, while minimizing the effort required to manage the database infrastructure.

Now let's talk about the situation when Cloud SQL is the best choice.

Situations When Cloud SQL Is the Best Choice

There are several situations when using Cloud SQL is the best choice:

- *When you have a variable workload*: Cloud SQL is a good choice when you have a variable workload, as you pay only for the resources you use and can easily scale up or down as needed.
- *When you need a fully managed relational database*: Cloud SQL is a fully managed service, so you don't have to worry about managing and maintaining the underlying infrastructure, such as servers and storage. This allows you to focus on developing and deploying your application.
- *When you need high availability*: Cloud SQL automatically replicates data across multiple zones to ensure that your data is always available, even in the event of a zone failure.
- *When you need automatic backups*: Cloud SQL automatically takes daily backups of your data, so you don't have to worry about manually backing up your databases.
- *When you need to integrate with other GCP services*: Cloud SQL easily integrates with other GCP services, such as Cloud App Engine, Cloud Dataflow, and BigQuery, making it easy to build and deploy applications that use data stored in Cloud SQL.
- *When you need a cost-effective solution*: Cloud SQL can be more cost-effective than running a self-managed database, especially when you have a variable workload. You pay only for the resources you use, and you can easily scale up or down as needed.
- *When you need a flexible solution*: Cloud SQL supports different types of SQL databases, allowing you to choose the database that best meets your needs.

- *When you need to comply with specific compliance requirements*: Cloud SQL can be used to store and manage data that is subject to specific compliance requirements, such as HIPAA and PCI DSS.

Cloud SQL is a great option for organizations that want the benefits of a relational database without the operational overhead and costs of managing and scaling the infrastructure. It is best used when you need a fully managed, scalable, and high-available relational database solution that integrates with other GCP services and can be used for a wide range of applications and workloads.

Using Java to Interact with Cloud SQL

Java is a popular programming language that can be used to interact with Cloud SQL. To use Java to interact with Cloud SQL, you will need to use a JDBC driver that supports the database you are using (e.g., MySQL or PostgreSQL) and the version of the database you are using.

Here is an example of how to connect to a Cloud SQL instance running MySQL using Java:

1. Add the MySQL JDBC driver to your classpath. You can download the driver from the MySQL website.

2. Use the JDBC driver to create a connection to the Cloud SQL instance. This can be done using the following code:

```
String url = "jdbc:mysql://" + hostname + ":" + port + "/" + dbName;
Connection connection = DriverManager.getConnection(url, username, password);
```

3. Once the connection is established, you can use standard JDBC calls to interact with the database. For example, to execute a SQL query, you can use the following code:

```
Statement statement = connection.createStatement();
ResultSet resultSet = statement.executeQuery("SELECT * FROM myTable");
```

4. After you have finished interacting with the database, you should close the connection by calling the following code:

```
connection.close();
```

There are also several libraries and frameworks that can be used to interact with Cloud SQL in Java. For example, Spring Framework provides an abstraction layer that makes it easy to interact with databases, including Cloud SQL. As another example, Hibernate is an object-relational mapping (ORM) framework that can be used to interact with databases in a more object-oriented way, it can be integrated with Spring to make it more efficient.

You can use the JDBC driver for the database you are using, along with standard JDBC calls, to interact with Cloud SQL in Java. Additionally, you can use libraries and frameworks, such as Spring and Hibernate, to make interacting with the database even easier.

Creating Tables in Cloud SQL Using Java

To create tables in Cloud SQL, you can use standard SQL commands. The syntax for creating tables will depend on the database management system (DBMS) you are using (e.g., MySQL or PostgreSQL). Here is an example of how to create a table in a Cloud SQL instance running MySQL:

```
CREATE TABLE myTable (
  id INT PRIMARY KEY,
  name VARCHAR(255) NOT NULL,
  age INT NOT NULL
);
```

This example creates a table called `myTable` with three columns: `id`, `name`, and `age`. The `id` column is set as the primary key and cannot contain null values. The `name` and `age` columns cannot contain null values either.

You can also add additional constraints to the table. For example, you can add a unique constraint to a column like this:

```
CREATE TABLE myTable (
  id INT PRIMARY KEY,
  name VARCHAR(255) NOT NULL UNIQUE,
  age INT NOT NULL
);
```

You can also create tables with foreign key constraints, indexes, and more. The syntax for these additional features will depend on the DBMS you are using.

You can also create tables using a programming language like Java. The process will be similar to the process of interacting with Cloud SQL using Java, as I described earlier: you'll need to open a connection to your Cloud SQL instance, create a statement, and execute the query.

```
String createTableSQL = "CREATE TABLE myTable ("
            + "id INT PRIMARY KEY, "
            + "name VARCHAR(255) NOT NULL, "
            + "age INT NOT NULL)";

        Statement createTable = connection.createStatement();

        // execute the query, and get a boolean indicating whether it
        returned a result set
        createTable.execute(createTableSQL);
```

It's important to note that creating tables can also be done using the Cloud SQL web console, the Cloud SQL command-line tool, and the `gcloud` command-line tool.

In short, to create tables in Cloud SQL, you can use standard SQL commands or a programming language like Java. Depending on your use case and the database management system you are using, you may find it more convenient to use one method over the other.

Inserting Data into Cloud SQL Tables Using Java

To insert data into a table in Cloud SQL, you can use the standard SQL `INSERT` command. The following is an example of how to insert data into a table called `myTable` in a Cloud SQL instance running MySQL:

```
INSERT INTO myTable (id, name, age) VALUES (1, 'John', 25);
```

This example inserts a new row into the `myTable` table with the values 1 for the `id` column, `John` for the `name` column, and 25 for the `age` column.

You can also insert multiple rows at once using the following syntax:

```
INSERT INTO myTable (id, name, age) VALUES (1, 'John', 25), (2, 'Mike',
30), (3, 'Sara', 35);
```

You can also insert data into a table using a programming language like Java. Listing 5-1 shows an example of how to insert data into a table called `myTable` using Java.

Listing 5-1. Inserting Data into a Table Using Java

```
PreparedStatement insertData = connection.prepareStatement("INSERT INTO
myTable (id, name, age) VALUES (?, ?, ?)");

insertData.setInt(1, 1);
insertData.setString(2, "John");
insertData.setInt(3, 25);

insertData.execute();
```

This example uses a prepared statement to insert data into the `myTable` table. The `setInt()` and `setString()` methods are used to set the values for the `id`, `name`, and `age` columns. The `execute()` method is used to execute the prepared statement and insert the data into the table.

You can also insert data into a table using the Cloud SQL web console, the Cloud SQL command-line tool, and the `gcloud` command-line tool.

In short, to insert data into a table in Cloud SQL, you can use the standard SQL `INSERT` command or a programming language like Java. Depending on your use case, you may find it more convenient to use one method over the other.

Running Queries on a Cloud SQL Instance Using Java

To run queries on a Cloud SQL instance, you can use the standard SQL `SELECT` command. Here is an example of how to run a query to select all data from a table called `myTable` in a Cloud SQL instance running MySQL:

```
SELECT * FROM myTable;
```

This query will return all rows and columns from the `myTable` table.

You can also use SQL statements with a `WHERE` clause to select specific data from a table. The following is an example:

```
SELECT name, age FROM myTable WHERE id = 1;
```

This query will return the name and age columns from the `myTable` table where the `id` equals 1.

You can also use SQL statements with `JOIN` clauses to select data from multiple tables. The following is an example:

```
SELECT myTable.name, myTable.age, otherTable.address FROM myTable JOIN
otherTable ON myTable.id = otherTable.id;
```

This query will return the name, age, and address columns from the myTable and otherTable tables where the id columns match.

You can also run queries using a programming language such as Java. The following is an example of how to run a query to select all data from a table called myTable using Java:

```
PreparedStatement selectData = connection.prepareStatement("SELECT * FROM
myTable");
ResultSet result = selectData.executeQuery();
```

This example uses a prepared statement to select data from the myTable table. The executeQuery() method is used to execute the prepared statement and return the results as a ResultSet object. You can then iterate over the ResultSet object to access the returned data.

You can also run queries using the Cloud SQL web console, the Cloud SQL command-line tool, and the gcloud command-line tool.

In short, to run queries on a Cloud SQL instance, you can use the standard SQL SELECT command or a programming language like Java. Depending on your use case, you may find it more convenient to use one method over the other.

Using Cloud SQL for Data Storage in a Java Application

Listing 5-2 shows a detailed example of how you can use the Google Cloud SQL JDBC driver to connect to a Cloud SQL instance running MySQL and perform some basic CRUD operations in a Java application.

Listing 5-2. Using Google Cloud SQL JDBC Driver to Connect to a Cloud SQL Instance Running MySQL

```
import java.sql.Connection;
import java.sql.DriverManager;
import java.sql.PreparedStatement;
import java.sql.ResultSet;
```

```
import java.sql.SQLException;
import java.sql.Statement;

public class CloudSQL {

    // Replace with your Cloud SQL instance connection name
    private static final String INSTANCE_CONNECTION_NAME = "my-gcp-
    project:us-central1:my-cloud-sql-instance";

    // Replace with your Cloud SQL instance username
    private static final String USERNAME = "myusername";

    // Replace with your Cloud SQL instance password
    private static final String PASSWORD = "mypassword";

    // Replace with your database name
    private static final String DATABASE_NAME = "mydatabase";

    // JDBC URL format: jdbc:mysql://[HOST]:[PORT]/[DB_NAME]
    private static final String JDBC_URL = String.format("jdbc:mysql://
    google/%s?cloudSqlInstance=%s&"
            + "socketFactory=com.google.cloud.sql.mysql.SocketFactory",
            DATABASE_NAME, INSTANCE_CONNECTION_NAME);

    public static void main(String[] args) throws SQLException {
        // Connect to the Cloud SQL instance
        Connection connection = DriverManager.getConnection(JDBC_URL,
        USERNAME, PASSWORD);

        // Create a table
        createTable(connection);

        // Insert some data
        insertData(connection);

        // Read the data
        readData(connection);

        // Update the data
        updateData(connection);
```

```
        // Delete the data
        deleteData(connection);

        // Close the connection
        connection.close();
    }

    private static void createTable(Connection connection) throws
    SQLException {
        Statement statement = connection.createStatement();
        statement.executeUpdate("CREATE TABLE mytable (id INT PRIMARY KEY,
        name VARCHAR(255))");
    }

    private static void insertData(Connection connection) throws
    SQLException {
        PreparedStatement statement = connection.prepareStatement("INSERT
        INTO mytable (id, name) VALUES (?, ?)");
        statement.setInt(1, 1);
        statement.setString(2, "John Doe");
        statement.executeUpdate();
    }

    private static void readData(Connection connection) throws
    SQLException {
        Statement statement = connection.createStatement();
        ResultSet resultSet = statement.executeQuery("SELECT * FROM
        mytable");
        while (resultSet.next()) {
            int id = resultSet.getInt("id");
            String name = resultSet.getString("name");
            System.out.println("ID: " + id + ", Name: " + name);
        }
    }
```

```
    private static void updateData(Connection connection) throws
    SQLException {
        PreparedStatement statement = connection.prepareStatement("UPDATE
        mytable SET name = ? WHERE id = ?");
        statement.setString(1,"Jane Doe");
                        statement.setInt(2, 1);
                        statement.executeUpdate();
                        }
       private static void deleteData(Connection connection) throws
       SQLException {
           PreparedStatement statement = connection.
           prepareStatement("DELETE FROM mytable WHERE id = ?");
           statement.setInt(1, 1);
           statement.executeUpdate();
       }
}
}
```

This example assumes you have a Cloud SQL instance running MySQL and that you have created a database named mydatabase. You will need to replace the INSTANCE_CONNECTION_NAME, USERNAME, PASSWORD, and DATABASE_NAME variables with the appropriate values for your Cloud SQL instance.

The example starts by connecting to the Cloud SQL instance using the JDBC URL, username, and password, and then creates a table named mytable with two columns: id and name.

It then inserts a single row of data into the table, reads the data back, updates the data, and finally deletes the data.

It is important to note that you will need to add the Google Cloud SQL JDBC driver to your application's classpath for this example to work. You can download the driver from the following link: https://github.com/GoogleCloudPlatform/cloud-sql-jdbc-driver.

Also, you will need to enable the Cloud SQL API and create a service account with the appropriate permissions to access your Cloud SQL instance.

In this example, I am storing the password in a variable and providing inline database connection string. In production code, you should follow the best practice for storing password and connection strings in secrets.

Summary

In this chapter, you learned about using Google Cloud SQL, a fully managed database service, to store and manage data in the cloud. We discussed the benefits of using Cloud SQL, the types of databases supported, and how to create and manage instances using the Cloud Console, `gcloud` command-line tool, and API. We also explored how to interact with Cloud SQL using programming languages such as Java and how to create tables, insert data, and run queries on Cloud SQL instances. Finally, we walked through an example of using the Google Cloud SQL JDBC driver to connect to a Cloud SQL instance running MySQL and perform basic CRUD operations in a Java application.

Summary

[illegible]

CHAPTER 6

Advanced GCP Services

In this chapter, we will explore the practical aspects of GCP's advanced services. It covers key topics such as Big Data and Machine Learning, Cloud Pub/Sub, Cloud Dataflow, Cloud Dataproc, and Cloud Functions. Through real-world examples, the chapter showcases the use of these services in building scalable, resilient, and data-driven applications. By the end of this chapter, readers will understand how to leverage Cloud Pub/Sub, Cloud Dataflow, Cloud Dataproc, and Cloud Functions to design and implement powerful solutions on GCP.

Let's go through the advanced services of GCP.

GCP Advanced Services

There are many advanced services offered by Google Cloud Platform (GCP) that can be used to build and deploy complex applications. We will discuss some of these services in this section.

Big Data and Machine Learning

Cloud Dataflow allows you to build, deploy, and execute data pipelines for batch and streaming data. It can process data using both batch and streaming execution models and can be used for data integration, data transformation and data analysis. For example, you can use Cloud Dataflow to process data from a real-time streaming service like Twitter and perform sentiment analysis on the tweets.

Cloud Dataproc allows you to create, configure, and manage clusters of virtual machines that are preconfigured with popular big data tools like Apache Hadoop and

A. Shashi, *Designing Applications for Google Cloud Platform*, https://doi.org/10.1007/978-1-4842-9511-3_6

Apache Spark. It can be used to process large amounts of data with the help of Hadoop and Spark jobs. For example, you can use Cloud Dataproc to process a large dataset of customer records and perform customer segmentation.

Cloud Datalab is an interactive tool for data exploration, visualization, and machine learning on GCP. It runs on top of a Jupyter Notebook and allows you to connect to various GCP services such as BigQuery and Cloud Storage. For example, you can use Cloud Datalab to connect to a BigQuery dataset, perform SQL queries, visualize the results, and build a machine learning model to predict customer churn.

Vertex AI allows you to build, deploy, and manage machine learning models on GCP. It provides a fully managed TensorFlow environment and also allows you to train models on a cluster of machines and deploy models to a variety of locations including the cloud, on-premises, and edge devices. For example, you can use Cloud Machine Learning Engine to train a deep learning model on a large dataset of images and deploy it to a mobile app to perform object recognition.

Kubernetes and Containers

Kubernetes Engine allows you to easily create, configure, and manage Kubernetes clusters on GCP. It provides features such as automatic scaling, load balancing, and automatic upgrades. For example, you can use Kubernetes Engine to deploy and manage a microservices-based application.

Cloud Run allows you to easily deploy containerized applications on GCP. It provides features such as automatic scaling, load balancing, and automatic updates. For example, you can use Cloud Run to deploy a web service that processes images and performs object detection.

Container Registry allows you to store and manage container images on GCP. It provides features such as image storage, versioning, and access control. For example, you can use Container Registry to store and manage the container images for your microservices-based application and easily deploy them to Kubernetes Engine or Cloud Run.

Cloud Build allows you to automate the build, test, and deploy your applications. It can be used to build container images, deploy to various environments, and also integrate with other GCP services such as Container Registry and Kubernetes Engine. For example, you can use Cloud Build to automate the build, test, and deploy a pipeline for your microservices-based application.

Security and Identity

Cloud Identity and Access Management (IAM) enables you to manage access to GCP resources. It provides features such as role-based access control, identity-aware proxies, and security key enforcement. For example, you can use Cloud IAM to set up fine-grained access control for a BigQuery dataset, allowing only certain users to query the data.

Cloud Key Management Service (KMS) allows you to manage and use encryption keys on GCP. It provides features such as key storage, key rotation, and key versioning. For example, you can use Cloud KMS to encrypt data at rest in Cloud Storage and also use the encryption keys to encrypt data in transit.

Cloud Security Command Center (CSCC) helps you gain deeper insights into security across your GCP environment. It provides features such as asset inventory, vulnerability management, and threat detection. For example, you can use Cloud CSCC to monitor your GCP resources for security threats and vulnerabilities and take appropriate action.

These are a few examples of the many advanced GCP services available. Each service has its own specific use cases and can be used in combination with other services to build powerful and scalable solutions on GCP.

Popular GCP Advanced Services

In this section, we will talk about four GCP services in detail. These four GCP services are used more frequently than the previous ones and are included in most applications.

- Cloud Pub/Sub
- Cloud Dataflow
- Cloud Dataproc
- Cloud Functions

Cloud Pub/Sub

Cloud Pub/Sub is a messaging service provided by GCP that allows you to send and receive messages between independent systems. It provides features such as message ordering, at-least-once delivery, and support for both push and pull messaging.

An example use case for Cloud Pub/Sub is decoupling microservices in a distributed system. You can use Pub/Sub to send messages between different microservices, allowing them to communicate without being tightly coupled. This can make your system more resilient to change and easier to scale.

Another example use case is real-time data processing. You can use Cloud Pub/Sub to ingest high-volume data streams, such as logs or sensor data, and then use a separate service such as Dataflow or Cloud Functions to process the data in real time.

You can also use Cloud Pub/Sub in conjunction with other GCP services such as Cloud Storage, BigQuery, and Cloud Dataflow. For example, you can use Cloud Pub/Sub to trigger a Cloud Functions when a new file is uploaded to Cloud Storage, which then processes the file and loads the data into BigQuery.

Cloud Pub/Sub is a powerful messaging service that can be used in a variety of ways to enable real-time data processing, decouple microservices, and make your system more resilient to change.

Reason to Use Cloud Pub/Sub

There are several reasons why Cloud Pub/Sub is an important service in GCP.

- *Decoupling*: Cloud Pub/Sub allows you to decouple systems by sending and receiving messages between them. This allows you to change or update one system without affecting the others, making your overall system more resilient to change.
- *Real-time processing*: Cloud Pub/Sub allows you to process high-volume data streams in real time. This is useful for tasks such as log analysis, monitoring, and alerting.
- *Scalability*: Cloud Pub/Sub is designed to handle high throughput and low latency, making it suitable for handling large amounts of data and traffic.
- *Flexibility*: Cloud Pub/Sub supports both push and pull messaging, which allows you to choose the most appropriate messaging model for your use case.
- *Integration*: Cloud Pub/Sub can be integrated with other GCP services such as Cloud Storage, BigQuery, and Cloud Dataflow, allowing you to build powerful and efficient data processing pipelines.

- *Cost-effective*: Cloud Pub/Sub is a cost-effective service that charges you only for the messages you publish and consume.

All these features make Cloud Pub/Sub a powerful messaging service that can be used in a variety of use cases to enable real-time data processing, decouple microservices, and make your system more resilient to change.

Drawbacks of Using Cloud Pub/Sub

Like any service, Cloud Pub/Sub also has some drawbacks.

- *Latency*: While Cloud Pub/Sub is designed to handle high throughput and low latency, some use cases may still experience higher latency because of factors such as network conditions or message size.
- *Durability*: While Cloud Pub/Sub guarantees at-least-once delivery of messages, it does not guarantee exactly-once delivery. This means messages may be delivered multiple times in some cases, which can lead to duplicates.
- *Complexity*: Cloud Pub/Sub can be complex to set up and manage, especially for large-scale, high-throughput use cases. It requires a good understanding of its features and how to use them effectively.
- *Cost*: While Cloud Pub/Sub is a cost-effective service, it can become expensive for large-scale, high-throughput use cases that involve a lot of data transfer and message processing.
- *Limited retention*: By default, Cloud Pub/Sub retains messages for 7 days, after which they are deleted. If you need to retain messages for a longer period, you need to configure it explicitly.
- *Limited support for big messages*: The maximum size of a message that can be sent to a topic is 10 MB. So if you have big messages that need to be transmitted, you need to split them or consider alternative options.
- *Pub/Sub sequencing*: Cloud Pub/Sub sequencing can lead to increased latency and reduced throughput.

It's important to understand these limitations when planning to use Cloud Pub/Sub for your use case. It might not be the best solution for all types of problems, but it's a powerful service when used correctly.

Use Case Where Cloud Pub/Sub Is Bad Choice

A wrong use case for Cloud Pub/Sub would be a scenario where low latency and exactly-once delivery are critical requirements, but Cloud Pub/Sub does not guarantee exactly-once delivery and may have some latency.

Another wrong use case for Cloud Pub/Sub would be a scenario where data needs to be stored for a long time, but Cloud Pub/Sub retains messages for only 7 days by default. If you need to retain messages for a longer period, you need to configure it explicitly.

Another case where Cloud Pub/Sub might not be the best fit is if you have a small number of messages with large payloads, as Cloud Pub/Sub has a maximum message size of 10 MB.

Additionally, if you don't need to process data streams in real time and you can afford some delay, other services such as Cloud Storage and BigQuery may be more appropriate.

It's important to understand that Cloud Pub/Sub is a powerful service, but it's not a one-size-fits-all solution, and it may not be the best fit for every use case. It's essential to understand the requirements of your use case and select the appropriate GCP services to meet those requirements.

Using Cloud Pub/Sub in Java Application

Listing 6-1 shows an example of how you can use Cloud Pub/Sub in a Java application. These are the steps:

1. First, create a project in the GCP Console and enable the Cloud Pub/Sub API.

2. Next, create a topic and a subscription in the Cloud Pub/Sub Console.

3. In your Java application, add the following dependencies to your `pom.xml` file.

Listing 6-1. Using Cloud Pub/Sub in a Java Application

```
<dependency>
    <groupId>com.google.cloud</groupId>
    <artifactId>google-cloud-pubsub</artifactId>
    <version>1.103.0</version>
</dependency>
```

4. As shown in Listing 6-2, create a Pub/Sub client and set the project ID and credentials. The project ID and credentials should not be hard-coded in production code and should follow the best practices to store and access it from there.

Listing 6-2. Creating a Pub/Sub Client and Setting the Project ID and Credentials

```
import com.google.cloud.pubsub.v1.Publisher;
import com.google.cloud.pubsub.v1.Subscriber;
import com.google.cloud.pubsub.v1.TopicAdminClient;
import com.google.cloud.pubsub.v1.SubscriptionAdminClient;
import com.google.pubsub.v1.ProjectTopicName;
import com.google.pubsub.v1.ProjectSubscriptionName;
import com.google.auth.oauth2.GoogleCredentials;
import java.io.FileInputStream;

GoogleCredentials credentials = GoogleCredentials.fromStream(new
FileInputStream("path/to/credentials.json"))
    .createScoped(Collections.singletonList("https://www.googleapis.com/
    auth/pubsub"));

String projectId = "your-project-id";
String topicId = "your-topic-id";
String subscriptionId = "your-subscription-id";

ProjectTopicName topicName = ProjectTopicName.of(projectId, topicId);
ProjectSubscriptionName subscriptionName = ProjectSubscriptionName.
of(projectId, subscriptionId);

TopicAdminClient topicAdminClient = TopicAdminClient.create(credentials);
SubscriptionAdminClient subscriptionAdminClient = SubscriptionAdminClient.
create(credentials);
```

5. Use the publisher to publish messages to the topic, as shown in Listing 6-3.

Listing 6-3. Use the Publisher to Publish Messages

```
Publisher publisher = Publisher.newBuilder(topicName).build();


ByteString data = ByteString.copyFromUtf8("Hello, Cloud Pub/Sub!");
com.google.pubsub.v1.PubsubMessage pubsubMessage = com.google.pubsub.
v1.PubsubMessage.newBuilder().setData(data).build();

ApiFuture<String> future = publisher.publish(pubsubMessage);
String messageId = future.get();
System.out.println("Published message with ID: " + messageId);

publisher.shutdown();
```

6. Use the subscriber to receive messages from the subscription, as demonstrated in Listing 6-4.

Listing 6-4. Using the Subscriber to Receive Messages

```
Subscriber subscriber = Subscriber.newBuilder(subscriptionName, new
MessageReceiver()).build();
subscriber.startAsync();

class MessageReceiver implements MessageReceiver {
    @Override
    public void receiveMessage(com.google.pubsub.v1.PubsubMessage message,
    AckReplyConsumer consumer) {
        System.out.println("Received message: " + message.getData().
        toStringUtf8());
        consumer.ack();
    }
}
```

7. Finally, don't forget to clean up resources when you're done using them by deleting the topic and subscription, as shown in Listing 6-5.

Listing 6-5. Deleting the Topic and Description

```
topicAdminClient.deleteTopic(topicName);
subscriptionAdminClient.deleteSubscription(subscriptionName);
```

This is a basic example of how you can use Cloud Pub/Sub in a Java application to publish and receive messages. In a real-world application, you may want to handle errors, retries, and other edge cases. You may also want to use other features provided by the Cloud Pub/Sub API such as batching, flow control, and message attributes.

Additionally, you may want to use Cloud Pub/Sub in combination with other GCP services such as Cloud Dataflow, Cloud Functions, and BigQuery to process and analyze your data streams in real time.

The code examples here in this section use the default settings, which may not be appropriate for your specific use case. You should carefully read the documentation and choose the appropriate settings for your use case, such as message retention, ordering, and delivery semantics.

Let's run Cloud Dataflow in the next section.

Cloud Dataflow

Cloud Dataflow is a fully managed service for data processing on the Google Cloud Platform. It can be used to create data pipelines that can process large amounts of data from various sources, such as Cloud Storage, BigQuery, and Cloud Pub/Sub, and output the results to various destinations, such as Cloud Storage, BigQuery, and Cloud Datastore. It supports both batch and streaming data processing.

Here's an example of how you might use Cloud Dataflow to process a batch of data stored in a Cloud Storage bucket:

1. Create a new Cloud Dataflow job using the Dataflow API or the Cloud SDK.
2. Define the input and output sources and destinations for the job. For example, you can use the `TextIO` class to read text files from a Cloud Storage bucket and write the output to another bucket.
3. Define the data processing logic using the Dataflow SDK. For example, you can use the `ParDo` class to perform a transformation on the data, such as filtering, mapping, or aggregating.
4. Run the Dataflow job.

Listing 6-6 presents an example of a simple pipeline that reads data from a Cloud Storage bucket, performs a transformation on the data, and writes the output to another bucket:

Listing 6-6. Reading Data from a Storage Bucket and Writing Output to Another Bucket

```
Pipeline pipeline = Pipeline.create();

PCollection<String> input = pipeline.apply(TextIO.read().from("gs://input-
bucket/*.txt"));


PCollection<String> output = input
    .apply("ExtractWords", ParDo.of(new ExtractWordsFn()))
    .apply("CountWords", Count.perElement());

output.apply(TextIO.write().to("gs://output-bucket/counts.txt"));

pipeline.run();
```

Cloud Dataflow also provides a way to process streaming data with the same API, by simply replacing `TextIO` with `PubSubIO` to read from a Pub/Sub topic and replacing `TextIO.write()` with `PubsubIO.write()` to write to a Pub/Sub topic.

Cloud Dataflow also provides a way to automatically scale the resources based on the size of the data and to handle errors and retries.

Another benefit of Cloud Dataflow is its ability to integrate with other GCP services, such as BigQuery, Cloud Storage, Cloud Pub/Sub, and Cloud Bigtable. This allows you to easily read and write data from and to these services and perform complex data processing and analysis tasks using Dataflow's built-in transforms and windowing capabilities.

Dataflow provides a web-based UI called the Dataflow Monitoring Interface, which allows you to monitor the progress and status of your Dataflow jobs, view job metrics, and debug any issues that may arise.

Additionally, Cloud Dataflow has built-in support for Apache Beam, which is an open-source programming model for data processing pipelines. This allows you to write Dataflow pipelines using the Beam API, which is available in multiple programming languages, including Java, Python, and Go.

However, Cloud Dataflow has certain drawbacks, such as a steeper learning curve compared to some other data processing tools and higher costs for certain types of jobs.

Another drawback is that it may not be the best fit for certain use cases, such as low-latency, real-time data processing, where other tools such as Cloud Stream might be more appropriate.

Cloud Dataflow is a powerful tool for data processing and analysis on the GCP, with many built-in features and integrations with other GCP services. It is well-suited for large-scale, batch, or streaming data processing tasks, and it can be a good choice for organizations that need a highly scalable and fault-tolerant data processing platform.

Java Example of Cloud Dataflow

Let's look at a Java example of a dataflow that will be triggered by Cloud Storage, when any file is dropped in to a Cloud Storage bucket. Cloud Dataflow reads the file from the Cloud Storage bucket and, based on the identifier data it reads from the file, the Cloud Dataflow pipeline stores the file data into different BigQuery table.

In Cloud Dataflow, a pipeline is a directed acyclic graph of data transformations, where each node in the graph represents a processing step that takes one or more inputs and produces one or more outputs. A DoFn (short for "do function") is a user-defined function that processes input elements and emits output elements. A ParDo is a Dataflow transform that applies a DoFn to each element in a `PCollection`, producing zero or more output elements for each input element.

Listing 6-7 depicts an example of a Java dataflow that is triggered by a file being added to a Cloud Storage bucket.

Listing 6-7. A Java Dataflow Triggered by a File Added to the Cloud Storage Bucket

```
import com.google.cloud.dataflow.sdk.Pipeline;
import com.google.cloud.dataflow.sdk.io.TextIO;
import com.google.cloud.dataflow.sdk.options.DataflowPipelineOptions;
import com.google.cloud.dataflow.sdk.options.Default;
import com.google.cloud.dataflow.sdk.options.Description;
import com.google.cloud.dataflow.sdk.options.PipelineOptionsFactory;
import com.google.cloud.dataflow.sdk.transforms.DoFn;
import com.google.cloud.dataflow.sdk.transforms.ParDo;
import com.google.cloud.dataflow.sdk.transforms.GroupByKey;
import com.google.cloud.dataflow.sdk.values.KV;
```

```
public class DataflowExample {
    public static class ExtractIdentifierFn extends DoFn<String, KV<String,
    String>> {
        @Override
        public void processElement(ProcessContext c) {
            String line = c.element();
            // Extract the identifier from the file data
            String identifier = extractIdentifier(line);
            c.output(KV.of(identifier, line));
        }
    }

    public static class WriteToBigQueryFn extends DoFn<KV<String,
    Iterable<String>>, Void> {
        @Override
        public void processElement(ProcessContext c) {
            String identifier = c.element().getKey();
            Iterable<String> lines = c.element().getValue();
            // Write the data to the appropriate BigQuery table based on
            the identifier
            writeToBigQuery(identifier, lines);
        }
    }

    public static void main(String[] args) {
        DataflowPipelineOptions options = PipelineOptionsFactory.
        fromArgs(args).as(DataflowPipelineOptions.class);
        options.setStreaming(true);
        Pipeline p = Pipeline.create(options);

        p.apply(TextIO.Read.from("gs://<bucket_name>/*"))
                .apply(ParDo.of(new ExtractIdentifierFn()))
                .apply(GroupByKey.<String, String>create())
                .apply(ParDo.of(new WriteToBigQueryFn()));

        p.run();
    }
}
```

This example uses the Cloud Dataflow SDK to create a pipeline that reads data from a Cloud Storage bucket, extracts an identifier from the file data, groups the data by the identifier, and writes the data to the appropriate BigQuery table based on the identifier.

Note that the example uses the `TextIO` class to read data from the Cloud Storage bucket, but you could also use the `BigQueryIO` class if you want to read data directly from BigQuery.

Also, the example uses some methods that are not implemented here, like `extractIdentifier()` and `writeToBigQuery()`, which should be implemented by you and contain the logic for extracting the identifier from the data and writing the data to the BigQuery table, respectively.

Listing 6-8 is an example of the `extractIdentifier()` method that could be used in the `ExtractIdentifierFn` class.

Listing 6-8. Using the extractidentifier() Method

```
private static String extractIdentifier(String line) {
    // Example logic for extracting the identifier from the file data
    String[] parts = line.split(",");
    return parts[0];
}
```

This example uses the `split()` method to split the line of data with a comma and then returns the first element as the identifier.

Listing 6-9 shows an example of the `writeToBigQuery()` method that could be used in the `WriteToBigQueryFn` class:

Listing 6-9. Using the writeToBigQuery() Method

```
private static void writeToBigQuery(String identifier, Iterable<String>
lines) {
    // Example logic for writing the data to BigQuery
    // Initialize the BigQuery client
    BigQuery bigquery = BigQueryOptions.getDefaultInstance().getService();
    // Create the table reference
    TableId tableId = TableId.of("<project_id>", "<dataset_id>",
    identifier);
    Table table = bigquery.getTable(tableId);
    // Write the data to the table
```

```
    bigquery.insertAll(
        InsertAllRequest.newBuilder(tableId)
            .addRow("1", lines)
            .build());
}
```

This example uses the BigQuery client library to initialize the BigQuery service, create a table reference based on the identifier, and insert the data in the table using the insertAll() method.

You can also use other libraries or services like Apache Beam to write data to BigQuery.

In the next section, let's discuss Cloud Dataproc.

Cloud Dataproc

Cloud Dataproc is a fully managed cloud service provided by Google Cloud Platform for running Apache Hadoop, Apache Spark, and Apache Pig workloads on a scalable and cost-effective infrastructure. It allows users to easily create, manage, and delete Hadoop and Spark clusters, and it automatically handles tasks such as cluster scaling, updates, and security.

The following are some of the key features of Cloud Dataproc:

- *Fast cluster creation and deletion*: Cloud Dataproc allows you to create Hadoop and Spark clusters in just a few minutes using a simple API call or web console.
- *Automatic scaling and management*: Cloud Dataproc automatically handles tasks such as cluster scaling, updates, and security. It also allows you to set autoscaling policies for your clusters.
- *Cost-effective*: Cloud Dataproc is designed to be cost-effective, using preemptible VMs and on-demand pricing for cluster nodes.
- *Integrations*: Cloud Dataproc integrates with other GCP services such as Cloud Storage, BigQuery, and Cloud SQL, making it easy to access, process, and analyze data stored in these services.

The following are some common use cases for Cloud Dataproc:

- *Data processing*: Cloud Dataproc is commonly used for data processing tasks such as data extraction, transformation, and loading (ETL), as well as machine learning (ML) and analytics workloads.
- *Data warehousing*: Cloud Dataproc can be used to move data from various sources into a data warehouse such as BigQuery and then perform analytics on that data.
- *Batch processing*: Cloud Dataproc can be used to process large batch jobs, such as processing log files or generating reports.

Listing 6-10 shows an example of how to create a new Cloud Dataproc cluster using the Google Cloud SDK.

Listing 6-10. Creating a New Cloud DataProc Cluster

```
gcloud dataproc clusters create my-cluster \
    --region=us-central1 \
    --zone=us-central1-a \
    --master-machine-type=n1-standard-2 \
    --worker-machine-type=n1-standard-1 \
    --num-workers=2
```

This command creates a new Cloud Dataproc cluster called `my-cluster` in the `us-central1` region and `us-central1-a` zone, with a master node of machine type `n1-standard-2` and two worker nodes of machine type `n1-standard-1`.

You can also use the web console, Cloud SDK, and the Cloud Dataproc RESTful API to manage and monitor your clusters and jobs.

Cloud Dataproc is a powerful, scalable, and cost-effective service for running big data workloads on GCP, and it can be used for a wide variety of use cases, from data processing to machine learning and analytics.

Java Example for Cloud Dataproc

Listing 6-11 shows an example of a Java program that uses Cloud Dataproc to create a new cluster, submit a job, and then delete the cluster.

Listing 6-11. Using Cloud Dataproc to Create a New Cluster, Submit a Job, and Delete the Cluster

```
import com.google.cloud.dataproc.v1.Cluster;
import com.google.cloud.dataproc.v1.ClusterConfig;
import com.google.cloud.dataproc.v1.ClusterControllerClient;
import com.google.cloud.dataproc.v1.ClusterControllerSettings;
import com.google.cloud.dataproc.v1.Job;
import com.google.cloud.dataproc.v1.JobControllerClient;
import com.google.cloud.dataproc.v1.JobControllerSettings;
import com.google.cloud.dataproc.v1.JobPlacement;
import com.google.cloud.dataproc.v1.JobReference;
import com.google.cloud.dataproc.v1.JobType;
import com.google.cloud.dataproc.v1.SoftwareConfig;
import com.google.cloud.dataproc.v1.SubmitJobRequest;
import com.google.cloud.dataproc.v1.SubmitJobResponse;
import com.google.cloud.dataproc.v1.ClusterConfig.Builder;
import com.google.common.collect.ImmutableList;
import java.io.IOException;

public class CloudDataprocExample {

  public static void main(String[] args) throws IOException {
    // Create a Dataproc cluster
    ClusterControllerSettings clusterControllerSettings =
    ClusterControllerSettings.newBuilder().build();
    try (ClusterControllerClient clusterClient = ClusterControllerClient.cr
    eate(clusterControllerSettings)) {
      String projectId = "my-project-id";
      String region = "us-central1";
      String clusterName = "my-cluster";
      Builder configBuilder = ClusterConfig.newBuilder();
      configBuilder.setMasterConfig(configBuilder.getMasterConfigBuilder().
      setMachineTypeUri("n1-standard-2"));
      configBuilder.setWorkerConfig(configBuilder.getWorkerConfigBuilder().
      setMachineTypeUri("n1-standard-1").setNumInstances(2));
      Cluster cluster = Cluster.newBuilder()
```

```
        .setClusterName(clusterName)
        .setProjectId(projectId)
        .setConfig(configBuilder.build())
        .setClusterUuid(clusterName)
        .setJobPlacement(JobPlacement.newBuilder().
        setClusterName(clusterName).build())
        .build();
    clusterClient.createCluster(projectId, region, cluster);
    System.out.println("Cluster created: " + clusterName);
}

// Submit a job to the cluster
JobControllerSettings jobControllerSettings = JobControllerSettings.
newBuilder().build();
try (JobControllerClient jobClient = JobControllerClient.
create(jobControllerSettings)) {
    String projectId = "my-project-id";
    String region = "us-central1";
    String clusterName = "my-cluster";
    String jobId = "my-job";
    JobReference jobRef = JobReference.newBuilder().
    setProjectId(projectId).setJobId(jobId).build();

                JobPlacement placement = JobPlacement.newBuilder().
                setClusterName(clusterName).build();
    SoftwareConfig softwareConfig = SoftwareConfig.newBuilder().
    setImageVersion("1.4").build();
    Job job = Job.newBuilder()
        .setReference(jobRef)
        .setPlacement(placement)
        .setSoftwareConfig(softwareConfig)
        .setType(JobType.HADOOP)
        .build();
    SubmitJobRequest submitJobRequest = SubmitJobRequest.newBuilder().
    setJob(job).build();
    SubmitJobResponse submitJobResponse = jobClient.submitJob(projectId,
    region, submitJobRequest);
```

```
      String jobName = submitJobResponse.getJob().getReference().
      getJobId();
      System.out.println("Job submitted: " + jobName);
    }

    // Delete the cluster
    ClusterControllerSettings clusterControllerSettings =
    ClusterControllerSettings.newBuilder().build();
    try (ClusterControllerClient clusterClient = ClusterControllerClient.cr
    eate(clusterControllerSettings)) {
      String projectId = "my-project-id";
      String region = "us-central1";
      String clusterName = "my-cluster";
      clusterClient.deleteCluster(projectId, region, clusterName);
      System.out.println("Cluster deleted: " + clusterName);
    }
  }
}
```

This example demonstrates the basic steps for creating a cluster, submitting a job, and then deleting the cluster. You will need to replace the placeholders such as `my-project-id` and `my-cluster` with your actual project ID and cluster name. Additionally, you will need to specify the job type, such as Hadoop, Spark, Pig, etc., and set up the job details like the main class, JAR file, arguments, etc.

Let's define a few terms that I have used here.

- *MR job* stands for MapReduce job. It is a processing model used in big data processing that involves processing large amounts of data in parallel across a cluster of nodes.
- A *job* is a unit of work submitted to a Dataproc cluster for processing. A job can be a MapReduce job, a Spark job, a Hive job, or any other type of job that can run on a Hadoop or Spark cluster.
- *Job placement* refers to the rules that determine where a job runs in a Dataproc cluster. For example, you can specify that a job should run on a specific set of nodes or that it should run on nodes with specific characteristics such as a certain amount of memory or a certain number of CPU cores.

- A *job reference* is a unique identifier for a job in Dataproc. It can be used to monitor the status of a job, retrieve information about a job, or cancel a job.
- *Job type* refers to the type of job being run on a Dataproc cluster. For example, a job can be a MapReduce job, a Spark job, a Hive job, or any other type of job that can run on a Hadoop or Spark cluster.
- *Job configuration* refers to the settings that control how a job runs on a Dataproc cluster. This includes settings such as the number of worker nodes to use, the machine types to use for the worker nodes, the type of software to use (such as Hadoop or Spark), and many other options that can be customized to fit the specific needs of a job.

Note The Cloud Dataproc may require additional configuration and error handling depending on the specific use case.

Configuring Cloud Dataproc

When using Cloud Dataproc, there are several configuration options that you can set to customize your cluster and jobs. Here are a few examples:

- *Cluster configuration*: You can specify the number of worker and master nodes in the cluster, the machine type for each node, and the amount of memory and CPU to allocate to each node. Additionally, you can configure the network and firewall settings and set up autoscaling to automatically add or remove nodes based on the workload.
- *Software configuration*: You can specify the version of Hadoop, Spark, Pig, or other software that you want to use on the cluster. You can also configure the environment variables and initialization actions to run before the job starts.
- *Job configuration*: For each job, you can specify the main class, JAR file, and arguments to run. You can also configure the job placement, such as the cluster to run the job on and the number of worker nodes to use.

- *Security configuration*: You can configure the authentication and authorization settings for your cluster and jobs. You can also set up encryption for data at rest and in transit.

Listing 6-12 demonstrates how to configure a cluster with four worker nodes and two master nodes, using machine type `n1-standard-4` and installing a specific version of software.

Listing 6-12. Configuring a Cluster

```
ClusterConfig clusterConfig = ClusterConfig.newBuilder()
            .setMasterConfig(InstanceGroupConfig.newBuilder()
                    .setMachineTypeUri("n1-standard-4")
                    .setNumInstances(2)
                    .build())
            .setWorkerConfig(InstanceGroupConfig.newBuilder()
                    .setMachineTypeUri("n1-standard-4")
                    .setNumInstances(4)
                    .build())
            .setSoftwareConfig(SoftwareConfig.newBuilder()
                    .setImageVersion("1.4")
                    .build())
            .build();
```

I hope you now have got good insight into Dataproc. Let's discuss Cloud Functions in the next section.

Cloud Functions

Cloud Functions is a serverless compute service offered by Google Cloud Platform that allows you to run code without having to provision or manage servers. With Cloud Functions, you can write and deploy code in a variety of languages, including JavaScript, Python, Go, and Java. Once your code is deployed, Cloud Functions automatically scales and manages the underlying infrastructure for you.

Here are some of the key features and use cases of Cloud Functions:

- *Event-driven*: Cloud Functions allows you to trigger your code to run in response to specific events, such as changes to data in a Cloud Storage bucket or a new message in a Cloud Pub/Sub topic. This makes it easy to build event-driven architectures that respond to changes in your data in real time.
- *Serverless*: Cloud Functions abstracts away the underlying infrastructure so you can focus on writing code. You don't have to worry about provisioning or managing servers, and you pay only for the resources that your code actually uses.
- *Integration with other GCP services*: Cloud Functions integrates seamlessly with other GCP services, such as Cloud Storage, Cloud Pub/Sub, and Firebase. This allows you to easily build complex, multistep workflows that involve different GCP services.
- *Easy deployment*: Cloud Functions allows you to deploy your code to multiple regions with a single command, and you can use versioning and rollback to easily manage different versions of your code.

Listing 6-13 is a simple Java function that is triggered by a new file being added to a Cloud Storage bucket.

Listing 6-13. A Java Function Triggered by a New File Added to the Cloud Storage Bucket

```
import com.google.cloud.functions.BackgroundFunction;
import com.google.cloud.functions.Context;
import java.io.IOException;

public class ProcessFile implements BackgroundFunction<StorageObject> {
  public void accept(StorageObject object, Context context) throws
  IOException {
    // Your code here to process the file
    String bucket = object.getBucket();
    String file = object.getName();
    System.out.println("Processing file: " + file + " in bucket " + bucket);
  }
}
```

In this example, the function `accept` is triggered by a new file being added to the specified bucket. The `StorageObject` passed as an argument contains information about the added file. In this example, it just logs the information about the added file.

You can customize the function to suit your needs, for example, by processing the file and storing the processed data in another GCP service like BigQuery or Datastore.

Use Cases for Cloud Functions

The following are a few examples of use cases for Cloud Functions:

- *Data processing*: You can use Cloud Functions to process data in real time as it is added to a Cloud Storage bucket or a Cloud Pub/Sub topic. For example, you can write a function that automatically resizes images as they are uploaded to a bucket or that reads data from a topic and stores it in a BigQuery table.
- *Automation*: You can use Cloud Functions to automate tasks that are triggered by specific events. For example, you can write a function that sends an email when a new file is added to a bucket or that automatically creates a new instance in Compute Engine when a button is clicked in a mobile app.
- *Integration*: You can use Cloud Functions to integrate different GCP services together. For example, you can write a function that reads data from a Firebase Realtime Database and stores it in BigQuery or that listens for changes in a Cloud Spanner table and updates a Firebase Cloud Firestore.
- *Web applications*: Cloud Functions can be used to build web applications by writing functions that handle HTTP requests and respond with JSON.

Limitations of Cloud Functions

The following are the limitations of Cloud Functions:

- *Execution time*: Cloud Functions has a maximum execution time of 9 minutes. If your function needs to run for longer than that, you will need to use a different service.

- *Memory and CPU*: Cloud Functions has a maximum memory and CPU allocation per instance, which is generally enough for simple functions. However, if your function requires more resources, you may need to use a different service.
- *Cold starts*: Cloud Functions may experience "cold starts" when they haven't been used in a while, which can cause a delay in the initial execution of the function. This can be mitigated by keeping the function warm by triggering it regularly or by using a different service that can handle longer idle periods.
- *Traffic shaping*: Cloud Functions does not provide any built-in mechanisms for traffic shaping, such as rate limiting or autoscaling. This means that if you expect a lot of traffic, you may need to use a different service that provides these features.

Cloud Functions is a serverless computing service, and it is designed to handle small, short-lived tasks. It is not meant to be used as a replacement for other compute services such as Compute Engine or Kubernetes Engine.

Java Example of Cloud Functions

Listing 6-14 shows a Cloud Functions function written in Java that is triggered by a REST call and retrieves random 10 questions (5 easy and 5 hard) from a Quiz database (Firestore database).

Listing 6-14. A Cloud Function Written in Java Triggered by a REST Call to Retrieve Questions from a Quiz Database

```
import com.google.cloud.firestore.Firestore;
import com.google.cloud.firestore.QueryDocumentSnapshot;
import com.google.cloud.firestore.QuerySnapshot;
import com.google.firebase.cloud.FirestoreClient;
import java.util.ArrayList;
import java.util.List;
import java.util.Random;

import com.google.gson.Gson;
import com.google.gson.JsonObject;
```

```
import java.io.IOException;

import javax.servlet.http.HttpServletResponse;

import com.google.cloud.functions.HttpFunction;
import com.google.cloud.functions.HttpRequest;
import com.google.cloud.functions.HttpResponse;

public class GetQuizFunction implements HttpFunction {
    private Firestore db;
    private Random random;
    private Gson gson;

    public GetQuizFunction() {
        db = FirestoreClient.getFirestore();
        random = new Random();
        gson = new Gson();
    }

    @Override
    public void service(HttpRequest request, HttpResponse response) throws
    IOException {
        List<JsonObject> easyQuestions = new ArrayList<>();
        List<JsonObject> hardQuestions = new ArrayList<>();

        // Get all questions from the Firestore database
        QuerySnapshot questionsSnapshot = db.collection("quiz").
        get().get();
        for (QueryDocumentSnapshot question : questionsSnapshot) {
            JsonObject jsonQuestion = gson.fromJson(question.toJson(),
            JsonObject.class);
            String difficulty = jsonQuestion.get("difficulty").
            getAsString();
            if (difficulty.equals("easy")) {
                easyQuestions.add(jsonQuestion);
            } else if (difficulty.equals("hard")) {
                hardQuestions.add(jsonQuestion);
            }
        }
```

```
// Select 5 random easy questions
List<JsonObject> selectedEasyQuestions = new ArrayList<>();
for (int i = 0; i SPi-Amp-LessThan 5; i++) {
    int index = random.nextInt(easyQuestions.size());
    selectedEasyQuestions.add(easyQuestions.get(index));
    easyQuestions.remove(index);
}

// Select 5 random hard questions
List<JsonObject> selectedHardQuestions = new ArrayList<>();
for (int i = 0; i SPi-Amp-LessThan 5; i++) {
    int index = random.nextInt(hardQuestions.size());
    selectedHardQuestions.add(hardQuestions.get(index));
    hardQuestions.remove(index);
}

// Combine the selected easy and hard questions
List<JsonObject> selectedQuestions = new ArrayList<>();
selectedQuestions.addAll(selectedEasyQuestions);
selectedQuestions.addAll(selectedHardQuestions);

// Convert the selected questions to JSON and set the content
type to JSON
String json = gson.toJson(selectedQuestions);
response.setContentType("application/json");
response.setStatusCode(HttpServletResponse.SC_OK);
                    response.getWriter().write(json);
            }
}
```

This example uses the Firestore client library to connect to a Firestore database and retrieve all questions from a collection called `quiz`. It then uses a `Random` object to select five random easy questions and five random hard questions from the retrieved questions. The selected questions are then combined into a single list and converted to a JSON string using the Gson library. The JSON string is then returned as the response to the REST call, and the content type is set to `application/json`.

Note the following about this program:

- Listing 6-14 uses the Firebase Admin SDK; you will have to configure the credentials of your function to access the Firestore database.
- Listing 6-14 does not include error handling. It's recommended to include error handling for production.
- I have assumed the field name `difficulty` in the Firestore document to be `easy` or `hard`.
- You can use the `.whereEqualTo()` method to filter the documents by the `difficulty` field.

Summary

In this chapter, you learned about powerful services offered by Google Cloud Platform: Cloud Pub/Sub, Cloud Dataflow, Cloud Dataproc and Cloud Functions. Cloud Pub/Sub can be used to decouple microservices and send/receive messages between independent systems. Cloud Dataflow can be used to create a data pipeline that can process large amounts if data by creating a batch or stream data processing. Cloud Dataproc is a managed Hadoop and Spark service that allows you to easily process large amounts of data using open-source tools. The chapter covered how to create a cluster, submit a job, and configure various aspects of the cluster and job. Cloud Functions is a serverless compute service that allows you to run code in response to specific events. The chapter covered some of the key features, use cases, and limitations of Cloud Functions and provided an example of how to write a Java function that retrieves random quiz questions from a Firestore database.

CHAPTER 7

Deployment and Scaling

This chapter focuses on designing and building scalable and resilient architectures on Google Cloud Platform (GCP). The chapter begins by introducing the principles of scalable and resilient design, including fault tolerance, elasticity, and scalability. You will learn about the key components of scalable and resilient architectures on GCP, including load balancing, autoscaling, and distributed databases. The chapter also covers best practices for building scalable and resilient architectures on GCP, including using managed services, designing for failure, and monitoring and alerting. Overall, this chapter provides a comprehensive guide to building scalable and resilient architectures on GCP, with practical examples and real-world use cases.

Deployment and scaling in GCP refers to the process of making your application or service available to users and ensuring that it can handle the expected load.

There are several ways to deploy and scale your application or service in GCP.

In this chapter, we will explore the deployment and scaling GCP services and applications.

Deploying a Java Application on GCP Using Various Options

There are several options for deploying a Java application on GCP.

- *App Engine*: To deploy a Java application on App Engine, you need to create a WAR file of your application and deploy it to App Engine using the `gcloud` command-line tool or the GCP Console. You can also use the Maven or Gradle plugin to deploy your application from your build tool directly to App Engine. App Engine provides two environments: standard and flexible. Standard is a fully managed

A. Shashi, *Designing Applications for Google Cloud Platform*, https://doi.org/10.1007/978-1-4842-9511-3_7

environment that automatically scales your application based on traffic. Flexible is a container-based environment that allows you to customize the runtime and dependencies of your application.

- *Kubernetes Engine*: To deploy a Java application on Google Kubernetes Engine (GKE), you need to create a Docker container image of your application and push it to a container registry, such as Google Container Registry. Then, you can use the Kubernetes deployment YAML file to deploy the container image to the GKE cluster. You can also use Helm, a package manager for Kubernetes, to simplify the deployment process and manage the configuration of your application.
- *Compute Engine*: To deploy a Java application on Compute Engine, you need to create a virtual machine (VM) instance and install the necessary software and dependencies for your application. You can choose from various Linux and Windows images provided by Compute Engine or create your own custom image. You can also use the startup script to automate the installation and configuration of your application on the VM.
- *Cloud Run*: To deploy a Java application on Cloud Run, you need to package your application into a container image and then deploy it to Cloud Run using the `gcloud` command-line tool, Cloud Console, or API. You can use any container image that meets the Cloud Run requirements, including the Jib container image, which is a containerization tool for Java applications.
- *Cloud Functions*: To deploy a Java application on Cloud Functions, you need to package your application code and its dependencies into a JAR file and deploy it using the `gcloud` command-line tool, the Cloud Console, or the API. You can trigger your function in response to events, such as changes to a Google Cloud Storage bucket or a Cloud Pub/Sub topic message. Cloud Functions supports the Java 17 runtime.

Each of these options has its own advantages and disadvantages, and the choice of which to use depends on the specific requirements of your application and organization.

Let's discuss the deployment of Java application on GAE in the next section.

Deploying a Java Application on App Engine Manually

Here's a step-by-step guide to deploying a Java application on App Engine:

1. Create a new project in the Google Cloud Console and enable the App Engine API.
2. Install the Google Cloud SDK and set up the SDK on your local machine.
3. Create a new App Engine application by running the command `gcloud app create` at the command line.
4. Create a new Maven or Gradle project for your application. If you are using Maven, add the App Engine plugin to your `pom.xml` file.
5. Configure the `appengine-web.xml` file in the `WEB-INF` directory of your project. This file contains the configuration settings for your App Engine application.
6. Add the necessary dependencies to your project, such as the App Engine API, the Servlet API, and any other dependencies required by your application.
7. Build your application using Maven or Gradle.
8. Deploy your application to App Engine using the command `gcloud app deploy` at the command line.
9. Verify that your application is running on App Engine by visiting the URL provided in the output of the `deploy` command or by visiting the App Engine dashboard in the Cloud Console.

In addition to these steps, there are other configurations and settings that you can specify in the `appengine-web.xml` file, such as the runtime and instance class for your application, the number of instances, and more. You should also be familiar with the App Engine quota and limits and how to configure them.

Also, App Engine supports several Java runtime environments, such as Java 8, Java 11, and Java 14. You will need to configure the runtime in the `appengine-web.xml` file accordingly.

You can also use tools such as Eclipse or IntelliJ to deploy your application on App Engine. These tools have built-in support for deploying to App Engine and can simplify the deployment process.

Google App Engine is a fully managed service, so it automatically scales your application based on traffic and handles tasks such as patching the underlying infrastructure, monitoring, and logging.

Deploying a Java Application on GAE Automatically

Deploying a Java application on App Engine using automation can be done using the following steps:

1. Create an App Engine standard environment for Java in the Google Cloud Console.
2. Install and configure the Google Cloud SDK on your local machine.
3. Use the App Engine Maven or Gradle plugins to build and deploy your application. These plugins handle tasks such as building the application, creating the `app.yaml` configuration file, and deploying the application to App Engine.
4. Set up continuous integration/continuous deployment (CI/CD) using a tool like Jenkins or Travis CI. This will automate the process of building, testing, and deploying your application whenever changes are made to your codebase.
5. Use the App Engine flexible environment if you want more control over the runtime environment and the ability to use custom libraries.
6. Use the Google Cloud Build for automating the process; it is a fully managed service for building and testing your application, and it can be integrated with other GCP services such as GitHub, Bitbucket, and your local development environment.
7. Monitor your application's performance and resource usage using App Engine's built-in monitoring and logging features or using external tools such as Operations Suite.
8. Scale your application up or down as needed using the App Engine dashboard in the GCP Console.

Google App Engine standard environment is optimized for applications that are stateless and have a high number of requests, while the App Engine flexible environment is more suitable for applications that need to run custom libraries or that require more control over the runtime environment. Also, the App Engine flexible environment is a more expensive option.

Additionally, you should familiarize yourself with the App Engine quotas and limits and how to configure them.

You can also use tools such as Spinnaker or Terraform to automate the deployment process on App Engine. These tools can help you to manage your deployments and handle the infrastructure.

Deploying a Java Application on GKE

Here's a general overview of the steps involved in deploying an application on Kubernetes Engine:

1. Create a new Kubernetes Engine cluster on GCP. You can choose from various configurations such as the number of nodes, machine types, and regions.

2. Create a container image of your application using a tool such as Docker. This image will be used to deploy your application on the cluster.

3. Push the image to a container registry such as Google Container Registry or Docker Hub.

4. Create a Kubernetes Deployment resource that describes how to deploy your application on the cluster. The Deployment resource defines the number of replicas, the container image to use, the ports exposed by the application, and more.

5. Create a Kubernetes Service resource that defines how to access your application. The Service resource creates a stable endpoint for your application and can also load balance traffic among replicas.

6. Use the `kubectl` command-line tool to create and manage the Deployment and Service resources on the cluster.

7. Monitor the status of your application using Kubernetes Engine's built-in monitoring and logging features or using external tools such as Prometheus and Grafana.

8. Scale the number of replicas up or down as needed using the `kubectl` command-line tool or the Kubernetes Engine dashboard in the GCP Console.

It is important to note that, before deploying your application, you'll need to have a running Kubernetes cluster and the `kubectl` command-line tool installed on your local machine.

You can also use Kubernetes Engine's Deployment Manager to automate the process of deploying your application. Deployment Manager uses a simple declarative syntax to define the resources needed to deploy your application and can help you manage and organize your deployments.

Also, Kubernetes Engine supports several configurations and settings for your cluster, such as the number of nodes, machine types, and regions. You should also be familiar with the Kubernetes Engine quota and limits and how to configure them.

You can also use tools such as Skaffold or Helm to deploy your application on Kubernetes Engine. These tools help to automate the deployment process and can simplify the process.

Google Kubernetes Engine is a powerful tool for deploying and managing containerized applications. It provides a highly scalable, reliable, and secure environment for running your Java applications. In the next section, we will discuss how to deploy a Java application on GKE through automation.

Deploying a Java Application on GKE Through Automation

Deploying a Java application on Kubernetes Engine through automation can be done using the following steps:

1. Create a Kubernetes cluster on GCP using the Kubernetes Engine in the Google Cloud Console with the `gcloud` command, as shown in Listing 7-1.

Listing 7-1. Creating a Kubernetes Cluster on GKE

```
gcloud container clusters create [CLUSTER_NAME] --num-nodes=[NUMBER_OF_NODES]
```

2. Build a Docker container for your Java application using a Dockerfile. Create a Dockerfile in your root directory, as given in Listing 7-2. Replace myapp with your application name.

Listing 7-2. Dockerfile

```
FROM openjdk:8-jdk-alpine
COPY . /usr/src/myapp
WORKDIR /usr/src/myapp
RUN ./gradlew build
CMD ["java", "-jar", "build/libs/myapp.jar"]
```

3. Create a Kubernetes deployment and service objects for your application using a YAML file, as shown in Listing 7-3.

Listing 7-3. YAML File for Kubernetes Deployment and Service

```
apiVersion: apps/v1
kind: Deployment
metadata:
  name: myapp-deployment
spec:
  replicas: 3
  selector:
    matchLabels:
      app: myapp
  template:
    metadata:
      labels:
        app: myapp
    spec:
      containers:
      - name: myapp
        image: gcr.io/[PROJECT_ID]/myapp:v1
        ports:
        - containerPort: 8080
---
apiVersion: v1
```

```
kind: Service
metadata:
  name: myapp-service
spec:
  selector:
    app: myapp
  ports:
  - name: http
    port: 80
    targetPort: 8080
  type: LoadBalancer
```

4. Use Helm to automate the process of deploying and managing your application on the cluster, as shown in Listing 7-4.

Listing 7-4. Helm Chart

```
helm install myapp charts/myapp
```

5. Use Helm values file to customize your deployment, as shown in Listing 7-5.

Listing 7-5. Using Helm Values

```
replicaCount: 3
image:
  repository: gcr.io/[PROJECT_ID]/myapp
  tag: v1
```

6. Use a CI/CD tool such as Jenkins or TravisCI to automate the process of building, testing, and deploying your application. Listing 7-6 shows the Jenkin `pipeline` command for building, testing, and deploying.

Listing 7-6. Jenkins Pipeline with Build, Test, and Deploy Stage

```
pipeline {
    agent any
    stages {
```

```
        stage('Build') {
            steps {
                sh './gradlew build'
            }
        }
        stage('Test') {
            steps {
                sh './gradlew test'
            }
        }
        stage('Deploy') {
            steps {
                sh 'kubectl apply -f k8s/'
                sh 'helm upgrade --install myapp charts/myapp'
            }
        }
    }
}
```

You can also use Spinnaker or Terraform to automate the deployment process on Kubernetes Engine. These tools can help you to manage your deployments and rollbacks and handle the infrastructure.

You will need to have the necessary permissions and credentials to perform these steps and also have the necessary resources available on your GCP account.

In the next section, we will discuss deploying the application on a virtual machine provided through Google Compute Engine.

Deploying a Java Application on Google Compute Engine

Google Compute Engine (GCE) is a scalable and flexible virtual machine environment for deploying applications. To deploy a Java application on GCP Compute Engine, you can follow these steps:

1. Create a virtual machine instance on GCP Compute Engine with the desired configuration (e.g., operating system, CPU, memory, storage).

2. Connect to the virtual machine instance via SSH.

3. Install the required software and dependencies, such as the Java Development Kit (JDK).
4. Transfer the Java application files to the virtual machine instance, either by uploading the files or by cloning a repository.
5. Start the Java application, either through manual execution or through a startup script.

Google Compute Engine Automation for Deployment

GCE is a service that provides virtual machine instances for running applications. You can use automation tools such as Google Cloud Deployment Manager or Terraform to deploy a Java application on GCE. You can create an instance group in GCE for high availability.

Let's talk about the instance group. An instance group is a collection of virtual machine (VM) instances that are created from a common instance template and managed as a single entity. Instance groups are designed to provide scalability, high availability, and load balancing for your applications.

There are two types of instance groups in GCP: managed instance groups and unmanaged instance groups.

Managed instance groups are a type of instance group that are managed by GCP. They are designed to automatically adjust the number of instances based on traffic demand, perform rolling updates, and provide automatic failover in the event of an instance failure. Managed instance groups can also integrate with other GCP services, such as load balancing, autoscaling, and container orchestration.

Unmanaged instance groups, on the other hand, are created and managed by the user. They are designed to provide more control and flexibility over the configuration and management of the instances, but they require more manual intervention for tasks such as scaling, updating, and failover.

Instance groups can be used in various use cases, such as web serving, batch processing, data processing, and machine learning. They can be accessed through the GCP Console, the `gcloud` command-line tool, or the GCP API.

To create an instance group in GCP, you first need to create an instance template, which defines the configuration settings for the instances, such as the machine type, disk size, image, and metadata. You can then use the instance template to create the instance group, specifying the number of instances, the autoscaling policy, and the load-balancing configuration.

Once the instance group is created, you can monitor and manage the instances using various GCP tools and services, such as Cloud Monitoring, Cloud Logging, and Compute Engine Autoscaler. You can also perform common tasks such as scaling, updating, and failover using the GCP Console, the `gcloud` command-line tool, or the GCP API.

Deployment can be done in two ways.

- Use a configuration management tool such as Terraform, Chef, or Puppet to automate the creation of virtual machine instances and the provisioning of software and dependencies.
- Use a CI/CD tool such as Jenkins or Google Cloud Build to automate the deployment process.

Listing 7-7 is an example of a Terraform script to automate the creation of a virtual machine instance and deployment of a Java application.

Listing 7-7. Terraform Script for Creating VM Instance

```
provider "google" {
  version = "2.0"
  project = "my-project"
  region  = "us-central1"
}

resource "google_compute_instance" "default" {
  name         = "my-instance"
  machine_type = "f1-micro"
  zone         = "us-central1-a"

  boot_disk {
    initialize_params {
      image = "ubuntu-1604-xenial-v20201117"
    }
  }

  connection {
    type        = "ssh"
    host        = self.network_interface.0.access_config.0.nat_ip
    user        = "ubuntu"
```

```
    private_key = file("~/.ssh/id_rsa")
  }

  provisioner "remote-exec" {
    inline = [
      "sudo apt-get update",
      "sudo apt-get install -y openjdk-8-jdk",
      "sudo apt-get install -y maven",
      "git clone https://github.com/my-repo/my-java-app.git",
      "cd my-java-app",
      "mvn clean install",
      "nohup java -jar target/my-java-app.jar &"
    ]
  }
}
```

This Terraform script creates a virtual machine instance running Ubuntu, installs the JDK and Maven, clones a Java application repository, builds the application, and starts the application in the background. This script can be executed to automatically deploy the Java application on GCP Compute Engine, streamlining the deployment process and reducing manual intervention.

Additionally, here are some other considerations for deploying Java applications on GCP Compute Engine:

- *Load balancing*: Load balancing can be achieved by creating multiple virtual machine instances and using a load balancer to distribute incoming traffic. GCP provides built-in load balancing options, such as TCP Load Balancer and HTTP(S) Load Balancer.
- *Custom domains*: Custom domains can be mapped to the load balancer through GCP DNS.
- *Resource quotas*: GCP has resource quotas for various components such as CPU, memory, and storage. These quotas can be increased through a support request.
- *Monitoring*: GCP provides detailed performance metrics and logging through Cloud Operations Suite. Custom metrics can also be added to track application-specific data.

- *Maintenance*: GCP provides automatic software updates and security patches for the operating system, freeing developers from these tasks.
- *Pricing*: GCP pricing is based on resource usage, including CPU, memory, storage, and outgoing network traffic.

In conclusion, deploying a Java application on GCP Compute Engine provides a scalable and flexible environment for deploying and running applications. By leveraging the various automation options and tools available on GCP, organizations can streamline their deployment processes and focus on building and enhancing their applications.

To configure Google Compute Engine for high availability, you can follow these steps:

1. *Deploy multiple virtual machine instances*: Deploy multiple virtual machine instances in different zones within a region to ensure high availability.
2. *Load balancing*: Use a load balancer to distribute incoming traffic across multiple virtual machine instances. GCP provides built-in load balancing options, such as TCP Load Balancer and HTTP(S) Load Balancer.
3. *Automated failover*: Use instance groups and managed instance groups to ensure automatic failover in the event of an instance failure. Managed instance groups automatically manage the creation and deletion of instances to maintain the desired number of instances.
4. *Persistent disk storage*: Use persistent disk storage to ensure that data is not lost in the event of an instance failure. Persistent disks can be attached to multiple virtual machine instances for data replication and backup.
5. *Monitoring and alerting*: Use Cloud Monitoring to set up alerts for critical resource thresholds and receive notifications in the event of an issue.
6. *Backups*: Regularly back up important data to a safe location, such as Cloud Storage or a different region, to ensure data recovery in the event of a disaster.

7. *Software updates*: Keep virtual machine instances updated with the latest security patches and software updates to ensure a secure and stable environment.

Here's an example of a high availability architecture using multiple virtual machine instances, load balancing, and managed instance groups.

In this example, incoming traffic is distributed across multiple virtual machine instances through a load balancer. Managed instance groups ensure automatic failover in the event of an instance failure, by automatically creating and deleting instances to maintain the desired number of instances. Persistent disk storage is used for data storage, and Cloud Monitoring is used for monitoring and alerting.

By following these steps, organizations can configure their Google Compute Engine environment for high availability, ensuring a robust and resilient environment for their applications.

Deploying a Containerized Java Application on Google Cloud Run

Google Cloud Run is a serverless, fully managed compute platform for deploying containerized applications. It provides a quick and easy way to deploy and run Java applications with automatic scaling, load balancing, and monitoring.

Here are the steps to deploy a Java application on Cloud Run:

1. *Containerize the application*: Package the Java application and its dependencies in a Docker container.

2. *Upload the container to a container registry*: Store the container in a container registry, such as Google Container Registry or Docker Hub.

3. *Deploy to Cloud Run*: Use the Cloud Run web console, `gcloud` command-line tool, or Cloud Run API to deploy the container to Cloud Run.

4. *Configure environment variables*: Configure environment variables for the application as needed.

5. *Test the deployment*: Test the deployment by accessing the generated URL.

Listing 7-8 shows an example of deploying a Java application on Cloud Run using the `gcloud` command-line tool.

Listing 7-8. gcloud Command to Deploy an Application on Cloud Run

```
# Build and push the Docker container to Google Container Registry
docker build -t gcr.io/<PROJECT_ID>/<IMAGE_NAME> .
docker push gcr.io/<PROJECT_ID>/<IMAGE_NAME>

# Deploy the container to Cloud Run
gcloud run deploy <SERVICE_NAME> \
  --image gcr.io/<PROJECT_ID>/<IMAGE_NAME> \
  --platform managed
```

In this example, the Docker container is built and pushed to Google Container Registry and then deployed to Cloud Run using the `gcloud run deploy` command. The `--platform managed` option specifies that Cloud Run should manage the deployment and infrastructure.

By using Cloud Run, organizations can deploy Java applications quickly and easily, with automatic scaling, load balancing, and monitoring. This can help organizations focus on building and enhancing their applications, without having to worry about infrastructure management.

Additionally, Cloud Run also provides several other features and options that can enhance the deployment and management of Java applications.

- *Custom domains*: Associate a custom domain name with the Cloud Run deployment to make the application accessible via a branded URL.
- *HTTPS*: Automatically secure incoming traffic to the application with HTTPS.
- *Environment variables*: Pass configuration values to the application through environment variables, making it easier to manage configuration without changing code.
- *Concurrency control*: Control the maximum number of concurrent requests to the application to prevent overloading.

- *IAM*: Control access to the Cloud Run deployment with fine-grained Identity and Access Management (IAM) policies.
- *Logging*: Monitor and debug the application with Cloud Logging, which integrates with other Operations Suite tools.
- *Tracing*: Identify performance issues and optimize the application with Cloud Trace.
- *Monitoring*: Monitor the health and performance of the application with Cloud Monitoring.

Organizations can use these features and options to deploy and manage Java applications on Cloud Run with more control and flexibility, ensuring a robust and scalable environment for their applications.

Deploying a Java Application on Cloud Functions

Google Cloud Functions is a serverless compute platform that allows you to run your code in response to events, without having to manage the underlying infrastructure. You can deploy Java applications on Cloud Functions and trigger them in response to events, such as changes to a Google Cloud Storage bucket or a message on a Cloud Pub/Sub topic.

Here are the steps to deploy a Java application on Cloud Functions:

1. *Write the function code*: Write the Java code for the function, using the Java 8 runtime.
2. *Package the function*: Package the Java code and its dependencies into a JAR file.
3. *Deploy the function*: Use the `gcloud` command-line tool, Cloud Functions web console, or API to deploy the function to Cloud Functions.
4. *Trigger the function*: Configure the function to be triggered by an event, such as a change to a Google Cloud Storage bucket or a message on a Cloud Pub/Sub topic.

Listing 7-9 shows an example of deploying a Java function to Cloud Functions using the `gcloud` command-line tool.

Listing 7-9. Deploying a Cloud Function

```
# Package the function code and dependencies into a JAR file
./gradlew build

# Deploy the function to Cloud Functions
gcloud functions deploy <FUNCTION_NAME> \
  --runtime java8 \
  --trigger-http \
  --entry-point <CLASS_NAME>.<METHOD_NAME> \
  --jar <JAR_FILE>
```

In this example, the function code is packaged into a JAR file using Gradle and then deployed to Cloud Functions using the `gcloud functions deploy` command. The `--runtime java8` option specifies that the Java 8 runtime should be used, and the `--trigger-http` option specifies that the function should be triggered by an HTTP request. The `--entry-point` option specifies the class and method name of the function entry point, and the `--jar` option specifies the JAR file that contains the function code and dependencies.

By using Cloud Functions, organizations can deploy and run Java applications quickly and easily, with automatic scaling and monitoring. This can help organizations focus on building and enhancing their applications, without having to worry about infrastructure management. Additionally, organizations can take advantage of the event-driven architecture provided by Cloud Functions to build highly scalable, efficient, and responsive applications.

Another feature of Cloud Functions is that it supports environment variables, which can be used to pass configuration values to the function at runtime, as shown in Listing 7-10.

Listing 7-10. Deploying a Cloud Function with Setting Environment Variables

```
gcloud functions deploy <FUNCTION_NAME> \
  --runtime java8 \
  --trigger-http \
  --entry-point <CLASS_NAME>.<METHOD_NAME> \
  --jar <JAR_FILE> \
  --set-env-vars <ENV_VAR_NAME>=<ENV_VAR_VALUE>
```

In Listing 7-10, the `--set-env-vars` option is used to set the value of an environment variable named `ENV_VAR_NAME` to `ENV_VAR_VALUE`. The function code can then access this value using `System.getenv("ENV_VAR_NAME")`.

Cloud Functions also provides several other features and options that can enhance the deployment and management of Java applications, including the following:

- *Custom domains*: Associate a custom domain name with the Cloud Functions deployment to make the function accessible via a branded URL.
- *HTTPS*: Automatically secure incoming traffic to the function with HTTPS.
- *IAM*: Control access to the Cloud Functions deployment with fine-grained IAM policies.
- *Logging*: Monitor and debug the function with Cloud Logging, which integrates with other Operations Suite tools.
- *Tracing*: Identify performance issues and optimize the function with Cloud Trace.
- *Monitoring*: Monitor the health and performance of the function with Cloud Monitoring.

Organizations can use these features and options to deploy and manage Java applications on Cloud Functions with more control and flexibility, ensuring a robust and scalable environment for their functions.

Another important aspect of deploying Java applications on Cloud Functions is testing and debugging. To test the function locally, you can use the `gcloud` command-line tool or the Cloud Functions Emulator, which provides a local environment that mimics the Cloud Functions environment. This allows you to test and debug your function before deploying it to the cloud.

For example, to test the function locally using the `gcloud` command-line tool, see Listing 7-11.

Listing 7-11. Trigger a Cloud Function Using the gcloud Command

```
gcloud functions call <FUNCTION_NAME>
```

In Listing 7-11, the `gcloud functions call` command is used to trigger the function locally. The command-line output will show the result of the function execution.

Another option is to use a local IDE, such as IntelliJ or Eclipse, to debug the function code. You can use a remote debugger to connect to the running function in the cloud and step through the code, set breakpoints, and inspect variables. This can help you identify and resolve issues more efficiently.

Finally, it is recommended to implement automated testing for your functions to ensure that they behave as expected, even after changes are made to the code. You can use a testing framework, such as JUnit, to write test cases for your functions and run them automatically as part of your continuous integration and deployment pipeline.

In conclusion, deploying Java applications on Cloud Functions can provide several benefits for organizations, including automatic scaling, monitoring, and automatic management of the underlying infrastructure. By following best practices for testing, debugging, and deploying functions, organizations can ensure a robust and scalable environment for their Java applications on Cloud Functions.

Scaling a Java Application on GCP

Scaling a Java application on Google Cloud Platform involves increasing the capacity of your application infrastructure to handle an increase in demand. You can achieve this by using various GCP services and tools, including the following:

- *Google Kubernetes Engine*: You can use GKE to run and manage containers that host your application. You can scale your application by increasing the number of replicas of your application containers in your cluster.
- *Google App Engine*: You can use Google App Engine to host your application in a managed environment. App Engine automatically manages scaling and resources for you, so you don't have to worry about managing infrastructure.
- *Google Compute Engine*: You can use Google Compute Engine to host virtual machines that run your application. You can scale your application by adding or removing virtual machines as needed.

- *Google Cloud Load Balancing*: You can use Google Cloud Load Balancing to distribute incoming traffic across multiple virtual machines or containers running your application. This helps to improve application performance and reliability by spreading the load evenly across multiple resources.
- *Autoscaling policies*: You can use autoscaling policies to automatically adjust the number of resources (such as virtual machines or containers) in your application infrastructure based on performance metrics, such as CPU utilization or incoming traffic.

When selecting a solution for scaling your Java application on GCP, you should consider the specific requirements of your application, such as performance, reliability, cost, and ease of management.

Steps for Scaling Applications

Scaling a Java application on Google Cloud Platform involves increasing the capacity of your infrastructure to handle an increase in demand. Here are some detailed steps and examples of how to scale a Java application on GCP:

- *Monitor application performance*: You should monitor the performance of your Java application using various GCP tools and services, such as Cloud Monitoring, Cloud Trace, or Cloud Logging. You can use these tools to monitor the resource usage, performance, and error rates of your application.
- *Identify areas where additional capacity is needed*: Based on the monitoring data, you should identify the areas where additional capacity is needed, such as increased CPU utilization, increased incoming traffic, or increased error rates.
- *Choose a scaling solution*: Depending on your specific requirements and the characteristics of your Java application, you can choose one or more scaling solutions, such as Google Kubernetes Engine, Google App Engine, Google Compute Engine, or Google Cloud Load Balancing.

Scaling a Java Application on Google Kubernetes Engine

You can use the gcloud CLI or the GCP Console to create a GKE cluster. You can specify the number of nodes and the machine type for each node, as shown in Listing 7-12.

Listing 7-12. Creating a Kubernetes Cluster Using the cloud Command

```
gcloud container clusters create my-cluster --num-nodes=3 --machine-
type=n1-standard-1
```

To deploy a Java application to the GKE cluster, you can use a Dockerfile to build a container image of your Java application and then use the kubectl CLI to deploy the container image to the GKE cluster, as given in Listing 7-13.

Listing 7-13. Deploying the Container Image to a Kubernetes Cluster

```
kubectl apply -f deployment.yaml
```

To create a horizontal pod autoscaler (HPA), you can use the kubectl CLI to create an HPA that automatically adjusts the number of replicas of your application containers based on CPU utilization, as shown in Listing 7-14.

Listing 7-14. Kubernetes Autoscaling

```
apiVersion: autoscaling/v2beta1
kind: HorizontalPodAutoscaler
metadata:
  name: my-app-hpa
spec:
  scaleTargetRef:
    apiVersion: apps/v1
    kind: Deployment
    name: my-app
  minReplicas: 1
  maxReplicas: 10
  metrics:
  - type: Resource
    resource:
      name: cpu
      targetAverageUtilization: 50
```

Scaling a Java Application on App Engine

You can use the gcloud CLI or the GCP Console to deploy your Java application to App Engine, as in Listing 7-15. You can specify the scaling type (automatic or manual) and the instance class for your application.

Listing 7-15. Deploying the Application

```
gcloud app deploy
```

You can use the app.yaml configuration file to enable automatic scaling for your App Engine application. You can specify the minimum and maximum number of instances and the CPU utilization target for automatic scaling, as shown in Listing 7-16.

The app.yaml file should be placed in the root directory of your application. When you deploy your application to App Engine, the app.yaml file is used to configure various settings, such as the runtime environment, scaling settings, and other application-specific settings.

Listing 7-16. Autoscaling

```
runtime: java
instance_class: F4
automatic_scaling:
  min_num_instances: 1
  max_num_instances: 10
  target_cpu_utilization: 0.5
```

Scaling a Java Application on Compute Engine

You can use the gcloud CLI or the GCP Console to create a Compute Engine instance, as shown in Listing 7-17. You can specify the machine type, disk size, and other configuration parameters for the instance.

Listing 7-17. gcloud CLI create instances Command

```
gcloud compute instances create my-instance --machine-type=n1-standard-1
```

You can use Google Cloud Load Balancer to distribute incoming traffic to multiple Compute Engine instances. You can choose from different types of load balancers, such as Network Load Balancer, HTTP(S) Load Balancer, or TCP Load Balancer, as shown in Listing 7-18.

Listing 7-18. Setting Up a VM

```
gcloud compute firewall-rules create allow-http --allow tcp:80
gcloud compute target-pools create my-target-pool
gcloud compute target-pools add-instances my-target-pool --instances=my-
instance-1,my-instance-2
gcloud compute forwarding-rules create http-load-balancer --port-range=80 \
  --target-pool=my-target-pool --region=us-central1
```

- *Automate the creation and deletion of Compute Engine instances*: You can use Google Cloud Deployment Manager or Terraform to automate the creation and deletion of Compute Engine instances. You can define the desired configuration in a YAML or Terraform file and use a script to create or delete instances as needed.
- *Use cases*: Scaling a Java application on GCP can be used in various use cases, such as e-commerce, content delivery, social media, or gaming. For example, if you run an e-commerce website, you can use App Engine or Compute Engine to scale your website during peak traffic periods and use Kubernetes to manage the deployment and scaling of your application containers.

Scaling a Java application on GCP involves monitoring application performance, choosing a scaling solution, and automating the scaling process. The specific steps and configurations will vary depending on your specific requirements and the characteristics of your Java application.

Monitoring Performance and Autoscaling

To monitor the performance of your Java application on GCP, you can use tools such as Cloud Monitoring, Cloud Logging, and Cloud Trace. These tools allow you to monitor the resource utilization, log data, and trace requests of your application in real time.

To choose a scaling solution, you need to consider factors such as the type of application, the expected traffic patterns, and the required level of customization. For example, if you have a simple web application that experiences predictable traffic patterns, you can use the App Engine's standard or flexible environment. If you have a more complex application that requires more customization, you can use Compute Engine or Kubernetes Engine.

Once you have chosen a scaling solution, you can use automation tools such as Google Cloud Deployment Manager or Terraform to automate the scaling process. For example, you can use Deployment Manager to create and delete Compute Engine instances as needed, or you can use Terraform to define and manage the infrastructure for your application.

Additionally, you can use tools such as Kubernetes Engine or App Engine to manage the deployment and scaling of your containers. These tools allow you to deploy and manage your containers in a scalable and efficient manner.

Overall, scaling a Java application on GCP requires a combination of monitoring, choice of solution, and automation. With these tools and best practices in place, you can ensure that your Java application is able to handle growing traffic and changing demand with ease.

Scaling in Serverless

Scaling in serverless architecture, such as Google Cloud Functions, is managed automatically by the platform. When your function receives a new request, the platform creates a new instance of the function to handle the request. When the request is completed, the instance is terminated. As each function execution is independent and does not depend on the previous execution or external state, the cloud function should be stateless.

The platform automatically manages the number of instances based on the number of requests. If the number of requests increases, the platform creates more instances to handle the load. If the number of requests decreases, the platform terminates some instances to conserve resources.

This means you don't have to worry about scaling your serverless applications manually. The platform takes care of it for you, providing the necessary resources to handle incoming requests and ensuring that your functions are highly available and scalable.

Additionally, you can set concurrency limits for your functions to control the maximum number of instances that can be created at any given time. This can help you avoid overloading your back-end resources and maintain the performance of your application.

Summary

In this chapter, you learned about deploying and scaling Java applications on GCP. You learned about different GCP services and tools, such as GKE, Google App Engine, and Google Compute Engine, that can be used to scale a Java application. The chapter also covered monitoring application performance, identifying areas where additional capacity is needed, and choosing a scaling solution based on the application's specific requirements. You also learned about automatic scaling in serverless architecture, such as Google Cloud Functions. Finally, the chapter covered testing and debugging best practices for Java applications deployed on GCP. Overall, the chapter provided a comprehensive overview of how to deploy and scale Java applications on GCP.

CHAPTER 8

Troubleshooting and Optimization

This chapter focuses on optimizing the performance of Java applications running on Google Cloud Platform (GCP). The chapter covers various techniques and best practices for improving performance, including optimizing Java virtual machine (JVM) settings, using caching, implementing load balancing, monitoring and logging, and optimizing the network. By implementing these techniques, you will learn how to improve the performance and reliability of your Java applications on GCP, providing a better experience for your users.

Troubleshooting and optimizing Java applications on GCP requires a thorough understanding of the underlying infrastructure and a robust set of tools and best practices. Here are some tips for troubleshooting and optimizing Java applications on GCP:

- *Monitoring*: GCP provides a range of monitoring and logging tools, including Operations Suite, that can help you keep track of the health and performance of your Java applications. You can use Operations Suite to monitor the performance of your Java applications, identify potential issues, and track resource utilization. For example, you can set up custom dashboards to monitor the performance of your Java applications in real time and use Cloud Logs to troubleshoot issues.
- *Load balancing*: Load balancing is a crucial aspect of optimizing Java applications on GCP. GCP provides several load balancing options, including TCP/IP load balancing and HTTP(s) load balancing with appropriate routing algorithm. You can use load balancing to distribute incoming requests across multiple instances of your Java application, ensuring that your application is scalable, is available,

A. Shashi, *Designing Applications for Google Cloud Platform*, https://doi.org/10.1007/978-1-4842-9511-3_8

and performs optimally. For example, you can use TCP/IP load balancing to distribute incoming requests to multiple instances of your Java application based on network performance metrics.

- *Scaling*: Scaling is another important aspect of optimizing Java applications on GCP. You can use GCP's autoscaling capabilities to automatically adjust the number of instances based on the demand for your application. For example, you can use autoscaling to automatically increase the number of instances during periods of high traffic and decrease the number of instances during periods of low traffic.
- *Performance tuning*: Performance tuning involves adjusting configuration settings and optimizing resource utilization to improve the overall performance of your Java applications on GCP. For example, you can optimize the memory and CPU settings of your Java instances to ensure that your applications perform optimally. You can also optimize the configuration of your database and network stack to ensure that your Java applications are able to access the resources they need.
- *Cost optimization*: Cost optimization is critical for ensuring that your Java applications on GCP are cost-effective. You can reduce resource utilization and waste by using cost-saving features such as reserved instances and by using resource-saving practices, such as using smaller instances when possible and optimizing the utilization of your instances or using Spot VM wherever it is suitable.
- *Debugging*: Debugging Java applications on GCP can be challenging, but several tools are available that can help you diagnose and resolve issues. For example, you can use the Cloud Debugger to examine the state of your Java applications and to identify the root cause of issues. Additionally, you can use log analysis tools, such as Cloud Logging, to help you troubleshoot issues with your Java applications.
- *Code profiling*: Profiling your Java code can help you identify performance bottlenecks and areas for optimization. You can use code profiling tools, such as JProfiler or YourKit, to understand how your Java applications are performing and to identify areas

for improvement. Remote profilers typically require additional configuration to allow them to connect to the application being profiled. This may involve setting up network configuration to allow the profiler to communicate with the application, configure security settings, and perform other related tasks. The specific steps will depend on the profiler and the application's environment.

- *Continuous integration and deployment (CI/CD)*: CI/CD is a software development practice that involves continuously integrating and deploying code changes to production. This can help you quickly and efficiently deploy updates to your Java applications on GCP, while reducing the risk of introducing new issues. You can use tools such as Jenkins or Travis CI to automate your CI/CD pipeline on GCP.
- *Error handling*: Error handling is a critical aspect of troubleshooting Java applications on GCP. You should ensure that your Java applications are designed to handle exceptions and errors effectively and that you have a robust error handling strategy in place. For example, you can use Stackdriver Error Reporting to capture and track errors in your Java applications.
- *Test automation*: Test automation is a crucial aspect of troubleshooting and optimizing Java applications on GCP. You can use automated testing tools, such as JUnit or TestNG, to validate the functionality of your Java applications and to identify and resolve issues.

By monitoring your applications, load balancing, scaling, performance tuning, and cost optimization, you can ensure that your Java applications are running smoothly and efficiently on GCP.

Troubleshooting Java Applications on GCP

Troubleshooting Java applications running on GCP can be a complex process, but there are several tools and best practices that can help you resolve issues quickly and effectively. Let's look at an example of how you might troubleshoot a Java application running on GCP.

Let's say you have a Java application running on a Compute Engine instance on GCP and you're receiving reports of slow performance and errors. Here's how you might troubleshoot the issue:

- *Monitor the application*: First, you'll want to monitor the performance of your Java application. You can use the Cloud Performance Monitoring tool to view real-time performance data, such as CPU and memory utilization, to understand how your application is performing.
- *Analyze logs and traces*: Next, you'll want to analyze the logs of your Java application to identify the root cause of the issue. You can use the Cloud Logging tool to view log entries for your application, including any errors or exceptions that have been thrown.
- *Debug the application*: If you're unable to identify the issue from log analysis, you can use the Cloud Debugger tool to examine the state of your Java application and identify the root cause of the issue. This tool allows you to pause the execution of your application and examine variables, stack traces, and other data to determine what might be causing the problem.
- *Optimize the code*: Once you've identified the root cause of the issue, you can optimize the code of your Java application to resolve the problem. You can use code profiling tools, such as JProfiler or YourKit, to identify performance bottlenecks and optimize your code accordingly.
- *Update the configuration*: Finally, you may need to update the configuration of your Compute Engine instance or your Java application to resolve the issue. For example, you might adjust the amount of memory or CPU resources available to your application to improve performance.

The key to effectively troubleshooting Java applications running on GCP is to use a combination of monitoring, log analysis, debugging, code optimization, and configuration updates. By following these best practices, you can quickly and efficiently resolve issues with your Java applications on GCP.

Let's run through some issues you might encounter and how to resolve them.

Example 1: Slow Response Time

A Java application deployed on GCP is running slow and causing frustration among users. The following steps can be taken to troubleshoot the issue:

1. *Check the load*: The first step is to check the CPU and memory utilization of the instances running the Java application. If the utilization is high, the instances might need to be scaled to handle the increased load. You can use Cloud Matrics, which is a monitoring service offered by Google Cloud Platform to collect, process, and visualize metrics and metadata from various Google Cloud services and custom data sources.

2. *Monitor the network*: Monitor the network to ensure that there is no significant latency in communication between the instances and the database. If there is a latency issue, it can be resolved by increasing the number of instances, optimizing the database, or adjusting the firewall rules.

3. *Debug the code*: Debug the Java code to identify any performance bottlenecks or bugs that are causing slow response times. Use Cloud Debugger to examine the state of the Java application at runtime and identify the root cause of the issue.

4. *Optimize the database*: If the slow response time is caused by a database issue, optimize the database configuration, indexing, and queries to improve performance.

Example 2: Exception Handling

A Java application deployed on GCP is throwing exceptions and causing issues for users. The following steps can be taken to troubleshoot the issue:

1. *Monitor the logs*: Use Cloud Logging to monitor the logs of the Java application for any errors or exceptions that are being thrown.

2. *Debug the code*: Use Cloud Debugger to identify the source of the exception and debug the Java code to resolve the issue.

3. *Check the dependencies*: Check the dependencies of the Java application to ensure that they are all up-to-date and functioning correctly.

4. *Update the configuration*: If the exception is caused by a configuration issue, update the configuration of the instances or the Java application to resolve the problem.

Example 3: Memory Leak

A Java application deployed on GCP is causing memory leaks, leading to performance degradation over time and crashes over time after going to out-of-memory. The following steps can be taken to troubleshoot the issue:

1. *Monitor the memory*: Use Cloud Performance Monitoring to monitor the memory utilization of the instances running the Java application. If the utilization is consistently high, it is likely that a memory leak is occurring.

2. *Debug the code*: Use Cloud Debugger to identify the source of the memory leak and debug the Java code to resolve the issue.

3. *Optimize the garbage collector*: Optimize the garbage collector configuration to ensure that it is collecting unused objects in a timely and efficient manner.

4. *Update the configuration*: If the memory leak is caused by a configuration issue, update the configuration of the instances or the Java application to resolve the problem.

These steps are examples of how you might troubleshoot Java applications running on GCP. By using the tools and best practices outlined, you can quickly and effectively resolve issues with your Java applications on GCP.

Optimizing a Java Application Running on GCP

Optimizing a Java application running on GCP can help to improve its performance, reliability, and scalability. Here are some best practices and examples of optimizing Java applications on GCP:

- *Scaling*: Scaling the instances running the Java application can help to improve performance and ensure that the application can handle increased load. Use the built-in autoscaling capabilities of GCP, such as the Managed Instance Group, to automatically add or remove instances based on the load.
- *Caching*: Caching can greatly improve the performance of Java applications by reducing the number of database queries that need to be made. Use a caching service such as Cloud Memorystore or a caching library such as Guava to cache frequently used data in memory.
- *Load balancing*: Load balancing helps to distribute the load of incoming requests evenly across multiple instances of the Java application. Use the built-in load balancing capabilities of GCP, such as the HTTP(S) Load Balancer, to balance the load of incoming requests.
- *Optimizing database queries*: Optimizing database queries can greatly improve the performance of a Java application by reducing the amount of time and resources needed to retrieve data from the database. Use the Cloud SQL Performance Insights tool to analyze the performance of database queries and optimize them for better performance. Using interleaving is recommended for Cloud Spanner, and caution is advised to avoid exploding indexes when working with Cloudstore.
- *Using managed services*: Using managed services, such as Cloud Datastore or Cloud Spanner, can help to reduce the operational overhead of running a Java application. Managed services provide automatic backups, scalability, and high availability, making it easier to maintain a reliable and scalable Java application on GCP.

Example 1: Improving Response Time

A Java application deployed on GCP is running slow and causing frustration among users. The following steps can be taken to improve the response time:

1. *Scale the instances*: Scale the instances running the Java application to ensure that they have enough resources to handle the increased load. Use the Managed Instance Group to automatically scale out the instances as needed. When scaling up instances, you can consider various factors such as CPU usage, memory usage, and network bandwidth utilization. The specific factors to consider may depend on the nature of your application and its resource requirements. For example, if your application is CPU-intensive, you may want to scale up instances based on CPU usage. If your application requires a lot of memory, you should scale up instances based on memory usage. In general, it's a good idea to monitor and analyze resource utilization to determine the optimal scaling strategy for your application.

2. *Cache data*: Implement caching in the Java application to cache frequently used data in memory. This can reduce the number of database queries that need to be made and improve the performance of the application.

3. *Load balance the requests*: Use the HTTP(S) Load Balancer to load balance incoming requests and distribute the load evenly across multiple instances of the Java application.

4. *Optimize the database queries*: Use the Cloud SQL Performance Insights tool to analyze the performance of database queries and optimize them for better performance.

5. *Upgrade to managed services*: Upgrade to a managed service such as Cloud Datastore or Cloud Spanner to take advantage of automatic backups, scalability, and high availability. If you are using a self-managed database, you should implement a backup and recovery strategy that meets your business requirements. This may involve setting up regular backups, testing the backups to ensure they can be restored successfully, and implementing

a disaster recovery plan in the case of an outage or failure. You should also monitor the health and performance of the database and take appropriate actions to optimize it as needed. Additionally, you may want to consider using third-party tools or services to help with monitoring and management of the database.

Example 2: Improving Reliability

A Java application deployed on GCP is experiencing issues with reliability. The following steps can be taken to improve the reliability of the application:

1. *Scale the instances*: Scale the instances running the Java application to ensure that they have enough resources to handle the increased load and avoid downtime.

2. *Implement failover*: Implement failover for the Java application to ensure that it can automatically switch to a backup instance in the event of an instance failure. Refer the automatic failover in Chapter 5 for details.

3. *Use managed services*: Use a managed service such as Cloud Datastore or Cloud Spanner to take advantage of automatic backups, scalability, and high availability.

4. *Monitor the application*: Use Cloud Monitoring to monitor the performance of the Java application and receive notifications in the event of an issue.

5. *Automate the deployment process*: Automate the deployment process for the Java application to ensure that updates and patches are deployed quickly and reliably. Use tools such as Cloud Deployment Manager or Terraform to automate the deployment process and reduce the risk of manual errors.

6. *Implement disaster recovery*: Implement a disaster recovery plan for the Java application to ensure that it can recover quickly in the event of a disaster. Use tools such as Cloud Backup or Cloud Storage to back up data and ensure that it is available in the event of a disaster.

7. *Implement redundancy*: Implement redundancy for the Java application to ensure that it can continue to function in the event of an instance failure or network outage. Use tools like Cloud Load Balancer or Cloud VPN to ensure that incoming requests are redirected to a backup instance in the event of a failure.

Example 3: Improving Scalability

A Java application deployed on GCP is experiencing issues with scalability. The following steps can be taken to improve the scalability of the application:

1. *Scale the instances*: Scale the instances running the Java application to ensure that they have enough resources to handle the increased load and avoid downtime.

2. *Implement autoscaling*: Implement autoscaling for the Java application to automatically add or remove instances based on the load. Use the Managed Instance Group to implement autoscaling.

3. *Optimize database queries*: Optimize database queries to ensure that they are optimized for performance and scalability. Use the Cloud SQL Performance Insights tool to analyze the performance of database queries and optimize them for better performance.

4. *Implement load balancing*: Implement load balancing for the Java application to distribute the load evenly across multiple instances and ensure that incoming requests are handled quickly and efficiently.

5. *Upgrade to managed services*: Upgrade to a managed service such as Cloud Datastore or Cloud Spanner to take advantage of automatic backups, scalability, and high availability.

Example 4: Improving Security

A Java application deployed on GCP is experiencing security issues. The following steps can be taken to improve the security of the application:

1. *Secure the network*: Ensure that the network is properly secured by using tools such as Cloud VPN or Cloud Interconnect to connect securely to the GCP network. Checking firewall rules and configuring ingress are important steps for securing the network on GCP. Firewall rules can be used to control traffic to and from instances and network endpoints, and ingress can be used to control traffic coming into the network from external sources. By configuring firewall rules and ingress, you can help ensure that your network is secure and protected from unauthorized access.

2. *Implement encryption*: Implement encryption for the data stored by the Java application to ensure that it is protected from unauthorized access. Use tools such as Cloud Key Management Service or Cloud Storage to store encrypted data. End-to-end encryption is a technique where the data is encrypted at the source and remains encrypted until it reaches its final destination, which can help protect the data from unauthorized access. Transport Layer Security (TLS) is a protocol that provides encryption and authentication for data in transit between applications over a network. Implementing TLS for your Java application can help ensure that the data is encrypted in transit and protected from eavesdropping or tampering. Other encryption techniques, such as encryption at rest, can also be used to protect data that is stored in databases or other storage systems. Cloud Key Management Service (KMS) can be used to manage cryptographic keys and implement encryption for your Java application on GCP.

3. *Secure the database*: Ensure that the database is properly secured by using tools such as Cloud SQL or Cloud Datastore to store data securely. Securing the database is a crucial step in ensuring the security of a Java application running on GCP. This involves implementing proper access controls and authentication mechanisms, monitoring and logging database activity, and encrypting sensitive data. Tools like Cloud SQL

and Cloud Spanner provide built-in security features such as encryption at rest and in transit, automated backups, and access controls. Regularly reviewing and updating the security settings of the database can help ensure the ongoing security of the Java application.

4. *Enforce authentication and authorization*: Enforce authentication and authorization for the Java application to ensure that only authorized users can access the application and its data. Use tools such as Cloud Identity-Aware Proxy to enforce authentication and authorization.

5. *Monitor and log*: Monitor the Java application and its environment to detect security incidents and log all activity to detect and respond to security incidents. Use tools such as Cloud Monitoring or Cloud Logging to monitor and log activity.

Example 5: Improving Performance

A Java application deployed on GCP is experiencing performance issues. The following steps can be taken to improve the performance of the application:

1. *Optimize the code*: Optimize the code of the Java application to ensure that it is running efficiently and effectively. Use tools such as Stackdriver Profiler or Cloud Debugger to analyze the performance of the application and identify opportunities for improvement.

2. *Implement caching*: Implement caching for the Java application to improve performance by storing frequently accessed data in memory. Use tools such as Cloud Memorystore to implement caching.

3. *Optimize database queries*: Optimize database queries to ensure that they are optimized for performance and scalability. Use the Cloud SQL Performance Insights tool to analyze the performance of database queries and optimize them for better performance.

4. *Scale the instances*: Scale the instances running the Java application to ensure that they have enough resources to handle the increased load and avoid downtime.

5. *Implement load balancing*: Implement load balancing for the Java application to distribute the load evenly across multiple instances and ensure that incoming requests are handled quickly and efficiently.

By following these best practices and examples, you can optimize your Java application running on GCP to ensure that it is performing optimally and meeting the needs of your users.

Tips and Tricks for Optimizing Performance

There are a number of steps you can take to optimize the performance of your applications. Here are the ones I consider to be most important:

- *Caching*: Caching can be an effective way to improve the performance of the Java application. By storing frequently accessed data in memory, it can reduce the number of round-trips to the database and improve the speed of the application. There are different types of caching, including in-memory caching, disk caching, and database caching. In-memory caching is the fastest type of caching, but it requires a lot of memory. Disk caching is slower than in-memory caching but uses less memory. Database caching is the slowest type of caching but requires the least amount of memory.

- *Code optimization*: Code optimization is an important step in improving the performance of the Java application. Developers can use profiling tools such as Stackdriver Profiler to identify slow-running methods and optimize them for better performance. Profiling tools can help to identify methods that take a long time to execute, methods that are executed frequently, and methods that consume a lot of memory. Developers can use this information to optimize the code and improve the performance of the application.

- *Database optimization*: Optimizing the database can help to improve the performance of the Java application. One way to optimize the database is to use Cloud SQL Performance Insights to analyze the performance of database queries and identify opportunities for improvement. Cloud SQL Performance Insights can help to identify slow-running queries, identify queries that are executed frequently, and identify queries that consume a lot of memory. Developers can use this information to optimize the database and improve the performance of the application.
- *Autoscaling*: Autoscaling is a key feature that can help to ensure that the Java application has enough resources to handle increased load and avoid downtime. Cloud Autoscaler can be used to implement autoscaling. Autoscaling allows the number of instances of the Java application to increase or decrease based on demand. When the demand for the application increases, the number of instances increases, and when the demand decreases, the number of instances decreases. This helps to ensure that the Java application has enough resources to handle the load and avoids downtime. In GCE it will scale based on the configuration of the managed instance group.
- *Load balancing*: Load balancing is another key feature that can help to improve the performance of the Java application. Cloud Load Balancer can be used to balance the load across multiple instances of the Java application. Load balancing helps to ensure that the application remains available even if one or more instances fail. When one instance fails, the load balancer redirects traffic to another instance to ensure that the application remains available.
- *Monitoring and logging*: Monitoring and logging are important tools that can help to identify and resolve performance issues with the Java application. Cloud Monitoring and Cloud Logging can be used to monitor the performance of the Java application and log important events. Monitoring and logging can help to identify performance issues and resolve them in a timely manner. Developers can use the information from monitoring and logging to identify areas for improvement and optimize the performance of the application.

- *Right-sizing instances*: Right-sizing the instances running the Java application is another important step in optimizing performance. Instances that are too small may not have enough resources to handle the load, which can impact performance. Instances that are too large may be wasting resources, which can impact cost. Developers should ensure that the instances running the Java application are of the right size and have enough resources to handle the load. Right-sizing is important not only for instances but also for some services such as Cloud SQL. For example, there are guidelines for the disk size, number of vCPUs, and memory for different types of CloudSQL instances based on their usage and workload. It is important to choose the right size for these services to optimize performance and cost. Overprovisioning can lead to higher costs, while underprovisioning can cause performance issues. Therefore, it is important to consider the workload requirements and usage patterns before choosing the right size for these services.
- *Network optimization*: Network optimization is another important step in improving the performance of the Java application. Cloud VPN or Cloud Interconnect can be used to optimize the network and reduce latency if the application is spread across GCP and on-premises. Network optimization helps to improve the performance of the application by reducing the time it takes for data to travel between instances and services.
- *Implementing microservices*: Implementing microservices can improve application performance by distributing the load and deploying it separately in small services. GCP offers various services that are useful for implementing microservices architecture, including Google Kubernetes Engine (GKE), Cloud Functions, Cloud Load Balancing, and Stackdriver. GKE is a managed Kubernetes service that makes deploying and managing microservices in containers easy. Cloud Functions is a serverless computing platform that allows developers to write and deploy microservices that run in response to events. Cloud Load Balancing helps to distribute incoming traffic among multiple instances of microservices, improving performance and reliability. Stackdriver is a cloud

monitoring and logging service that provides detailed insights into the performance of microservices, helping developers to detect and resolve issues quickly. These services help developers to implement and manage microservices architectures more efficiently and effectively.

By following these tips and tricks, you can help ensure that your Java applications running on GCP perform optimally and meet the needs of your users. In the next section, we'll look at each of these recommendations in greater detail.

Architecture Concepts

In this section, let's discuss each tips and tricks to optimize the performance of Java applications running on GCP in detail.

Caching

Caching is an important technique for optimizing the performance of Java applications on GCP. By caching frequently accessed data, you can reduce the number of database queries and improve the responsiveness of your application.

There are several types of caching that can be used to improve the performance of Java applications on GCP, including the following:

- *In-memory caching*: In-memory caching stores data in the application's memory, allowing for fast access to frequently used data. You can use in-memory caching solutions such as Hazelcast or Redis to implement in-memory caching for Java applications on GCP.
- *Disk caching*: Disk caching stores data on disk, allowing you to persist cached data between application restarts. You can use disk caching solutions such as Ehcache to implement disk caching for Java applications on GCP.
- *CDN caching*: Content delivery network (CDN) caching stores data on edge servers, allowing for fast access to frequently used data from anywhere in the world. You can use CDN services such as Cloud CDN to implement CDN caching for Java applications on GCP.

To implement caching for your Java application on GCP, you'll need to do the following:

1. *Choose the right caching solution*: Choose the right caching solution based on your specific needs and requirements. Consider factors such as cache size, persistence, and data access patterns when making your decision.
2. *Configure the cache*: Configure the cache by setting the cache size, eviction policy, and other settings.
3. *Integrate the cache with your application*: Integrate the cache with your application by using caching APIs and libraries. You may need to write some custom code to handle the caching of specific data elements.
4. *Monitor cache performance*: Monitor cache performance using tools such as Stackdriver to ensure that the cache is working as expected and to identify and resolve performance bottlenecks.

By implementing caching for your Java application on GCP, you can improve the responsiveness of your application and reduce the load on your back-end databases, resulting in better overall performance.

Code Optimization

Code optimization is an important technique for improving the performance of Java applications running on GCP. There are several techniques for optimizing Java code that can be used to improve the performance of your application, including the following:

1. *Minimize object creation*: Object creation can be a performance bottleneck, especially in high-traffic applications. Minimizing the number of objects created and reused will help reduce memory pressure and improve performance.
2. *Use efficient algorithms*: Algorithm selection is important for performance optimization. Use algorithms that are known to be efficient for your specific use case, and consider using multiple algorithms to solve different parts of the problem.

3. *Use efficient data structures*: Data structures play an important role in the performance of Java applications. Use data structures that are optimized for your specific use case, such as hash tables for lookups or priority queues for scheduling.

4. *Optimize I/O operations*: I/O operations can be a performance bottleneck, especially in high-traffic applications. Optimize I/O operations by minimizing the number of I/O operations, using buffered I/O, and optimizing file and database access.

5. *Avoid blocking calls*: Blocking calls can cause performance problems by freezing the application while waiting for a response. Avoid blocking calls by using asynchronous I/O, nonblocking I/O, or event-driven architectures.

6. *Profile and measure performance*: Profiling and measuring performance is important for identifying performance bottlenecks and determining the root cause of performance issues. Use tools such as Stackdriver, JProfiler, or JVisualVM to profile and measure the performance of your Java application.

By optimizing your Java code, you can improve the performance of your application, reduce resource usage, and provide a better user experience for your users. Keep in mind that code optimization is an iterative process and requires continuous monitoring and tuning to ensure that your application continues to perform well.

Database Optimization

Database optimization is an important technique for improving the performance of Java applications running on GCP. There are several database optimization techniques that can be used to improve the performance of your application, including the following:

- *Proper indexing*: Proper indexing is critical for optimizing database performance. Indexes help the database quickly retrieve data based on specific search criteria. Make sure to index columns that are frequently searched or used in joins and to regularly analyze and optimize indexes. Note that over-indexing will have impact on the performance while running insert and update queries.

- *Query optimization*: Query optimization is important for improving database performance. Use `EXPLAIN` statements to analyze and optimize your SQL queries, and avoid using complex subqueries or `UNION` statements whenever possible.
- *Proper data modeling*: Proper data modeling is important for optimizing database performance. Make sure to model your data in a way that minimizes data redundancy, eliminates data anomalies, and optimizes database queries.
- *Caching*: Caching is an important technique for improving database performance. Consider using a caching layer such as Redis or Memcached to cache frequently accessed data, and make sure to properly configure and manage the cache to ensure it does not become a performance bottleneck.

By optimizing your database, you can improve the performance of your application, reduce resource usage, and provide a better user experience for your users. Keep in mind that database optimization is an iterative process and requires continuous monitoring and tuning to ensure that your application continues to perform well.

Autoscaling

Autoscaling is a crucial technique for optimizing the performance of Java applications running on GCP. It enables dynamic scaling of the number of instances of your application based on changing demand. With autoscaling, you can ensure that your application can handle sudden spikes in traffic and minimize downtime during periods of low traffic. This approach enables you to allocate resources efficiently to match the current workload and optimize costs by scaling down during low-demand periods. Overall, autoscaling provides a highly effective means of ensuring your Java application's smooth and efficient operation on GCP.

Here are a few tips for implementing autoscaling for your Java application on GCP:

- *Use managed services*: GCP provides several managed services that support autoscaling, including App Engine, Compute Engine, and Kubernetes Engine. These services automatically manage the scaling of your instances and make it easier to implement autoscaling.

- *Monitor your application*: To effectively implement autoscaling, you need to monitor your application to understand how it is being used. Use tools like Stackdriver Monitoring to monitor resource utilization, such as CPU, memory, and network usage.
- *Set scaling policies*: Once you have an understanding of your application's resource utilization, you can set scaling policies that define how and when your application should scale. For example, you might set a policy that automatically adds instances when CPU utilization exceeds 80 percent. GCP allows you to set up autoscaling based on various factors such as CPU utilization, load-balancing metrics, system metrics, schedules, and even machine learning–based predictions. This gives you the flexibility to choose the scaling method that best fits your application's requirements and ensures that your application has enough resources to handle changes in traffic demand.
- *Test your scaling policies*: Before deploying your autoscaling policies, it is important to test them to ensure that they work as expected. Test your policies in a development environment and monitor the performance of your application to ensure that it is scaling as expected.
- *Monitor and adjust*: After you have deployed your autoscaling policies, it is important to monitor and adjust them as needed. Regularly review the performance of your application and make adjustments to your scaling policies to ensure that your application continues to perform well.

By implementing autoscaling for your Java application on GCP, you can improve its performance, reduce downtime, and provide a better user experience for your users. Keep in mind that autoscaling is an iterative process and requires continuous monitoring and tuning to ensure that your application continues to perform well.

Load Balancing

Load balancing is another technique for optimizing the performance of Java applications running on GCP. Load balancing distributes incoming traffic across multiple instances of your application, which can help ensure that your application is able to handle high levels of traffic and minimize downtime.

Here are a few tips for implementing load balancing for your Java application on GCP:

- *Use managed services*: GCP provides several managed services that support load balancing, including App Engine, Compute Engine, and Kubernetes Engine. These services automatically manage the distribution of incoming traffic and make it easier to implement load balancing.
- *Choose the right load balancing method*: There are several methods for load balancing on GCP, including network load balancing, HTTP load balancing, and SSL/TLS load balancing. Choose the method that best fits the requirements of your application.
- *Monitor your application*: To effectively implement load balancing, you need to monitor your application to understand how it is being used. Use tools such as Stackdriver Monitoring to monitor resource utilization, such as CPU, memory, and network usage.
- *Test your load balancing configuration*: Before deploying your load balancing configuration, it is important to test it to ensure that it works as expected. Test your configuration in a development environment and monitor the performance of your application to ensure that it is distributing incoming traffic as expected.
- *Monitor and adjust*: After you have deployed your load balancing configuration, it is important to monitor and adjust it as needed. Regularly review the performance of your application and make adjustments to your load balancing configuration to ensure that your application continues to perform well.

By implementing load balancing for your Java application on GCP, you can improve its performance, reduce downtime, and provide a better user experience for your users. Keep in mind that load balancing is an iterative process and requires continuous monitoring and tuning to ensure that your application continues to perform well.

Monitoring and Logging

Monitoring and logging are essential for optimizing the performance of Java applications running on GCP. By monitoring and logging your application, you can gain insights into its behavior, identify potential issues, and resolve problems quickly.

Here are a few tips for implementing monitoring and logging for your Java application on GCP:

- *Use a centralized logging solution*: Use a centralized logging solution such as Stackdriver Logging to collect and store logs from your Java application. This makes it easier to search and analyze logs and identify patterns and trends, especially in microservices-based architectures.
- *Monitor application performance*: Use Stackdriver Monitoring to monitor the performance of your Java application, including CPU, memory, and network usage. This helps you identify performance bottlenecks and make informed decisions about how to optimize your application.
- *Log relevant information*: When logging information from your Java application, make sure to log information that is relevant to your application and its performance. This could include log messages from your application, error messages, and performance metrics such as response times.
- *Use logging frameworks*: Use logging frameworks like SLF4J or Logback to manage logs from your Java application. These frameworks provide a consistent logging interface and make it easier to configure and manage logs.
- *Use alerts*: Use Stackdriver Monitoring alerts to automatically notify you when certain conditions are met. For example, you can set an alert to notify you when the response time of your application exceeds a certain threshold.

To implement monitoring and logging in detail for a Java application on GCP, you can follow these steps:

1. *Set up Cloud Logging*: First, set up Stackdriver Logging for your Java application on GCP. This involves creating a Stackdriver Logging instance, enabling logs for your application, and configuring the log settings.
2. *Configure logging frameworks*: If you're using a logging framework such as SLF4J or Logback, configure the logging framework to log to Stackdriver Logging. You'll need to set up the logging framework in your Java application, configure the log levels, and specify the log format.
3. *Log relevant information*: When logging information from your Java application, make sure to log relevant information that can help you understand the performance of your application. For example, log information about the request and response, any errors, and performance such as response times.
4. *Set up Cloud Monitoring*: Next, set up Stackdriver Monitoring for your Java application on GCP. This involves creating a Cloud Monitoring instance, enabling monitoring for your application, and configuring the monitoring settings.
5. *Monitor performance metrics*: Use Cloud Monitoring to monitor the performance of your Java application, including CPU, memory, and network usage. You can set up dashboards, charts, and alerts to help you keep track of the performance of your application.
6. *Set up alerts*: Use Cloud Monitoring alerts to automatically notify you when certain conditions are met. For example, you can set an alert to notify you when the response time of your application exceeds a certain threshold.
7. *Analyze logs*: Regularly analyze the logs from your Java application to identify patterns, trends, and potential issues. Use Cloud Logging to search, filter, and aggregate logs to help you identify problems and resolve them quickly.

8. *Continuously monitor and log*: Monitoring and logging are ongoing processes and require continuous attention to ensure that your application continues to perform well. Make sure to continuously monitor the performance of your application, update the logging and monitoring settings as needed, and analyze the logs regularly to identify and resolve problems quickly.

By following these steps, you can implement monitoring and logging for your Java application on GCP and optimize its performance. Keep in mind that monitoring and logging are critical components of a well-architected Java application on GCP, and they require ongoing attention and maintenance.

Network Optimization

Network optimization is an important aspect of optimizing the performance of a Java application running on GCP. Here are some tips and best practices for network optimization:

- *Choosing the right network topology*: Choosing the right network topology, such as a custom VPC or shared VPC, can greatly affect the performance and security of the application. Consider factors such as network security, data privacy, and network performance when making this decision.
- *Minimizing latency*: Minimizing latency between the application and its dependencies, such as databases, can help improve performance. This can be achieved by deploying the application and its dependencies in the same region or using Google's private global network, Google Cloud Interconnect, to connect to GCP.
- *Load balancing*: Load balancing distributes incoming requests evenly across multiple instances of the application, improving reliability and performance. GCP offers several load balancing options, including Network Load Balancer, HTTP(S) Load Balancer, and TCP Load Balancer, to name a few.
- *Network optimization*: Optimizing the network can help improve application performance. This includes optimizing the TCP/IP stack and choosing the right instance types and sizes for the application, based on network performance requirements.

- *Monitoring network performance*: Monitoring the network performance and identifying bottlenecks can help with network optimization. GCP offers several tools for monitoring network performance, including Cloud Monitoring.
- *Implementing security features*: Implementing security features, such as firewall rules, to secure the network can also help improve network performance by reducing the load on the network caused by security-related activities.

By following these tips and best practices for network optimization, you can help ensure that your Java application on GCP runs smoothly and performs optimally.

Implementing Microservices

Implementing microservices is a common approach to performance optimization. By breaking down a large, monolithic application into smaller, independent services, you can take advantage of several benefits, including the following:

- *Scalability*: Microservices can be scaled individually, allowing you to address performance bottlenecks by scaling the specific service that's causing the issue.
- *Resilience*: Microservices are designed to be fault-tolerant, meaning that if one service fails, the others can continue to operate, resulting in improved overall system resilience.
- *Flexibility*: Microservices can be developed, deployed, and managed independently, giving you greater flexibility to update and modify your application as needed.
- *Improved efficiency*: Microservices can be written in different programming languages, using different frameworks and technologies and allowing you to choose the best tools for each specific service.

When implementing microservices for performance optimization on GCP, you can use the following tools and services:

- *Google Kubernetes Engine*: GKE is a managed Kubernetes service that makes it easy to deploy and manage microservices in containers.
- *Cloud Functions*: Cloud Functions is a serverless computing platform that makes it easy to write and deploy microservices that run in response to events.
- *Stackdriver*: Stackdriver is a cloud monitoring and logging service that provides detailed insights into the performance of your microservices and helps you detect and resolve issues quickly.
- *Cloud Load Balancing*: Cloud Load Balancing distributes incoming traffic among multiple instances of your microservices, helping to improve performance and reliability.

When optimizing performance with microservices, it's important to keep the following best practices in mind:

- *Monitor performance metrics*: Use Stackdriver, Operations Suite, or another monitoring tool to track performance metrics for each microservice so you can quickly identify and resolve performance bottlenecks.
- *Automate deployment*: Automate the deployment of microservices using tools such as GKE or Cloud Functions so you can quickly and easily update and deploy new versions.
- *Use caching*: Implement caching mechanisms to improve performance by reducing the number of requests made to the back-end database.
- *Keep services stateless*: Keep microservices stateless so they can be easily scaled and managed without the need to maintain state information.

Summary

In this chapter, you learned about optimizing the performance of Java applications running on Google Cloud Platform. The chapter covered several techniques for optimizing performance, including optimizing compute resources, using managed services, load balancing, monitoring and logging, optimizing networks, and implementing microservices. You also learned about the importance of monitoring and tuning these techniques to ensure that their application continues to perform well over time. By following these best practices for performance optimization, you can improve the performance of your Java applications on GCP, provide a better user experience, and reduce downtime.

Here are some resources for further reference:

- *Cloud-Based Microservices*: `https://link.springer.com/book/10.1007/978-1-4842-6564-2`
- *Google Cloud Documentation*: `https://cloud.google.com/docs`
- *GCP Pricing Calculator*: `https://cloud.google.com/products/calculator`
- *GCP resource hierarchy*: `https://cloud.google.com/resource-manager/docs/cloud-platform-resource-hierarchy`

CHAPTER 9

Conclusion

This chapter concludes the coverage of designing and building a Java application on Google Cloud Platform (GCP). In this chapter, you will learn about the key takeaways of designing and building a Java application on GCP. I'll discuss the different GCP services and tools available for Java application development; factors to consider when choosing services and tools; and techniques for optimizing performance, monitoring and logging, collaboration and teamwork, and keeping up with changes in the GCP platform. Additionally, you will find a list of additional resources and next steps to continue learning about GCP and Java development. By the end of this chapter, you will have a comprehensive understanding of how to design and build a Java application on GCP and deliver a scalable, reliable, and cost-effective solution that meets the needs of their business.

Designing an application for GCP using Java is a powerful way to build scalable, resilient, and secure cloud-based solutions. The wide range of services offered by GCP, combined with the vast ecosystem of libraries and tools available for Java, provide a robust platform for building and deploying applications.

By leveraging the features of GCP, such as autoscaling, load balancing, monitoring and logging, caching, and database optimization, you can optimize the performance and reliability of your application. Additionally, implementing microservices and following best practices for security can help secure your application and make sure it is able to meet the needs of your users.

Designing an application for GCP with Java requires careful consideration of your business requirements and a deep understanding of the services and tools available to you. However, with the right planning and implementation, you can create a powerful and flexible cloud-based solution that can meet the needs of your organization for years to come.

A. Shashi, *Designing Applications for Google Cloud Platform*, https://doi.org/10.1007/978-1-4842-9511-3_9

In addition, it is important to keep in mind that GCP is a constantly evolving platform, with new services and features being added regularly. Keeping up with these changes and incorporating them into your application can help ensure that your solution remains relevant and up-to-date.

It provides the ability to bring products and services to market more quickly. GCP provides a range of tools and services that make it easier to develop, test, and deploy applications at scale, allowing organizations to iterate and experiment with new features and functionality quickly. This agility is particularly valuable in today's fast-paced business environment, where companies need to stay nimble and responsive to changing customer needs. Additionally, GCP's global infrastructure and replication capabilities make it easier to deliver consistent experiences to customers around the world. In this chapter, we will explore how GCP enables quicker time to market, rapid experimentation, and globally replicable applications, and how these capabilities can help drive business success.

With any application development project, collaboration and teamwork are the keys to success. Whether working with in-house development teams or outsourcing to third-party developers, it is important to have clear communication and collaboration to ensure that everyone is working toward the same goal and that the final solution meets the needs of the business.

Designing an application for GCP with Java provides a powerful and flexible platform for building scalable, secure, and reliable cloud-based solutions. With the right approach and tools, you can create an application that meets the needs of your business and provides value for years to come.

Summary of Key Takeaways

Here are the key takeaways:

- GCP provides a wide range of services and tools for building, deploying, and managing Java applications, including App Engine, Compute Engine, Kubernetes Engine, and Cloud SQL.
- When choosing services and tools for your application, it is important to consider factors such as performance, scalability, reliability, and cost-effectiveness.

- Performance optimization is a key aspect of building a successful Java application on GCP. Techniques such as caching, code optimization, database optimization, autoscaling, load balancing, and network optimization can help ensure that your application runs efficiently and can scale as needed.
- Monitoring and logging are crucial for troubleshooting and improving the performance of your Java application. Tools such as Stackdriver and Logging can provide real-time insights into your application's performance and help you identify areas for improvement.
- Collaboration and teamwork are important for ensuring that the application is delivered on time and within budget and that it meets the needs of the business. Using tools such as GitHub and Stack Overflow can help facilitate collaboration and knowledge sharing.
- The GCP platform is constantly evolving, with new services and tools being added on a regular basis. Keeping up with these changes can help ensure that your Java application remains relevant and up-to-date.
- In conclusion, designing and building a Java application on GCP requires careful planning, a solid understanding of the platform, and a focus on performance optimization and collaboration. With the right tools and techniques, you can deliver a scalable, reliable, and cost-effective application that meets the needs of your business.

Additional Resources

There are many resources available to learn more about developing Java applications on Google Cloud Platform. The following are some of the resources:

- *Google Cloud documentation*: This is an extensive resource on all GCP services, including Cloud SQL, Cloud Spanner, Cloud Datastore, and others. The Google Cloud Documentation can be found at: `https://cloud.google.com/docs`.

- *Google Cloud tutorials*: There are a collection of step-by-step tutorials on how to use GCP services and build applications. The Google Cloud step-by-step quickstart tutorials can be found at: `https://cloud.google.com/docs/tutorials`.
- *Courses and certifications*: GCP offers various online courses and certifications in the areas of cloud computing and Java development. These can be found on the Google Cloud Platform website. `https://cloud.google.com/learn/certification`.
- *Online communities and forums*: There are many online communities and forums where you can ask questions, share your experiences, and learn from others. Some popular communities include the Google Cloud Platform Community (`https://www.googlecloudcommunity.com/gc/Google-Cloud/ct-p/google-cloud`) and Stack Overflow (`https://stackoverflow.com/questions/tagged/google-cloud-platform`).
- *YouTube videos and blog posts*: There are many YouTube videos and blog posts on GCP and Java development, which can be a good source of information and inspiration. Google Cloud YouTube channels can be found at: `https://www.youtube.com/googlecloud` and `https://www.youtube.com/@googlecloudtech` . The Google Cloud blogs can be found at: `https://cloud.google.com/blog`.
- *Books*: There are many books available on GCP and Java development, which can provide a comprehensive overview of the platform and its services. There are also some popular books related to microservices architecture you can consider. Here are a few of my recommended books **Cloud-Based Microservices by Chandra Rajasekharaiah, Microservices Patterns** by Chris Richardson, **Cloud Native Architecture and Design** by Shivakumar R Goniwada.

Next Steps for Learning More About GCP and Java Development

To become proficient designing and building Java applications on GCP, continuous learning and practice are essential. The recommendations for further learning include familiarizing yourself with the GCP platform and its services, building and deploying Java applications on GCP, studying microservices architecture and performance optimization, learning about logging and monitoring tools, and participating in online communities and attending events, webinars, and conferences. By following these steps and continuously honing your skills, you can become an expert in building scalable, secure, and reliable cloud-based solutions on GCP using Java.

To continue learning about GCP and Java development, you can follow these steps:

- Familiarize yourself with the GCP platform and its services by reading the official documentation and taking online tutorials or courses.
- Get hands-on experience by building and deploying Java applications on GCP. Start with simple applications and gradually build more complex applications as you gain more experience.
- Learn about microservices architecture and how it can be applied to Java applications on GCP. Read about the different tools and frameworks available for building and deploying microservices on GCP.
- Study the best practices for performance optimization of Java applications on GCP. This includes caching, code optimization, database optimization, autoscaling, load balancing, monitoring and logging, and network optimization.
- Learn about different tools and services available for logging, monitoring, and debugging Java applications on GCP. This includes Stackdriver, Cloud Debugger, and Cloud Trace.
- Participate in online communities and forums to connect with other developers and stay updated with the latest advancements and best practices in Java development on GCP.
- Attend GCP events, webinars, and conferences to stay updated with the latest advancements and best practices in GCP and Java development.

By continuously learning and practicing, you can develop a strong foundation in Java development on GCP and become an expert in optimizing performance and building scalable and reliable applications.

Summary

This chapter summarized the key takeaways for designing and building Java applications on Google Cloud Platform. The chapter emphasized the importance of GCP services and tools for building scalable, secure, and reliable cloud-based solutions using Java. It also highlighted the key factors to consider when choosing services and tools for your application, including performance, scalability, reliability, and cost-effectiveness. The chapter outlines various techniques for performance optimization, monitoring and logging, and collaboration, and provides a list of additional resources for learning more about GCP and Java development. Overall, this chapter and the entire guide aim to help you develop a solid foundation in Java development on GCP and become an expert in optimizing performance and building scalable and reliable applications.

Index

A

B

C

A. Shashi, *Designing Applications for Google Cloud Platform*, https://doi.org/10.1007/978-1-4842-9511-3

D

H

I

J

P

Q

R

S

T

U

V

W, X, Y, Z

Printed in the United States
by Baker & Taylor Publisher Services